GO...
MAKE...
RIPPLES

Jennifer Godwin

WESTBOW
PRESS®
A DIVISION OF THOMAS NELSON
& ZONDERVAN

WestBow Press books may be ordered through booksellers or by contacting:

WestBow Press
A Division of Thomas Nelson & Zondervan
1663 Liberty Drive
Bloomington, IN 47403
www.westbowpress.com
844-714-3454

Cover Design: Amanda Krumel @TandemHart

ISBN: 978-1-6642-6350-5 (sc)
ISBN: 978-1-6642-6352-9 (hc)
ISBN: 978-1-6642-6351-2 (e)

Library of Congress Control Number: 2022906822

Print information available on the last page.

WestBow Press rev. date: 5/20/2022

Contents

1

———❦❦❦———

This Explains the Ripples

What do diseases, floods, weddings and babies all have in common? Life . . . it's a journey. But here's the good news –- Jesus was with me every step of the way. And with every step it has made me more Christlike. Had I known everything that would happen in the three plus years it took to finish this book, I would have been overwhelmed. It seems like a lifetime ago that I wrote the next paragraph. (**It was the first one – and the only one NOT edited!**)

Ok, this is it! I'm going to write a book! Well I would, but just getting my computer to give me a blank page to write on is difficult. I am not an author nor am I a computer person, and I'm realizing my ninth grade typing teacher would not be impressed with my typing skills either. So, the monster cookie I ate right before starting was a reward for beginning. People say starting is the hardest part of any endeavor. It's a good thing my personality is one of fearlessness and never giving up. God has given me two gifts that I will need for this assignment: the gift of stepping out and trying something new and of perseverance to finish things to the end. Both are true gifts from God and will be the gifts I will need to finish! (HOW TRUE THAT LAST SENTENCE TURNED OUT TO BE!!!)

If you lack the courage to start, you have already finished. -- Joe Girard

I never dreamed about writing a book. It was never a desire of mine or a line on my bucket list. I *KNOW* it makes you want to read this now, doesn't it? This was written out of obedience to God! And to glorify Him!

Throughout my life, the Lord has impressed upon me several things I believe He has wanted me to do. Some of them I have done, and some, like this book, took me a while to finish. It was twenty years ago that I heard the Lord say, "You will write a book." I know it was God, because I would have *NEVER* come up with this idea on my own! God has such a sense of humor. I had never written an essay paper in high school, attended college, or used proper English. As I typed along, I wasn't sure I even knew where to put commas. I also "rabbit trail" while talking, so writing was a challenge. Stick with me, I will get to the main point eventually.

So, why did I write this book? Besides being obedient to God and wanting to sleep peacefully at night, I also wanted to share how I came to know Jesus as my best friend, the different adventures we have had together, and to encourage those of you reading this. I've read many books about how people have served the Lord. Maybe you have too! Ones that made us sit in awe of what the person accomplished. Pastors and missionaries who share the Lord with thousands of people. People who have started prison ministries, homes for pregnant women, or worked with teens in distress, people who adopted or fostered hundreds of children or people who ministered to the masses. It's incredible what people are doing in this world to make it a better place and ways they share the good news of Jesus. But after we're done reading, we may be discouraged thinking, *"What am I doing for God?"* Instead, we should be inspired! We can all make little changes in our lives to become better people and learn new ways to share Jesus with those we come in contact with.

This book is for those of you like me that live out loud and are not afraid to share the Gospel with anyone. It's also written for those of you that want to share but prefer to remain in the background, quietly spreading His word. This is a hurting world and the need for Jesus is getting stronger every day! If we all do our part as ordinary Christians, we as a group can make a BIG difference for The Kingdom!! Like all the small things that people did which helped my spiritual journey, I would love to share and encourage you in ways that you *can* make a difference! Hebrews 10:24-25 says, "Let us think of ways to motivate one another to acts of love and good works. And let us not neglect our meeting together, as some people do, but encourage one another, **especially now that the day of His return is drawing near.**"

Don't be nervous. I will be cheering you on and God will be with us every step of the way!

I was not raised in a Christian home, so I did not learn about God as a child. *Seriously!* I didn't even know Easter was a religious holiday until I was *fourteen years old,* let alone that the resurrection was a big deal!!! I started a relationship with Jesus in my teens, but my education about who God is and how to serve Him happened as an adult. I did most of my learning on my own. I don't have many hang-ups about churches. However, it can't be the only way that we learn about God. I am a person who believes that if you want to know someone, then you have to put the work into building that relationship. The relationship between God and yourself is no different. That's how you become best friends with Jesus – by spending time with Him. Think about any of your relationships with friends or spouses. Did you build those relationships by having someone tell you about your spouse or friends, what they did growing up, all their childhood stories, or what they like and dislike? NO!!! You spent time with them! Our world is all about "instant." We all want things now! We want to go to church one hour a week, but we all know relationships require more than an hour a week. *Relationships take time!* Do you feel like there's never enough time when you're with someone you love – like you always want more! That's how it should be. Jesus makes a great best friend. He is always ready when you are . . . no schedule conflicts on His side. He always wants the best for you. And He always loves you even when you mess up.

I am an encourager, even when I was a young girl. This skill probably came from watching movies like *Pollyanna.* The girl in that movie turned her bad thoughts into positive ones and encouraged a whole town to do the same. She was the girl who took lemons and made lemonade. I would love to encourage you to grow in your relationship with God and encourage you to share what you learn with others.

1 Thessalonians 5:11 states, "So encourage each other and build each

other up, just as you are already doing." I love to encourage others to grow in their faith and to share different ways to do good deeds inexpensively that show the love of Jesus. One of the titles I thought about for this book was, *"Good Deeds Done Dirt Cheap,"* which is kind of a play off the song "Dirty Deeds Done Dirt Cheap." (A lot of people didn't get it, oh well . . . next title!)

Something like *"Go . . . Just . . . Do . . . It."* I was a cheerleader in high school and loved to encourage the crowd to cheer a little louder, especially because I thought at least if we weren't winning, our crowd could be the best at encouraging. Our basketball team in high school didn't win one game my senior year. It was a *long* season! (The coach should have taught them a basic skill – free throws. I know . . . boring! But we might have won a few games that year when the scores were close! That's what we all need – the basics. We can't all be Michael Jordan, but we can help win the game with basic skills!) Even though we didn't win any games, not cheering for them ever entered my mind! Perseverance runs through my blood. Hey, that is what life is about sometimes; having someone cheer you on especially when things are not going your way. Praying for God's protection . . . Defense! Listening for God's help . . . Defense! Reading God's word . . . Defense! BUT, at some point we as Christians need to work on our offense! We all need to take a few shots for the team. "Go . . . Fight . . . Win!"

Another title I leaned towards was, "Are you a Thermometer or a Thermostat*?"* I told a few people, and someone asked me if I thought I could sell a book with that title? Bless you, nurse Nancy. Who knows? But that title does describe me. I am a thermostat for sure! I like to set the temperature around me, and *I like it HOT!* I want to be on fire for God, and I want the people around me to be that way too. A thermometer just tells you what the temperature is around you, and sometimes Christians are only warm. God tells churches (us) not to be lukewarm in (Revelation 3:16). "But since you are like lukewarm water, neither hot nor cold, I will spit you out of my mouth*!"* I don't want to be spit out! Do you? Christians need to turn up their thermostats. Listen, I'm not saying that by doing good deeds you can get into Heaven, but James 2:18 says "Now someone may argue, "Some people have faith; others have good deeds." But I say, "How can you show me your faith if you don't have good deeds? I will show you my faith by my good deeds."

What are you doing right now that requires faith? - Francis Chan

The last thing Jesus said before leaving this earth is in Matthew 28:19. "Therefore, go and make disciples of all the nations, baptizing them in the name of the Father and the Son and the Holy Spirit." It means to go tell people about Jesus. This was not a suggestion, but a command.

The Kingdom has been built by ordinary people with the help of the Holy Spirit. It started with fishermen, shepherds, and even people who were not model citizens. It will continue with us, but I want to be clear – the things mentioned in this book all came with time and came at different seasons of my life. Many of the ways I've tried to share Jesus have been successful, and others have failed miserably. God knows my heart and my desire for people to know Him as their personal Savior, for my brothers and sisters in Christ to grow more like Jesus and to glorify Him. In order to do that, we need to take an active part in showing others a better way of life and show them God's love. Here's my heart . . . I don't always come off warm and fuzzy! Sometimes I'm . . . what shall I say . . . aggressive. But stick with me; know that I love you. Coaches are not always warm and fuzzy, sometimes they have to push. If you don't like being pushed, think of me as a friend pulling your arm trying to get you to do something you don't want to do but knowing you will love it once you get there. *COME ON*, it will be an adventure!

Dictionary.com says the definition of ripple effect is "a spreading effect or series of consequences caused by a single action or event." Let's make a difference, and when we do, others will join us. Jesus was the first ripple and from there they haven't stopped! I am just one ripple responding to the pebbles thrown out before me. I now want to be someone that keeps throwing pebbles in the pond to keep the ripples going and would love for you to do the same. When this book was finished . . . the title on the cover made the most sense.

Here's one more thing I want to mention and don't take lightly!!!! (Matthew 6:1) "Watch out! Don't do your good deeds publicly, to be admired by others, for you will lose the reward from your Father in heaven." This book was written NOT to get praise from you, NOT to brag, and NOT to be admired! I am sharing with you so we together can further His Kingdom!

In the boxes I have suggested ways to make ripples in your own life and for those around you! Some may feel awkward at first, but with practice it gets easier! Why not try a few along the way? The easiest way to do this would be to grab a pen and a stack of index cards. Write down the ripples on your cards. Pray and ponder them. Think of ways you can make them your own. Put these cards in a place you will see them. Leave them visible until you try doing them! We won't all do things the same way, but at least try a few of them. Ask God to help you with each challenge. Go . . .Make . . . Ripples!!!

2

---oⁱᵒⁱᵒ---

A Handful of Pebbles

THE BEGINNING

From the beginning I did not *feel* like I grew up in a typical household. What is a typical household? My parents owned a motorcycle dealership and worked a lot of hours. They worked six days a week, 9:00 AM - 6:00 PM, and even later in the summertime. They had Sundays off only because the state law said they couldn't sell motor vehicles on that day. I was raised by several babysitters, school, and eventually I was a latch key kid. I am NOT complaining. I had a great childhood, just not a typical "Leave it to Beaver" or a "Brady Bunch" type of family. We did not go to church, nor did we talk about it. Of course, how could you talk about something you didn't know anything about?

My first memory of God . . . OK, *let's really be serious*, the first time I even *HEARD* God's name (when it wasn't being used as a curse word) was in kindergarten. I was over at my friend, Linda's house. Her mother had prepared dinner, and we were sitting down to eat at her kitchen table. I do not remember my family ever sitting down to eat dinner together, so it was all new and intimidating to me. I picked up my fork and started to eat because everyone was there and the food was getting cold. I'm sure I was hungry too. Then someone said, "We have to pray first." I put down my fork because I knew I was the only one that was eating. Then her dad said, "Let's pray." *WHAT???*

> **Ripple:** Praying in front of people for your food at dinner can really set you apart from other people. It was a small thing that started my salvation story! So start praying in front of people for your meals.

What did that mean? I had no clue, but everyone looked down and closed their eyes, so I did the same. Then he began talking to someone that I couldn't see. I opened my eyes to look for who he was talking to and to see what everyone was doing. But I didn't see anyone else in the room except us, and they still had their eyes closed. To say that I was confused is an understatement! (I still can picture this scene in my memory like I'm watching a movie.) After we prayed, everyone picked up their forks and started eating dinner. When Linda and I finished eating, we were allowed to leave the table. We went to play, while her parents cleaned up. After I had taken the time to think about what had happened at dinner, I asked her, "Who were you talking to before we ate?" She said, "Oh, we were praying to God." That was the best she could tell me. She couldn't explain it, and I didn't get it!!! I'm sure it made sense to her since she had been doing it all her life. Remember, we were only six years old. It was just something they did and something my family did not do. This was the first ripple someone started that pointed me to the Lord. It was the first time I had ever heard God's name and the first time that I witnessed someone talking to God. Imagine how many children grow up in homes that do not see or experience this. Prayer is a powerful thing to us as believers, and it can be to that person who may think they are all alone in this world. Imagine if they knew that they could call on Him anytime, day or night, that there is Someone who truly cares for them.

This same friend would later take me to church a few times and to Vacation Bible School (VBS). (I'm sure this was through the encouragement of her parents.) VBS was kind of like going to school. We had snacks, play and craft time, and of course, a story.

Ripple: Invite young children to AWANA, VBS, or church on Sunday. Children who don't have families that do these things, love to feel included! Invite people to church and have your children do this, too. It will be a skill that they will have for a lifetime.

The stories that were told at VBS were always in the middle of a larger story, like the flannel board stories about fishermen, and a man on a boat. Of course, what I was really intrigued about was that the flannel cut-out people stuck to the board. It amazed me. (Imagine old fashioned Bible characters and objects cut out and glued to felt. These were then placed on a board propped on an easel. Look it up!) Later in life, while reading my Bible, I could remember those cute cut-outs as though I was still sitting in the classroom. I now know the people in the cut-outs were Peter and Andrew leaving their fishing boats to follow Jesus and become His disciples. He would make them fishers of men. (Matthew 4:19) Isn't it *AMAZING*? The first Bible story told to me was about fishing for people (telling people about the good news of Jesus so others can become Christians). Fifty years later I'm writing a book about how to do just that. I don't remember much else about VBS except at the end of the week I received my first Bible.

Ripple: Suggest to your church that they should give kids and teenagers age appropriate Bibles to new visitors! You never know who may read it!! Help start a fund to purchase the Bibles.

Ripple: Give a Children's Bible as a baby gift to a new mother, or as birthday gifts to children.

(I did not receive even one Bible for any of my children for gifts! I made up for it and gave my first grandson five different Bibles when he was born! They were all different! A baby one that was soft, toddler ones that pointed to pictures, and three different children's Bibles.)

It was light blue with a father and his son on his shoulders. I really wanted a pink one with a girl on it but was excited about my Bible anyway. I don't know why I would be excited. I couldn't read it. It was an adult version of the New Testament. I'm sure they told me how important it was, but it didn't even have pictures in it. (I kept that Bible until I was a teenager.) I also remember telling my great-grandpa that I went to church. He was proud of me and gave me another Bible. It was in a wooden box. Inside the box it had a picture of Jesus. Now I had two Bibles, but when I tried to read them, I couldn't understand because they were a reading level above my head. But, I do remember thinking how special I felt about owning two Bibles. If they had given me a children's Bible back then, I would have had my parents read to me. Then all of us would have learned some of the basic stories.

When my children were little, that's what we did, and we all learned about God together. Noah, Jonah, and Moses were all names I had heard, but I only had the basics as to who or what their stories were.

> **Ripple:** Read a story in the Bible to your children or grandchildren before you read any other book. The Bible is the one book that will help them the most through life!

Christmastime was a bit of a mystery to me. I would look for ways to figure out how Santa and baby Jesus fit into Christmas together. I must have been either an inquisitive child or a doubter. Santa just didn't make sense to me. I remember asking my mother if Santa Claus was real, and of course, she always told me yes. (I did the Santa thing differently with my kids. Santa only gave the boring gifts. Clothes, socks, books, and anything else that wasn't exciting. I didn't want him to get the credit for the good gifts. I wanted our children to know that Dean and I gave them the good stuff, which made Santa not that exciting in our house. He was never put on a pedestal. Knowing what I know now, I'm not sure I would do the Santa Claus thing. I always felt like I was lying to my children . . . but that's just me!)

Growing up in simpler times, we didn't have the internet, so reading meant a trip to the library. My quest was to find out if Santa was real. I wanted to believe my mother, but I knew something wasn't right. Maybe it was the way she would smile when I asked my questions. It was as though she knew more than she was saying. So, cartoons became my mode of research. Of course cartoons were *not* as real looking back then as they are now. I figured Rudolph had to be fake because I knew that reindeer didn't talk . . . so maybe Santa Claus was fake too. How does one man that is bigger than a chimney slide down them? I could believe the Grinch could fit down a chimney but he didn't look real since he was green. How does Santa deliver all the presents in one night? How does that flying sleigh carry all those presents? Plus, if you looked at how many presents were in the sleigh, you knew that there weren't enough presents for all the kids in the world. I almost believed the elves making the toys, but why were there JCPenney and Sears catalogs with all the same toys in them? I did ask my mother several of these questions, but I was always answered with more fairy tale lies, or the standard answer, "You just have to believe in Santa to get your presents," which made you want to believe!

Cartoons were fun to watch but not very educational . . . especially when you are trying to gather the truth. Everything was make-believe, except . . ."The Little Drummer Boy" cartoon. This cartoon was more serious, there wasn't snow, and it had a funny look to it. – It wasn't animated like the other Christmas cartoons – the characters were movable figures that actually looked more real than the other shows. The young boy would eventually play his drum for a baby (Jesus) born in a barn. He was told that the baby was going to be a king. As I got older, it started making more sense, but I still didn't understand how it all fit together. It seemed there were two completely different stories going on at Christmas, a Santa Claus that gave out gifts and a baby in a manager that received gifts. Confusing!

> **Ripple:** The Christmas season is a great time to have a movie night at your house. Gather around with snacks and popcorn and encourage others to bring friends and show a REAL CHRISTMAS movie about Jesus!

At ten or eleven years of age, I understood that church and God went together, and that you went to church to learn about God. I think I got this information from my neighbor friend who I was hanging out with at the time. Every Saturday I would spend the night at my Catholic friend Jodi's house so we could go to church on Sunday mornings.

Ripple: Allow your children to have friends spend the night on Saturday nights with the understanding that EVERYONE, including guests, are going to church in the morning.

I thought everyone liked to go to church. I'm not so sure that kids who went to church every week really liked going to church. At least my friend didn't. I don't know if I liked church, but I knew that was where to get the answers to my questions about God and how to get to Heaven. Honestly, I don't know how I first understood the concept of heaven and hell. I knew if you believed in God, you would go to Heaven. If not, you would go to Hell. The problem was my friend really liked her sleep, so several times she told her mom that we stayed up too late, and needed to sleep. She just didn't want to go to church. Eventually her mother wouldn't let me spend the night on Saturdays because my friend would always use me as an excuse. Really, I was the one who *DID* want to go to church. When we did go to church, I wondered if they were even speaking English. We attended the adult service, and I didn't understand a thing that they were talking about. But, I did learn a few things. They had padded boards that pulled out from the church pews, that we knelt on to pray, which I thought was neat. I also learned how to cross myself, touch your forehead -- you say "Father," touch your heart – you say "Son," touch the front of your shoulder on the left – you say "Holy," touch your right front shoulder – and say "Spirit." It looked spiritual and when I did it, I felt like I fit in. They also did something with wine in a glass and bread on a plate at the front of the church. My friend said she didn't want to drink after everyone so she would not go forward. I'm sure now it's because I wasn't Catholic and I couldn't take communion. I didn't understand why people at church did this either, but it was something they did.

Another way God popped into my life was with more television. I remember watching TV programs like *The Waltons*. It was a nice family show. Remember those? It was about a family who had seven children, and there was something different about them besides the numbers. They did things very differently than my family; like having dinner together and praying for their food (*HUH!* This looks and sounds familiar). They also went to church. This is the way I wanted my family to be like. During certain episodes, someone in the family would do something wrong, feel guilty about what they did and confess, even before they got caught! I remember the show talking about God, church, and doing what was right. Unfortunately, I was only able to see half of those shows because my bedtime was halfway through the program. So again, I only had half of the story. When I watched these shows, it would stir something in my heart that I knew was missing. I had parents, a sibling, and love in my family. *What was I missing?*

> **Ripple:** Search for good family value shows, and watch them as a family. You could even spend time after the show having a great conversation about what you watched.

Then a show called *Little House on the Prairie* came out. It was set in an earlier era, but again they seemed like a "normal" family, and, *YES,* they prayed before dinner too. The episode I will never forget is the episode where Laura Ingalls, the main character, was jealous of her new baby brother. She didn't like that the baby took away her father's time and attention. Laura was her pa's favorite, and she wanted to keep it that way. She prayed to God that the baby would leave so Laura could have her pa's attention again. When the baby died, she thought that it was her fault. The death of the baby was so devastating to her family that she knew she had to do something to fix it. She wanted to take back her prayer, so she went to talk to God. She ran away and climbed up on a mountain to be closer to God. A gentleman (who was portrayed as an angel) appeared and talked to her. By the end of the show, she knew that the death of her baby brother wasn't her fault. Her pa came searching and rescued her on top of the mountain. He told her the same thing the angel had said, that it wasn't her fault and that he loved her. In the last scene of that show, a cross necklace floated down the stream that had broken off Laura's neck while she was lost.

If you're confused, I get it! I was totally confused about God, how to get to heaven, and now I was confused about angels? Just another piece of the puzzle I was trying to put together or a mystery I was trying to solve.

I'm just giving you insight into a young person's life who did not grow up in a Christian home. You see how other families are different from your own and try to figure out what they have that you don't. Again, my parents worked, which at that time only about half of my friends' parents both worked. We had nice things and were able to go on vacations. Both of my parents loved me, but again I felt something was missing from my life. As an adult, I think about all those children that grow up in homes of drug addicts, abusers, and who knows what else, so, I'm not complaining about my family. I knew deep within my soul that *something* was missing. I often wonder how many other children are out there searching for their missing piece?

> **Ripple:** Reach out to young children. Volunteer as a homeroom helper in a school working with children that need extra help. You can offer encouraging words as you take the time to really listen to them. Volunteer at an afterschool program where you help with reading and homework. Ask your church if this is something it can offer for people needing help with kids . . . children inside and outside the church. Maybe you are in an apartment house? Let parents know that you are available to host a Bible story time in a common area, or you're willing to help with homework. Show them Jesus's love and that you care.

During this time I somehow knew there was a God, but He was only giving me a small glimpse of Himself. It seemed as though He was everywhere, but nowhere I could find Him. I also knew He loved me because a lot of the cars in Des Moines in the 1970's had bumper stickers with a big yellow smiley face on them with the words "Smile, God Loves You." I took comfort in the fact that God loved me. (It's amazing what God will use to lead you to Himself.)

> **Ripple:** Bumper stickers – you read them and so do I. If you notice, there seem to be a lot more negative ones than positive ones out there. Why not put a sticker on the bumper of your car that has a positive message about God? Maybe one that leads people to a Christian radio station or maybe a "God Loves You" sticker. You never know how God can use that sticker to speak into someone's life.

When I was twelve or thirteen years of age and in middle school, someone important had predicted the end of the world. This was a serious thing, and a lot of people were talking about it. So by everyone, I mean pre-teens who don't know much about current events outside of school, but they heard about it somewhere. They even had it on the news. I remember asking my seventh grade teacher what she thought. She said that this was not a new thing. People have been predicting the end of the world since the beginning of time. She didn't seem worried, and I figured she knew more about these things than a bunch of pre-teens, so I went on with my day. That didn't mean that everyone stopped talking about it. They discussed when it would happen, and how it would be nice if it happened before their tests. Also, they asked each other if they thought they would go to Heaven or Hell. I didn't know much, but I knew I wanted to go to Heaven and not that other place.

The school bus ride home wasn't much better. Several neighborhood kids were talking about baptism. I was told that a pastor or priest would dunk people under water or would sprinkle them with water and then you would have done what you needed to do to get to Heaven. Great. This was NOT looking too promising for me. What was confusing is that nobody was baptized the same way. Some went to the river, some in a kind of bathtub, and some were sprinkled as a baby. I didn't know what this meant in connection to Heaven or God, but I had never been baptized in any method so my fear grew! When I got home that day, I called my Catholic neighbor friend who had heard the same things at school and was worried enough about me that she and her older sister baptized me in the kitchen sink. They ran the spray nozzle over my head and prayed. They were not being mean when they did this; they were worried I would go to Hell. I might have been confused about the whole Heaven and God thing, but I was sure that this was *NOT* how you got into Heaven. Needless to say.... the world did not end that day, which was a good thing since I was not ready to die yet!

> **Ripple:** Invite family and friends to church to see baptisms or talk about it to people. This is a great way to start a conversation at work. You can talk about how many people were baptized at church last weekend.

If my story seems to be a bit incomplete, and it all seems like bits and pieces, then I did my job getting you as confused as I was. I knew there was a God, and He loved me, that there were places called Heaven and

Hell, and that you had to be baptized. (I later found out that baptism does not get you into Heaven.) Ok, I was smart enough to know I wanted to go to Heaven and not burn in Hell with the devil. I asked my friends all sorts of questions, but even though they went to church, they seemed to be as clueless as I was. Can you tell I was determined to figure this out?

Ripple: Start conversations with the young people that are around you. Talk to them about church and God. Let them know if they have any questions, they can come to you.

AHA MOMENT

Skip ahead with me to 1981. I was now fourteen years old, three months short of fifteen. I thought I was so mature and that I knew everything. (Just like all teenagers.) I was about to finish my first semester of my ninth grade year of high school. On the weekends, I was drinking, smoking pot, and sneaking out. During the rest of the week, I was an average teenager going to high school and getting good grades. I was no longer thinking about God, Heaven, or Hell . . . only guys. Thank the Lord that most boys didn't like me yet, so I don't have too many regrets in that area! But, I was heading in the *WRONG* direction!

> *You'll never change your life until you change
> your choices. - John C. Maxwell*

The Friday or Saturday after Thanksgiving 1981, I spent the night with my friend Jill. We were in her room chatting about boys, when her sister Rhonda, (whom I had never met and have only seen once since that night) came into her room. She asked if we wanted to know how to go to Heaven. Let me stress, this was so far from where I was at during that moment of my life. In every way! I was no longer thinking about God. Our conversation wasn't anything about God. Seriously, I didn't even know that Jill had an older sister, let alone at home in the basement. *Honestly . . . this was as strange as if an alien would have walked into the room!* I also didn't know this family went to church or knew God. You would have thought that I had just listened to a whole sermon about Heaven and Hell! I responded so fast, I'm sure she was shocked! Of course, I said, *"Yes!!!"* Jill didn't want to go, so I went with Rhonda to her basement bedroom. She was home from Moody Bible Institute, a college in Chicago. I didn't even know this girl, but wanted to know what she knew.

Finally! Someone who may have the answers I had been looking for. I don't know why she would come to her sister's room and randomly ask her sister and her friend that question. Can you imagine walking into a teenage girl's room and asking that question? Seriously, if I wouldn't have said yes we probably would have sat there talking about how weird she was. We would have had a giggle session as soon as she shut the door behind her. Teenage girls can be mean, even if one of them is your sister. But I'm sure glad she had enough courage to ask the question! She gave me the best gift anyone can do for another human being. She told me how to have a personal relationship with Jesus Christ!

She must have gone back to college after Thanksgiving break and told her professors, give me an A+! I led a girl to Christ this weekend and all I had to do was ask. I really want you to understand how totally random this was! It would be like someone walking into your room right now and asking if you would like to go to the moon? You've thought about the moon, you have seen the moon, and you know the moon is in the sky . . . but someone knows how to get to the moon and wants to know if you want to go to the moon. That is how strange to me it was, that this gal walked into the room that night and said, "Do you want to know how to go to Heaven?" *IT WAS A GOD THING!!!*

Ripple: Sometimes all we have to do is ask people if they would like a relationship with Jesus. The seeds may have already been planted and all you have to do is water. Try to make it a point at least once a month to ask anyone if they want to know how to get to Heaven. I know that is not really a small thing, but it was in Rhonda's case. All she did was ask. The rest is my eternity!!! Or if that's too big, start a God conversation. "Wow did you see that sunset or sunrise this morning? God really is a master artist." Or "What do you think is happening in this world." This is a loaded question but opens a lot of avenues to input God. Anything that makes them think about God. If they are really searching, they may ask you how to get to Heaven?

I knew without hesitation that I wanted to know God . . . PERIOD! This is what I felt I had been searching for ALL fourteen years of my life. We both sat on her bed. She said that God loves me and has a plan for me. She opened the Bible and showed me John 3:16 "God so loved the world that He gave His one and only Son, [Jesus Christ], that whoever believes in Him shall not perish, but have eternal life." She told me that I was a sinner (a person who was breaking the 10 commandments). *Duh*, I understood that! She showed me Romans 3:23. "All have sinned and fall short of the glory of God." The way I was doing life, Heaven was *not* a possibility for me. I didn't even try to justify all the good I did. I knew I wasn't going to Heaven at that point of my life. She then told me that it didn't matter what I had done in my life, good or bad, I couldn't go to Heaven unless I had someone to pay the price for my sins. But the good news was Jesus had done all the work. He died to pay for my sins in my place on the cross so that through faith in Him, I could go to Heaven. Romans 5:8 says, "God demonstrates His love toward us in that while we were still sinners Christ died for us." I needed to confess my sins and accept that Jesus died for my sins and rose again, and that I wanted Him as my personal Savior.

This should have been the most confusing conversation that I had ever heard in my life. I had *NEVER* heard this kind of message before, but somehow God had been fitting all the pieces together. The Holy Spirit was in that room because I understood what Rhonda told me. So on the floor beside her bed, she led me in a prayer asking Jesus into my life. It was quick and easy, but that prayer changed my life forever, and I mean forever into *ETERNITY!!!* I didn't understand all of what I heard, but I had an overwhelming feeling that it didn't matter if I had all the answers to my questions. I had Jesus.

If you want to know Jesus as your personal Savior you can pray a prayer like this one. But remember it's not the exact words that are important, it's your heart's attitude towards God. It's more about wanting to do this so you can be right with Him.

"Dear God, I know I'm a sinner, and I ask for your forgiveness. I believe Jesus Christ is Your Son. I believe that He died for my sin and that you raised Him back to life. I want to trust Him as my Savior and follow Him from this day forward. Guide my life and help me to do your will. I pray this in the name of Jesus. Amen."

Give your life to Jesus: He can do more with it than you can! - DL Moody

I remember the two things that really stuck out to me that night. She told me that since I had now accepted what Jesus had done for me, I would want to confess my sins to Jesus in prayer and tell other people about the decision I had made.

Both of those sounded easy to do. So I went upstairs to my friend's room. I must have been in the basement for a while because my friend had gotten ready for bed. When I walked in, she turned off the lights and said, "Let's go to sleep." I don't remember my friend even asking me what happened when I was with her sister downstairs. But that was ok, because I had business to do.

That night as I laid in bed, I confessed all the things (sin) I was doing and had done in my life that were against God. Seriously, every sin that I could think of, I confessed! This took hours, I kept coming up with all sorts of sin. By the time I was done, I felt so good that all that "stuff" was behind me.

The next morning after accepting Jesus as my personal Savior, I couldn't stop smiling. I felt a joy that I had never felt before. I'm a pretty happy person typically, but this was different! I was no longer the same person. I felt so at peace . . . like I had all the answers to my questions, and I had a new best Friend. I wanted to *SHOUT* to the world just how great I felt! When I went home the next morning, I decided to work on the second thing that Rhonda told me I should do; tell someone about my salvation. When I arrived home, I told my family about accepting Jesus into my life, that I knew how to get to Heaven, and that they needed Jesus too. I'm pretty sure my parents thought I was out of my mind! They were used to me talking a lot, and I was not afraid to tell them anything, but I'm sure the God conversation was *NOT* what they were expecting out of me. They didn't ask me any questions or seem interested, so I went on my way. I had told someone about the good news, but they didn't want to hear it. (With time, I came to understand that this would be a normal response.) That was the first day I began witnessing!!!

"Yet preaching the Good News is not something I can boast about. I am compelled by God to do it. How terrible for me if I didn't preach the Good News!" - 1 Corinthians 9:16

Since Rhonda had taken the time to tell me how to get into Heaven, I feel a duty to do the same favor to all those people who are searching like I was. I want to help people who don't know enough to be searching, or that gave up a long time ago. I'm kind of like the Samaritan woman at the well. If you don't know this story, check it out in John 4:1-42. As soon as she knew the good news of Jesus, she couldn't keep it to herself. She became the first missionary for Jesus!

It took all sorts of people doing small things for me to come to know Christ as my Savior. First, Linda's family prayed in front of me and then took me to VBS. The person that created the "Smile God loves you" bumper sticker and the people that put the stickers on their cars. The person that wrote, directed, and produced television shows that talked about Christ. Other friends that talked about their faith in front of me. And a Christian college that encouraged Rhonda to share her faith. For me, none of these things were small because each one softened my heart enough to accept the gospel when I heard it. I believe that they will all be rewarded in Heaven by God or definitely by ME!!!

GROWING RELATIONSHIPS

During this same time, I had a crush on this cute boy who was in my typing class. While I was confessing all my sins that first night of my salvation, I decided to ask God to put that "Godwin boy" in my life. I had never prayed before, and I guess I didn't know what I was or wasn't allowed to ask for in my prayers. I just talked to God like He was my new best friend!! (Actually, I have done this ever since that night because He is my best friend.)

I always tell people to be careful what you pray for! About two weeks after I prayed for that Godwin boy to be in my life, we started dating . . . which is kind of a miracle in itself, but that's another story. Trust me, it really was a God thing!!! I giggle about this all the time. Well, sometimes I roll my eyes too. I just wanted that boy as a boyfriend. Of course, four decades later, he is still in my life — as my husband. When I get mad at him, I have nobody to blame that he's in my life but me! I prayed and God took me literally! So be careful how you pray!!! ☺

After my prayer for that "Godwin boy" to be in my life, Dean and I started dating. I found out that Dean was a Christian and that he attended church. Had I known this, I would have been even more serious about praying for him to be in my life! This was a win/win situation for me. I was excited to try the church thing again! When I expressed interest in going to church with him, he said, "Sure. We can go to the evening service." I'm not sure why he didn't want me to go to the morning church. (Evening church was a shorter, less formal church service.) But, knowing Dean as I do, I'm sure he thought I would find it boring. There also wouldn't be as many people in the evening, so not as many people would see him with me. He had been dating a girl from that church for about two years. She was also four years older than me, and I'm sure that he wasn't sure he wanted me in his life *YET.* He didn't want people asking questions about me. I was the little girlfriend for the time being.

I had entered into a relationship with God, and I didn't know how I was going to be able to attend church since I didn't drive at the time. I was sure my parents had no desire to take me to a church, so I thought God was very smart for giving me this guy so I could go to church!! I was now a Christian and Christians go to church, so this was *PERFECT!*

After I had been around awhile, Dean decided that he liked me enough to start taking me to the morning church service. This is when I figured out we had a problem — I didn't own any dresses! I know that sounds weird, but why would I need a dress? I didn't go to church, and my family didn't go to places I needed to wear a dress. Dean didn't think this was too big of a problem. He took me shopping, and I found a couple of dresses, so now I was ready to go to church.

> **Ripple:** Do you know people who don't attend because they still think you have to dress up to go? Start a God conversation and talk about what people wear to church. Or invite someone to church and let them know it's a casual thing. People who don't attend church don't know that!

The same problem happened at Dean's church that happened during my previous experience with church. I couldn't understand a thing they were saying. They were using Christian words I didn't understand and not putting the Bible passages into everyday circumstances. This was a very theological church, and they talked over my head. (Churches now have gotten much better about explaining the verses that they are talking about.)

I did not learn a lot about God at church, but I did learn how to "do church." You would come in, find a seat in the back row, and sit. Then you stood and the pastor prayed. Then you sat again. While sitting, they made a few announcements about what was happening at the church for the following week. Then you stood to sing. You then sat down and the choir sang. Then you stood up and sang again. Then you sat and the pastor talked and prayed. Then you stood and shook hands with the people around you. Since you were still standing, you sang again. After all your exercise, you sat and the pastor talked for half an hour or more. While he talked, you looked at your watch to see how much longer he's going to talk and then he finally prayed. While the choir sang, you passed around containers to collect the money for the church (the offering). Then you stood and sang a final song. After all that, the pastor prayed and dismissed you. I had only gone to church a few times earlier in my life, so this was still all very new to me. All I kept thinking was, this seems like a lot of exercise. (At least now when you go to church you stand for a while and sing and then sit for the pastor's message. It used to be an up-and-down event.) I'm not complaining. I really did learn a lot, just not a lot about God and Jesus. I learned how to sit still and not fidget, to be quiet and look forward. If you were kind of sick, you would try not to cough and you only blew your nose while you were singing. You would have thought with all this instruction, I was attending church with a strict parent. But I wasn't. I was with Dean, who was only seventeen years old but had been going to church since he was a baby. He knew this was how you were to act at church. I did not want him to be embarrassed by me – to his family or those attending church. So he acted like a parent. I love my parents, but they didn't give a lot of corrections to me as a child. Nothing about saying please, thank you, or sitting still and being quiet. The only time they wanted me to be quiet was on car rides. Their idea on how to get me to be quiet was to play this one particular game with me and my brother.

They would tell us they would give fifty cents to whoever could be the quiet the longest. I was greedy, so it worked at first. But I liked to talk more than earn money, and I soon came to the conclusion that it wasn't worth fifty cents to be quiet. I had things to say.

I did learn a lot from the hymns we sang at church though. Listen, you can learn a lot from a good Christian hymn, especially if you sing all the verses. I think we do a disservice to young people and new believers by not singing at least one hymn during the services. There is something that sticks with you when you sing a slower paced song. Also, choir directors should read the words of songs!! If they say nothing about God or anything that does not glorify Him, why sing it in church? I love the current upbeat contemporary songs, but they are not the same as a hymn. It's called balance!! I also remember the stories behind the hymns, why the person wrote it, and what verse in the Bible we were singing about. I also like when they do this on Christian radio stations! It gives people who don't know the Bible, pieces of the Bible in song form . . . .like the song *I will follow* by Chris Tomlin. It's about Ruth and Naomi in the Bible. It's a short book of the Bible, a great story, and worth the read.

While I attended this church, I was baptized. (Baptism is an outward sign to show people that you are now a follower of Christ.)

Ripple: If you have not been baptized, make that commitment and invite family and friends to watch. If you were sprinkled as a baby, this is still something you should do as an adult. What a great way to show others you are a believer!

I was married at this church, and had all three of my children, Abigail (Abby), Zachary (Zack) and Katelyn (Katie) while attending this church. But I was not growing spiritually. Every once in a while, they would have guest speakers and they would say something I understood, then I would be hopeful, until the next week. Honestly, I don't understand why I didn't understand church; I did listen. Maybe the pastor assumed that everyone there knew what he was talking about or they had a theology degree. It seemed like I was in a different century or they were talking in a foreign language. I finally figured out that I was not learning much at this church. I now know that satan (This is not a typo! I just don't believe that the name satan deserves a capitalization) didn't want me to grow in my faith. While writing this book, I questioned why things took me so long to figure out. I think it may be that while you are in the middle of a situation, satan lulls you along, keeping you busy thinking about everything except what is most important in life. I was young and was starting a family. We built a house, and I was running my photography business. We were busy with life and not putting God first. I think this is what a lot of people do. They build their families and careers, and God gets put on the back burner. I finally reached the point when I decided I needed to start building a relationship with God, but wasn't quite sure what that looked like yet.

I thought when you went to church you would learn about God and how to be a better person. That is not how I felt after church. I only felt confused and that I wasted my time. So I decided I would try to help in the children's church with my kids. If I wasn't learning with the adults, maybe I needed to start at the beginning of this Bible/Christian stuff with my children.

I asked the children's pastor if I could help in one of my children's classrooms. This church had a strict policy that if you were not attending morning church services, evening church services, Wednesday night church services and Sunday school, you could not help with the children's church classes. They said, "Not at this time." I really felt discouraged. I wanted to learn about God but didn't know how. (This was before the internet.)

Though no one can go back and make a brand new start, anyone can start from now and make a brand new ending. - Carl Bard

DISCUSSION QUESTIONS: (I need to confess! Even now while doing book studies with my group, I don't look all the way to the end. More often than I would like to admit, halfway through we realize that there are discussion questions in the back of the book. So this is why my questions are right after the chapter you read.) One more thing . . . I wish I could be with you to hear your answers!!! You will figure out that I love questions and answers. Enjoy your questions. Bonus question . . . Have you written any ripples on your note cards yet? Have you pulled out note cards?

QUESTIONS

1. How would you feel if God asked you to write a book? What would your title be?

2. Do you wait for people to ask you about God or do you ask them? How?

3. Do you pray for each of your meals? Has anyone ever noticed you praying for your meal while eating out and said something to you?

4. What church function were you invited to that made the biggest impression on you?

5. Was the Bible read to you when you were young? Have you ever given someone a Bible? Who?

6. What movie or show has made a spiritual impact on your life and why?

7. Have you ever been baptized? How old were you when you were baptized? Where were you baptized? River? Ocean? Tub? Pool?

8. Have any bumper stickers made you think about God?

9. How do you start God conversations?

10. Have you ever led someone to the Lord? How did it make you feel?

3

---∽∾∿---

Hold on! The Waves Are Coming

BIG CHANGES

Somewhere in my soul I knew it was time to look for a new church. I wasn't sure why other than I wanted to learn more and be satisfied after attending church. The decision to switch churches was not easy. My husband attended this church in his mother's womb and grew up there. Plus, we were the last kids in my husband's family to still be in the church where his father attended.

I shared with Dean how I felt and I know he felt the same way because most of the time while the pastor was talking, he was working on his small hand held pocket calculator. (This was before cell phones.) I told Dean that when you go to church, you are supposed to be happy. You also should learn how to apply what you learned from church to your life so you can live for God. I don't know where these thoughts came from. (I was telling this to a person that had attended church all his life!) No one told me this; I just felt it. I now know this had to be God planting these ideas in my head. Dean wasn't so sure about leaving this church, (This man is *NOT* big on change!!) but he told me, I could go look.

When he saw that I was really going to do this, he started to come around and said that his older brother's family was going to another church down the road and asked that we try that one first. God bless my husband! He has always supported or at least followed me. He wasn't going to let me go alone, so we all went scouting this church as a family.

Ripple: Visit a new church occasionally to see how others do things. I'm not promoting church hopping, just try something new sometimes. Look for great ideas for your church to try! If you go out of town, make it a point to go church while traveling. I've been to many GREAT churches across this country! And I'm always looking for better ways to do things, and then I pass the information along!

When Sunday rolled around, we went to the new church. We were greeted by a friendly man named Dale, who asked us if we were visitors. We told him that we were and he welcomed us like old friends, then he showed us where we could take our children. Our son used to get very nervous about being left in new places, and he really wanted his younger sister to stay with him. Sharon, the teacher, was so nice. She said that it would be fine if they stayed together in the same room. Zack and Katie liked her right away. Our oldest daughter is a little like me. Dale pointed down the hallway to where her classroom was (she couldn't wait to be escorted) and off she went to make new friends. Abby didn't even say goodbye or ask us to follow her. Then we were shown the auditorium where the church service was held.

After the service, we were amazed at how different this church was – it was a night and day difference! The words to the songs were projected on a large screen at the front of the church. They were not slow hymns out of a hymnal book. No! These were fast upbeat Christian songs. The order of the service was different also. Here's the exciting news . . . I actually understood what this pastor said! It was like listening to church in my own language! I could even understand how to apply it to my life. Can we say *WOW?* We walked out of the past and into the present.

We walked out of church with smiles on our faces that day. I learned more in that hour of church than I had for the previous eleven years. (That's an exaggeration, but close to the truth.) I couldn't wait until the next week! The younger kids were thrilled they were able to be in the same classroom and loved their teacher. Abby was excited that her cousin Amanda was in her same room. Oh, they didn't wear dresses either, just nice dress-up clothes. Even my husband did not look at his calculator during the entire service. We knew that we had found our new church home!

Like a puzzle, from that point on, the pieces were starting to fit nicely together. I had a lot to learn, but now I was hearing sermons that I could apply to my life. After attending for about a month, we took the pledge to join the church. After that service we were in the lobby chatting with people and were asked if we attended a Sunday School class yet (now called small groups). A couple told us they would love for us to attend their group. I, of course, was excited to go! I'm not sure about Dean, but he went along. I loved this Sunday School class! We were all different ages and it was small enough that we were able to get to know each other. We learned from people that had been doing church a lot longer than us and who had real experience with raising children. Plus, our children were excited to hang out longer with their new friends at church.

> **Ripple:** Invite someone to come to your small group.... friends, neighbors, or coworkers. Sometimes the small environment is less intimidating than going to a large church service. Once they get to know the people in the group, they will have friends they know when they attend the church service. Ask people even if they are in church. You never know if they are in a small group, and it's *ALWAYS* nice to be *ASKED!*

Being a Christian is more than just an instantaneous conversion - it is a daily process whereby you grow to be more and more like Christ. -- Billy Graham

This was the beginning of the learning process for me and God was making up for lost time! I was a sponge, soaking up two full hours of church a week. We joined the church in the spring and by that fall I was actually asked by some ladies to help in Awana clubs. Awana is based on the verse in 2 Timothy 2:15 and stands for *Approved Workmen Are Not Ashamed.* This is a church program designed for kids three to thirteen years of age. By the time we were in this church for six months, I was attending church *four* times a week. Sunday morning, Sunday school,

Sunday evenings, and now Wednesday evenings. Wow, it's amazing how inviting someone to be involved in church encourages them to attend more. What a concept!! It was so easy for this church to get us to come. They just kept *asking!* What a great way to get people involved in the community of church!

Volunteering on a Wednesday night was not an easy decision to make. I worked and taking out an entire evening of appointments from my schedule with my portrait business was a very *BIG* sacrifice. But I could tell God was leading me to do this, and would work things out. He did! I treasure those memories of Wednesday evenings with our kids and Awana. (I still have my uniform vest hanging in my closet.) The kids and I would usually eat out before we went to church and would wear our uniforms in the establishments. This was a great conversation starter about going to church.

Awana is where I learned all the well-known stories from the Bible: Moses and the ten plagues, Noah and the Ark, and more obscure ones like, Shadrach, Meshach, and Abednego and the fiery furnace. Remember . . . I did not grow up hearing these stories, and when you are not around church and the Bible, it's not easy to learn about God and Bible stuff. (Disclosure! This was all before internet searches! Of course, how do you search for something you don't know?) It's not as though this world is out to teach you about God, Jesus, and the kingdom of Heaven! This is how unchurched I was. At the age of sixteen, I didn't even know Easter was celebrated as a Christian holiday. Easter bunnies, egg hunts, and candy were all I had ever experienced. For some reason I did know that children went to church during Easter and received new outfits, but I didn't know why. It's very sad, but true. I didn't have a clue about what I didn't know. I wasn't going to let that happen in our family; our kids knew that Jesus's resurrection was way more important than all the other stuff.

I started with the Cubbies, (three to five year olds) with my two youngest children. When they moved to the next level to Sparkies, (Kindergarten to 2nd grade) so did I. Then came Chums, (3rd to 6th grade girls) so Zack and Katie were separated and I went with the girls. After several years of staying at home on Wednesday nights alone, I convinced Dean to volunteer to help in our son, Zack's 3rd-6th grade boys class.

When the kids graduated out of Awana, I was asked to be the co-commander of the program. This is where I got to be creative! We planned the "themed" evenings such as wacky hair night, Bible hero costume night, pajama night, and many others. We did this to get the kids excited about inviting friends to Awana. We also rewarded them with incentives. Rides across the several acres of the church property in army jeeps and big long decorated golf carts. One year, we even had a limo donated. We gave the kids pop and snacks and drove them around the block! They loved these incentives and attendance was always higher on these nights. Only God knows how many kids had seeds planted in their lives because they had an exciting experience at church.

Reaching children while they are young with the gospel is so important. Awana had many visitors because a section in their workbooks required them to invite a friend to church. I think they should have required inviting friends quarterly to church, but once was a great lesson to learn as a young person. The hope was that it would be a trait they continued even into adulthood. I would say that half of the kids who were invited to church functions would come more than once. (If you remember, I was probably only invited to church a few times but each of those times made a lasting impression on me. I can vividly remember each one. If my friends' parents would have kept taking me, I would have gone every week!) Inviting people to church and church functions is a good thing! Seriously, it bothers me that if Christians really believe that they have a better life and an eternity that will last forever in Heaven, *WHY?* . . . do they not invite people so that they can hear the Good News?

Another thing that I remember vividly from my youth is that while in the sixth grade, a group of girls at school were asking each other if they were going to Awana that night. I asked what this club was that they were talking about? They told me it was a church club and blew me off since I didn't belong in their group and was listening to a conversation that I wasn't included in. I would have been *THRILLED* to have been asked to go! I never forgot the name of that club but didn't figure out what it was until I was asked to help. I'm glad I was finally *ASKED!*

Ripple: Tell your children and grandchildren to ask and have conversations about Awana and other church functions with kids at their schools. Remind them that they like to be asked to go to activities and be included. Ask them to invite and be willing to pick their friends up. Suggest this to your church leaders: offer a huge reward to the young person that brought the most visitors throughout the year to Awana, Sunday School, VBS, and youth groups. Think about it-if they invite people while they are younger, they won't have as many hang-ups as an adult, and they will make this a lifetime habit that they will continue to do!

MY TURNING POINT

Our church gave parents the opportunity to send their children to camp each summer. The younger kids went with the youth pastor and a few parent volunteers as chaperones. Volunteers were needed, so they *asked* me if I could help out for a week at camp. OK ... *really???* There does come a time when you don't want to be asked to do *EVERYTHING!* I wasn't sure I was ready for church camp.

I never went to camp as a kid, especially one that was for a full week and overnight. I almost went to a Campfire Girls Camp, but my parents took me to see the camp and it looked dirty. I'm a naturally tidy person. I told my parents that I couldn't see myself going to that camp, and my parents said, "Ok." They didn't push the subject, not even a little! They were kind of "hands off" type of parents, which in turn did make me very independent.

Not only does God have a great sense of humor, He loves to push me out of my comfort zone. Unlike my parents, if God gets it in His mind that I need to do something that is good for me, I might as well just surrender!! He's NOT good at taking no for an answer. I'm not the only one that has had to do what God has asked them to do, just ask Jonah! You know the story in the Bible where the guy was swallowed by the whale? God asked Jonah to go to Nineveh to share the gospel with the people there, but he went in the opposite direction from where God told him to go. He was then swallowed by a whale. I'm not saying that if you disobey God, He makes your life miserable. But God can be very persistent! I'm sure Jonah got the hint as to what God wanted him to do, moments after he was hot, slimey, and smelling like a fish! The story ends with Jonah pouting, but Nineveh rejoicing! Read for yourself. (Jonah 1:1-17) Just like Jonah, I tried to get out of going!

Try and fail, but don't fail to try. -- *John Quincy Adams*

I told Bill, the youth pastor, that I couldn't sleep without air conditioning. I let him think I had allergies. Guess what? I think this is the only church camp with air conditioning in our area! I said that I couldn't go because I had two younger children, and I was responsible for their care. Guess what he said? Take them along. (They were old enough to do most of the activities with mom around.) I then told him I couldn't ride on the church bus. I didn't give a reason, but I think he assumed I suffered from motion sickness. Of course by now you guessed it, he said I could follow the bus in my van and thought it was a great idea because they needed the extra seats. Needless to say, I gave up . . . or at least I couldn't come up with any more excuses. So, with much uncertainty, I said goodbye to Dean, packed up the kids, and drove the eight hours behind the church bus to camp. God was pulling on my arm telling me, "Come on, this is good for you. We will have an adventure, and you will like it!"

Going to camp was *SOOO* out of my comfort zone! This was the first time that I had ever traveled without Dean for a whole week. I slept with a bunch of kids in dirty camp bunks in the same room and figured out that even kids can snore loudly. The showers had slimy floors, and showering with everyone wasn't much fun. There was not a day that the women's toilets didn't need help being unplugged. – *and* there was no privacy at all, at any time. Good thing I didn't drive all the way to Missouri to check it out first. I *could* have come up with a few more arguments! But, it's amazing how terrible things can seem while you're in the mess, but then look back and remember it fondly.

I'm still not sure who got more out of that week at camp, the kids attending or me. I was *radically* changed!! I believe it was the turning point in my spiritual life. The messages that week were about if you are on the fence about a decision that you have to make, you have already made a decision! Because NO decision is a decision. If you never ask Christ to be in your life and you die without asking Him, the decision is made. If you never read your Bible, the decision is made. If you don't do something God wants you to do, you are making a decision . . . a decision to not do it!

Even if you are on the right track, you will get run over if you just sit there. - Will Rogers

I became aware that I needed to mature as a Christian. I had been happy to grow spiritually at the same level as my children, but I *was* an adult. It was time to start growing faster and deeper in my spiritual life. The leaders also talked about who or what was on the top of the pedestal in your life? I didn't have to give that one much thought. It was my husband. Dean was more important to me than God. Most women will put their kids on the top pedestal of their lives and men will put their careers. I had put Dean. According to God, there should *NOT* be anyone or anything more important in your life than Him. Having Dean as the top priority in my life, caused me to worry about what I would do if he ever left me – in divorce or death. It almost made me not go to camp. Dean didn't have a problem with me going to camp with the kids, but I couldn't imagine leaving him at home alone and being away from him.

God was working on my heart and needed me to be isolated away from Dean in order to hear Him and get my priorities in order. God first, Dean second, and then the kids. When I made the decision to get the order right, peace settled in. God impressed upon me to stop worrying about what would happen if Dean was gone. The Lord was not going to leave me. He would be with me for the rest of my time on Earth and into eternity.

New decisions and priorities began to happen in my life by putting God first. Ones that would change how I conducted myself. I was no longer afraid of divorce, and was more relaxed about where Dean was during the day and what he was doing. (He checked on different job sites, and I never knew where he was.) I started making decisions based on what God thought I should do. I felt more confident, if that was even possible! Maybe . . . I was more at peace!

The second problem that needed to be worked out, was that I am not the one in charge or in control of my circumstances. It was not my schedule or my plans at the camp, which puts me out of my comfort zone. I was at the mercy of the ones in control. They told me when to get up, when to eat, and when to go to bed. What can I say? I like being in control of my little world. From the time I graduated high school and started my own business, I've set my own schedule. – Even with our kids – they went where I was going – whenever I wanted to go. They were on *my* schedule. I was not on theirs. Sure, I took their schedules into account, but they adapted to me.

When you think about your life, are you *really* in control? No! Everything that happens all day long is not in our hands. We can make our plans, but the Lord determines our steps (Proverbs 16:9). I knew that I was not letting God be in charge of my life. I wanted to be the one in charge! Slowly, during the week, I realized that having God be in control of my life was going to work out much better than charging ahead of Him. Waiting for God was something I was going to have to work on. (I'm still working on this!!!) But I'm not the only one in history that has moved ahead of God. Take for example Abraham and Sarah. They were making their plans on their time table, but look how that worked out. Read in Genesis 16:2 where Sarai said to Abram, (these were their names before God changed them) "Go sleep with my servant and have children with her." The Bible has some very scandalous parts to it! Read the full story in Genesis 16. We all need an example to remind us to wait on God. Our choices have consequences.

If you want to make God laugh, tell Him about your plans. - Woody Allen

Now, *DON'T* let all the negativity of what I said about camp scare you out of serving, because it's one of the best things I've done! God needed me to get away from all the distractions in my life in order focus on Him! Camp might have been geared for the kids, but I was the one who grew spiritually. (I will let you in on a little secret. When the campers and counselors all played hide and seek at camp, the bus and car section was off limits, but I snuck over and hid in my van just to feel closer to home! I needed a few minutes to know that I was going to be okay! So be kind to your kids when they get a little homesick. Even this adult got homesick!) Camp was over, and I had survived. I wished the church, camp, or youth pastor would have given me a t-shirt with *"I survived church camp"* written on it. I would have that shirt hanging in my closet right next to my Awana uniform!

Ripple: Why not sponsor one child to go to church camp? There are always children that can't afford to go. Or organize a scholarship fund at your church to help kids pay for camp. Children are like adults; they need to have time alone with God so they can see the direction they need to take in life. Or better yet!! Volunteer your time and go to church camp with the kids.

Another thing I learned at church camp was that Christians have really cool upbeat rock-type music. *Who knew?* My kids were still young and *nobody* told me. They played Steven Curtis Chapman at every service and before we left camp, I bought a CD and listened to it all the way home. I loved his song *"Dive"*.

A few weeks after camp, my friend Janet told me about a radio station that played upbeat Christian music. (We actually have three different Christian stations in our area). *WOW!!!* Call me clueless again! That was a game changer. I have listened ever since. Listen . . . Christian music isn't advertised everywhere. Yes, I have seen bumper stickers for these radio stations, but they don't promote "upbeat Christian" music on them! I seriously don't know how people find these stations unless they spend a lot of time scanning their channels. I learned through word of mouth. Christians ought to talk about these things more often. I know this is very basic, but not all Christians know these things, especially baby Christians and unbelievers. This is so true! While writing this book I introduced another Christian to this type of music, and she didn't know about it either! We are not talking about old gospel music. They have a lot of different genres--country sounding, rock, hip/hop, fast and slow. I love to crank it loud and dance and sing in my car while driving down the street or while dusting my house. There have been so many good lyrics that have spoken to my heart over the years that I could fill a book.

When I discovered this type of music, I had been listening to Disney CD's with our children for so long, I didn't even want to get in my van anymore!! Christian music is adult oriented but definitely kid friendly! Praise the Lord! Now when people ride in my van, it is always on. God's uplifting messages are sung through the lyrics, unlike the music that is played on secular radio where they sing about drugs, sex, and who they broke up with – and hate! Definitely not kid or adult friendly and definitely not *encouraging*!!!

Music and memories go together. Songs cause us to remember different moments of time in our lives. I love the memory of the moment, but when some songs are played, I'm embarrassed because of what the lyrics say. For example: "Achy Breaky Heart,"sung by Billy Ray Cyrus (this was my country phase). Our oldest daughter danced to that song when she was about two years old. (Terrible lyrics for young ears to listen to!) I love the memory of Abby dancing, but regret what she was listening to. I've listened to Christian music for years now, so my memories of different songs are not with regrets.

Many passengers have asked what I'm listening to and I'm always excited to tell them about my music. How powerful the messages are in the songs and how many times God has played the right song at just the right time – songs that helped me through several rough times in my life and songs that have encouraged me to live out my faith! There is so much negativity in this world. Do we really want more in the songs we listen to?

Ripple: Try Christian radio for a week? Why not make it a point to tell this story of how I didn't know these radio stations existed and let Christians know to spread the word about Christian radio stations. Contact your stations and tell them they should tell their listeners to tell other people about them. Try to tell five people about Christian radio stations in the next week. Also, listen to these stations at work and everywhere you are. You never know who may start listening.

NO TURNING BACK

The day I surrendered my life to God seems like yesterday. I'm not talking about the day I accepted Christ as my Savior. I'm talking about – *God, here's my life, take and use it however you choose!*

While attending church camp, I became friends with Melanie. We had great God talks after we returned home. During one of our talks, I was up on some scaffolding painting the ceilings of our home. Melanie asked me if I had surrendered my life to God. "Yes, He's my personal Savior." Was she confused? Couldn't she tell I was a Christian? "No," she said. "Have you surrendered your life to Christ? Will you serve the Lord anyway He wants or anywhere He wants?" My first thought was ***I'm not sure if I can*** *do that.* I don't tend to take things lightly when it comes to God stuff. I don't want to make a promise to Him that can't be kept.

I do not like being cold. I seriously fear being cold. That may be an understatement. *I really, really HATE being cold.* So my thoughts were, what if God sends me to Antarctica? Seriously, this was my first thought while thinking about surrendering my life to Christ. Some people don't want to go to Africa and live in the jungles with snakes and wild animals when they think of serving God. Not me. Give me snakes over being cold any day! (I've already put in my request with God, to be in the warmer section of Heaven!!) *IF...* I surrender to God, He could decide to send me somewhere cold. I know this was not logical reasoning! I was scared and told Melanie my arguments. She of course laughed, but she was gracious and reminded me that if God sent me to Antarctica, God could make me warmer on the inside or make it less cold there. Ok . . . I could not argue with that. She said that if God called me to go somewhere cold, He has my best interest at heart.

> *The will of God will not take us where the grace of God cannot sustain us. - Billy Graham*

I rationalized all the reasons why I should surrender my life and could only come up with one reason not to. The decision was made! I remember climbing down the scaffolding, getting on my knees, and telling God that He could have *ALL* of my life. *Wherever* He wanted to send me, *whatever* He wanted me to do, I was willing. If He wanted me to be poor, sick, or take my family, He is God and He knows best. (I'm a firm believer that God can do whatever He wants, so I'm not sure why I hesitated.) Jesus is a gentleman, and He won't force His will on us. He just wants us to join with Him in His mission to glorify His Father and to further His kingdom!

The next morning, I expected a call asking me to be a missionary to Antarctica. I know! I know!! But it did cross my mind. As you continue reading, you'll see I've had many opportunities to test myself to trust God with my life.

Many years later, the study group discussed Kay Warren's book, *Dangerous Surrender*. In it, Kay says, "Accepting God's will in our circumstances is the hardest thing He asks of us because it requires denying ourselves and taking up our crosses." Perhaps, this is a foreign concept to you. If you are truly committed to God, why would you not surrender to Him? You might have thought that accepting Jesus Christ as your Savior was the same thing. Surrendering is something that goes way beyond being saved from Hell. Consider what you are truly saying to God. I trust you with my life and everything I have. After making that commitment, you will still surrender your life to God as a daily exercise. It's like a marriage. When you get married you are committed, but you still surrender your way every day.

When we were done, I realized that over the years I had become more and more selfish with *MY* time and *MY* family. My time, what a joke! Time is a precious gift that you only get to use once. Writing this book has taken a lot of *MY* time away from things I would rather do – reading a good book and enjoying it, but I was being obedient. It hasn't been all bad. I've learned a lot about myself, and Max Lucado doesn't have anything to worry about as I don't see writing in my future, although, I didn't see myself writing *this one* either!

Have you ever stopped to think about the things that God has asked you to do? Do you regret any of them? Stopping by the hospital to see a sick friend, helping those that have been hit by a natural disaster, hosting a Bible study, working at a shelter? The list could go on and on. I'm not saying that you have to be serving all the time, but ask yourself, when was the last time God prompted your heart to do something for Him? In Kay's book she asks the question, "In what ways are you allowing God to *rearrange* your schedule, your finances, your affections, so that you can regularly interact with those He loves?" It was a really good question; one that prompted me into action as you will read later.

What you are is God's gift to you, what you become is your gift to God. - Hans Urs von Balthasar

What I'm talking about is that small voice inside of you that says, "I need help over here." or "Go be my hands and feet over there." Maybe you have stopped hearing that voice. Maybe you have never heard God ask you to help Him somewhere. Stop right now and ask God if there is something that you could be helping with that could further His kingdom. Matthew

25:34-45 says, "Then the King will say to those on his right, 'Come, you who are blessed by my Father, inherit the Kingdom prepared for you from the creation of the world. For I was hungry, and you fed me. I was thirsty, and you gave me a drink. I was a stranger, and you invited me into your home. I was naked, and you gave me clothing. I was sick, and you cared for me. I was in prison, and you visited me.' "Then these righteous ones will reply, 'Lord, when did we ever see you hungry and feed you? Or thirsty and give you something to drink? Or a stranger and show you hospitality? Or naked and give you clothing? When did we ever see you sick or in prison and visit you?' And the King will say, 'I tell you the truth, when you did it to one of the least of these my brothers and sisters, you were doing it to me!' Then the King will turn to those on the left and say, 'Away with you, you cursed ones, into the eternal fire prepared for the devil and his demons. For I was hungry, and you didn't feed me. I was thirsty, and you didn't give me a drink. I was a stranger, and you didn't invite me into your home. I was naked, and you didn't give me clothing. I was sick and in prison, and you didn't visit me.' Then they will reply, 'Lord, when did we ever see you hungry or thirsty or a stranger or naked or sick or in prison, and not help you?' And he will answer, 'I tell you the truth. When you refused to help the least of these my brothers and sisters, you were refusing to help me." Now that you read what Jesus said, ask that question again. 'Lord, is there anything that you would like me to help with?' . . . *Now, listen!*

After reading Kay's book and knowing I really wasn't doing anything to help "the least of these," I started volunteering at a women's shelter leading a Bible study.

Ripple: This is a really Big Thing. Surrender your life to God. Think about what that means. Moving if He wants you to move, fostering children if He wants you to foster, write a book if He asks you to do that!!! Ask other Christians if they have surrendered their lives to Christ, explain if necessary. All Melanie did was ask me. I was confused at first, but my life has never been the same since I surrendered my whole life to God.

IN HIS WORDS

After church camp, I wanted to know God more. That meant I needed to put the time and effort into building my relationship with Him. That's how you fall in love with God – spending time with Him. It was time to hear what God said about Himself directly. I decided to start reading my Bible. That sounds easy, but the only Bible I owned was a King James Version, which is written in old English. It has words like 'cometh, seeketh, or doeth'. (As I typed those words, my computer thought they were typos.) I needed modern English not Shakespeare words.

I struggled reading my Bible, and I had doubts I would even understand what I read. But, God must have wanted me to read His Word. While photographing a high school senior (I was a portrait photographer for twenty-four years) we got into a God-conversation about reading the Bible. I explained the trouble I had understanding all the Old English words, and that I was flustrated (No that's not a typing error. My book, my word.) He suggested the Bible version he read. I didn't understand what he was talking about at first. This young man proceeded to explain to me about the different kinds of versions in easy-to-read formats. (It's the same Bible; written in more modern English so you can understand what you are reading.) He suggested a few options to look for at the Family Christian Store. After looking through several Bibles, I settled on the New Living Translation. Bless that young man!! What a difference it made in reading the Bible. This is another thing nobody at the church told me. Who knew they make easy-to-read Bibles? (Disclosure: This was before Bible apps, and again I could have looked it up but, how do you look for something you don't know exists?)

> **Ripple:** Download the Bible app if you don't have it. Bible apps give you different translations of the Bible and different reading plans. If you commute to work, there's an option for the Bible to be read aloud while you drive! Share this knowledge with others. Start reading or listening today.

While I could now understand the words in my Bible, I still didn't know *how* to read the Bible. Where do I start? What am I reading? Did I ask anyone? No! Sometimes I just do things the hard way, on my own. I'm not sure where most people start reading their Bibles. The beginning was the logical place to start. So that's where I started – Genesis, the first book in the Bible. I read about Adam and Eve, Cain and Abel, Noah and the Ark, and Abraham, Isaac, and Joseph. It was a fast read. These were all the Bible stories we had read to our children. I wondered what other stories were left to read since most of the famous ones were all at the beginning.

Then came Moses in Exodus. I found out that there was a lot more to the Moses story in the adult Bible than in the children's version! A lot of details about the Tabernacle . . . way more! I didn't remember reading all the rules in Leviticus in the kid's Bible . . . too bad as it might have made them think my rules were easier to remember. And if the children's Bible would have had all those genealogies, the kids would have asked to go to bed early. It was nice to read stories I remembered from the children's Bible because now I knew the rest of the story and I felt more adultish.

> God meant for the Bible to be bread for our daily use, not
> just cake for special occasions. - Suzanne Woods Fisher

Moses had a lot of coverage in the Bible! Then I read the chapters of the measurements of how big the temple was and, *wow*, some of those chapters were *LONG!* Also, there were many things that happened in the Old Testament, that were a bit odd! Lot's daughters . . . what were they thinking??? Read for yourself, (Genesis 19:30-38) This story was definitely not in the kids' version. (People think we are living in strange times right now! Read your Bible! People have always been sinful. We just hear more about it now.)

When I had finally made it to the New Testament, it was familiar to me. I had heard enough sermons on this section, so I understood more of it. But by the time I got to Luke, I thought maybe I had been reading it too long. Every time I would read a new book in the Bible, I felt I was reading the same stories. So, I flipped through what I had already read, just to see if I was losing my mind. After finding several of the same stories in different books of the Bible, I decided to ask our children's pastor, Bill, the one who roped me into going to church camp. I said to him, "I don't understand the Bible. I keep reading the same stories over and over in different sections." He laughed! (What a nice Christian thing to do!) Then he explained that each section, Matthew, Mark, Luke and John, were all different books of the Bible. That were written by different authors about the same stories from their perspectives. That the Bible is sixty-six books combined into one and was written over a span of 1,500 years.

I know that pastors can't tell you everything, but some basics would be nice. A few years back, I was at a church where the pastor said that the message he was preaching about was a small piece of a larger story! He used the analogy of *Star Wars*. He said, "The Bible is one big story, but all the little stories along the way help give more background to the main story line." God wants to have a relationship with us and that is the main point He tries to get through to us from the beginning to the end. . . . That would have been helpful for me to know the first time I read the Bible.

When I started this journey, I had many questions about the Bible but didn't know where to turn. I could have asked someone, but I didn't know who to ask *or* what to ask! The churches I attended did not have new believer programs. Now there are different programs such as the Alpha and discipleship programs where you meet with a group of new believers or one-on-one with a leader. This is where people can go and hear an overview of the Bible, Jesus, God, and what the church is all about. These are programs where people can ask many of the questions I had. So, if you know someone that is new to the Lord, be sure to direct them to these types of classes. (Of course now there is the internet, BUT you cannot believe everything you read on the internet. Plus, *you don't always know what to ask.*)

Ripple: Start a Bible study in your home for new Christians or invite a few friends over to your house for a question and answer session on the Bible. People will ask questions if they know that they won't be laughed at.

Now that I understood the repetition thing, I kept reading. I figured out a few things that were said from the pulpit that weren't correct. Nothing big, but I had a pastor who was so in love with his wife that he said he would be married to her in Heaven. Wrong! I read the Bible about this, and it does not say we will be married to our spouses in Heaven. (Matthew 22:29-30) Another pastor told me that God did not know when we were going to die. Wrong! Now that I had read my Bible, I knew that God said He knew me in the womb and that all my days were numbered. (Psalm 139:16) After making these discoveries, I understood the importance of reading the Bible! Some other misconceptions – I was told that interracial marriages were being unequally yoked. But the Bible, clearly says in 2 Corinthians 6:14, "Do not be yoked together with unbelievers. For what do righteousness and wickedness have in common? Or what fellowship can light have with darkness?" I wondered how anyone could think it had anything to do with the color of your skin or what township you were from. When the Bible was written, it talked about people from certain towns that were not as good as people from other towns, which would still be a discrimination thing. But this verse is clearly saying that a believer in Jesus Christ should not get into a marriage with an unbeliever. I also heard a pastor say that God doesn't do miracles anymore as He did in the Old Testament. God does miracles every day! I've had plenty in my own life and in the lives of the people I know. Maybe it's your definition of a miracle. God can't be put into a box. He's God and He can do what He wants! I'm not saying that I haven't learned from pastors, because I have. Pastors have a hard job! They can't teach you everything because there isn't enough time. That's why it's important for *YOU* to read the Bible.

> **Ripple:** Pastors work 24 hours a day, 365 days a year and need to be encouraged. Send a thank you note to a current or previous pastor and encourage them by letting them know the ways they helped you grow spiritually. Also be sure to pray for your pastor every day!

God speaks to your heart when you read His Word. He illuminates what is important for you to know at the time. I've read through the Bible several times already in my life. I'm not an in-depth student of the Bible as I could be, but I read it and other books from people that have studied it. It's also not about how fast you read it – It's just that you do.

> *Success seems to be largely a matter of hanging on*
> *after others have let go. - William Feather*

People say they don't have time to read God's Word, *but is that true?* If you have time to watch commercials, go through junk mail, read the newspaper about things that don't matter for eternity, watch YouTube videos, and get on Facebook. If you do any one of those things, **you do have time.** If you have a phone that you carry with you, download a Bible app such as YouVersion. You can pick daily plans and what translation you prefer. I'm not talking about languages here, (but you can do that too), I'm talking about really modern speech of today like "The Message" version. Or if you prefer a more poetic version, "Old English" might be the version for you. I prefer the NLT (New Living Translation) which is easy to read. You can also have your Bible app read to you while you drive to work or on your way to pick up the kids from school. In time, you will get through the entire Bible. I promise! My plan is to keep on reading the Bible daily until the day I die. This could be your plan, too! So, before you look at another puppy or kitty video or read another unnecessary piece of junk mail, give God some of your time. This is me pulling you away from the less important stuff so you can make a ripple. Not only for yourself, but so that others might be inspired to read their Bible because you do. The knowledge you gain you can share with others.

> **Ripple:** Try reading your Bible, even if it's only ten minutes a day. It all adds up! As you read your Bible, you can use it as a conversation starter with co-workers or family members. You can say – wow, do you know what I read in the Bible today? Or wow, I had no clue that this happened in the Bible until I read it today in my daily reading. Also encourage other believers to read their Bibles. Hold each other accountable. We need to be prepared to give answers when people ask.

The Bible is His instruction book for our life. BIBLE – **B**asic **I**nformation **B**efore **L**eaving **E**arth! This is something that is worth your time here and for eternity.

Truly, it's really sad how many Christians have never read the Bible. Just ask ten people. Non-Christians, you may get one in ten that have read the entire Bible, but I doubt it. Christians, you might get three out of ten that have read the entire Bible. Be one of the three!!! If someone says they've read the entire Bible (and you don't believe them), ask them about Lot's daughters. If they've read the Bible, they will remember that story! I dare you to read all of Genesis. And then keep reading. Don't be a lukewarm Christian!

When all is said and done, more is often said than done! - Lou Holtz

QUESTIONS

1. Do you go to church when you are out of town? Did you feel welcomed? What was the best experience you've had?

2. Do you go to a small group? Have you ever invited someone to come to the small group?

3. Did you go to church camp? What pivotal moment did you have? Did you get homesick? Do you have fond memories of it?

4. Do you listen to Christian music? How did you find out about it? Have you told someone about Christian music?

5. Have you ever surrendered your life to God? Did you have concerns before you committed your life to Him?

6. Do you have a Bible app on your phone? Have you ever told someone about the Bible app?

7. Have you ever led a Bible study? Have you ever been asked to be in a study group?

8. Have you ever encouraged your pastor? How? Do you pray for your pastor daily?

9. Do you read your Bible? Have you ever read the entire Bible?

10. What is your favorite book of the Bible? Why?

4

—◦◦◦—

Throwing My Own Stones

ACTIVITY DIRECTOR

When I was about ten years old, there was a show on TV called *"The Love Boat."* One of the main characters, Julie, was the activity director on the cruise ship. I thought she had a great job. She loved being around people, and she planned all sorts of fun things for the guests on the ship to do. That was what I wanted to do when I grew up. Of course, someone would eventually tell me I had to move away from home since there were no cruise ships in Iowa, and that put an end to those plans.

I have tried my hand at being an activity director, but not at sea. I love to plan things for others. I want people to have fun and find joy from being around other believers. I have planned activities for Awana and the JOY group (Jesus.Older.Youths) and with other various groups I have been a part of. I'm always looking for opportunities to entertain. I'm open for suggestions . . . and God usually has some.

One year as camp was getting closer, the idea of hosting a church camp at my house was put on my heart. I don't think it came as a big surprise to Dean when I asked him about the idea. After driving eight hours to another state with third and fourth graders, I thought there had to be a better solution. I did suggest the camp an hour north of our church, but they chose not to pursue it at the time. So I suggested another solution to our church leaders. We could hold a camp at my house.

We had a pool, a pool house, and several acres of land. Did I mention . . . a great husband who doesn't discourage me, and good friends who will help me with my different ideas? This was simple – we will just have a church camp at my house with second through fourth graders. *How hard can it be?* Plus, I could get my nieces and nephews to go to camp as well as my children's friends.

I convinced the church leaders that this was in their best interest and mine. (I wouldn't have to go away to camp anymore, I could stay home in my own bed at night and send everyone home at the end of the day ☺. Since it was my plan (*really God's*) and my house – I would be in charge and make sure everything ran smoothly. Bill, the youth pastor said he would teach. (Good thing, since I was still learning this God stuff myself!) We would need someone for crafts and other adults to keep the kids entertained and corralled. I made a few calls and talked some friends into giving up a week in the summer to help. We had a few planning meetings where we worked out all the details . . . or so I thought. This is where my husband completes me. I'm the type of person who has the big idea, and I'm able to put most of it together. My husband is a detail person. He comes up with all the things I tend to think are not as important – until they are needed.

Dean only had two concerns. The first was that we only had one bathroom in the pool house, and we had about thirty kids coming to camp. My husband's solution was to rent a portable potty. He didn't just rent one, but he ordered two portable potties; one for the girls and one for the boys. (I told you he is good!)

The second concern was the home owner's insurance. Dean didn't want to get sued if something went terribly wrong at camp! So, I said I would make the necessary calls to make sure that the camp was covered with insurance. Who wants to do something good and have it turn out terrible? The church's insurance company said they would cover all the kids since it was a church function just as if they were traveling somewhere to another camp. Perfect! But just in case, I called our insurance company, too. During this same time frame, I operated my portrait studio out of our home so we had a million dollar umbrella policy that would cover my clients in case there were any accidents. Common sense would say I was covered, but when I talked to our insurance company, they said, *"NO."* I told them that the church's policy would cover it. Again they said, *"NO."* They said that I was not covered as a camp, and they didn't want the kids swimming in the pool. It made me question if they would even cover any accident that would happen if some child was over at my house and happened to drown. After several common sense arguments from me, she said, "Sure, that should be fine. You can have a camp and we will cover you." Finally, common sense prevails! All the planning was done and all the details were worked out. We were ready for camp!

On the first day of camp, I was at the church checking the kids in. Soon they would be jumping on the church bus and riding fifteen minutes to my house (church camp). While I waited for all the kids to check in, I received a call from Dean who told me that the insurance company had just canceled our home policy! *WHAT???* Are you kidding me? I have thirty plus children all ready to come to camp, and I don't have any insurance! This is when I realized that satan was real, and that he didn't like me or what we were trying to do.

This is how ludicrous the insurance company was. The camp was going to last one week. *ONE WEEK!* They have to cover me for thirty days after they cancel my policy!!! *30 DAYS!!* So even if they cancel my policy, they still have to cover the week of camp. As far as the kids were concerned camp had started and I didn't have home insurance. (Well . . . I did for thirty days.) I should have gotten the approval in writing. I'm sure at some point the person on the phone, listening to my reasoning as to why we should be covered, told me what I wanted to hear while she was typing up the cancellation notice!

This is where satan likes to attack me. He uses arguments between me and my husband. I get easily distracted from everything else when we are in a disagreement. Dean was very upset with the fact that we didn't have home insurance because of this ludicrous camp idea of mine. I felt terrible!

As the kids lined up to get on the bus, I drove home from the church, almost in tears. My husband was angry, we had no insurance, and our rates would probably go up! I *hate* spending more money on things that I know should be cheaper. I was holding a church camp for God and felt this was *not* supposed to happen while doing something good for The Kingdom.

(Later I figured out this is when satan wants to derail your plans for God!) When I arrived home, I went straight to my knees in prayer. *What else can you do?* There was no time to track down another insurance company, the campers would arrive shortly.

While I prayed, my wonderful husband was making calls to insurance companies, (which I didn't know). I was in crisis mode! How would I run a business out of our home with no coverage? What if the house burned down? So many thoughts ran through my head, but my thoughts should have been about the kids. (I was fighting a spiritual battle!)

Before the kids arrived, Dean called and said he had it handled! He talked with a different insurance company and explained about the church camp. Guess what my wonderful friend God did? Insurance! *Better coverage and cheaper!!!* Plus, Dean wasn't upset anymore! That's when I knew for sure God was so much bigger than satan. God had it handled. Everyone arrived and the fun began!

> **Ripple:** Look for ways to use your home for the church. Do you have a farm, pumpkin patch, pond or other asset? Or a skill like cooking, sewing, or mechanics? (The schools have cut these programs.) Offer the church to provide your assets or skills to kids or adults!!!

We were blessed with really great weather and time spent learning about Jesus. I loved seeing our home and yard being used to glorify God and people enjoying it. The time spent serving Him alongside friends was a blessing also. (The portable potties were necessary, but I was very glad when they left my yard!)

Church camp was a success in that nobody was seriously injured! (Okay, one child did receive stitches!) We had a great turnout of "church kids" who attended over the two years we offered camp. But when the second year was over and we could count the number of visitors on one hand, we decided it was too much work for kids that were already attending church every week.

All the time and effort on everyone's part to put on such a quality program made it disappointing that people did not use it as an outreach to others. I'm just saying that when given such an opportunity, why would you not invite people? We did charge for the camp, but I'm sure it was way below what daycare would cost for a week, and what a great experience. So why did they not invite their neighbor kids, friends, or cousins? This is something I don't understand.

During this stage of my life, kids were where I did my ministering. (My photography business was by appointment only, so I could schedule around different events.) The next thing I moved on to help with was Vacation Bible School (VBS). At this point, I'm sure you figured out that the youth pastor, Bill, saw a lot of me.

With all our children activities we went out of our way to create a lot of incentives to get the kids to bring visitors to church. At the end of the Awana season, we would hold an awards ceremony for the different accomplishments that the children completed. Children were to encourage their families to attend. VBS also held a parent night where the children put on a short program of songs they learned during the week. Both were ways to encourage the children to bring their families to church.

We were big on rewarding those who brought the most visitors. I would go out of my way to take all the kids in the neighborhood to all of the church functions. Of course, leaders couldn't win prizes, but I set a good example! The time to get Christians to step out of their shell is when they are young. When you grow up inviting your friends, it's just a natural thing to do as an adult. Both of our adult daughters invite people to Bible studies and church all the time. I'm sure they think this is a normal thing to do, since they have done this all their lives.

> **Ripple:** Look for opportunities to invite children to church – VBS, camp, Awana and many other activities that churches do. My good friend Jenni started going to church all because someone *asked* her children to Awana And because of that, all of the Clapper family accepted Christ as their Savior.

USING GOD'S TALENTS

My husband and I came from very average income homes and both of our parents owned businesses. So we knew it was possible for either of us to own a business also. I started my photography studio a year out of high school; I was nineteen. Dean bought a business three years out of school and was twenty-one. My parents set aside some money to help me use for college, a wedding, or however I chose. I really wanted to spend it on a cute little sports car; but when Dean and I discussed what would be a better plan, I opted to buy all the photography equipment for my studio. Dean received about the same that I did from his mother's trust. (She passed away when he was sixteen.) He purchased a small business with his money.

We both made good decisions with what God gave us. It's like the parable that Jesus told about a master (boss) giving bags of silver to his different servants. Each servant received what the master proportioned to their abilities. Not all of the servants were given the same amount and not all produced the same return for the master. (Matthew 25:14-30)

Humility is not thinking less of yourself, it's thinking of yourself less. - Rick Warren

Dean never struggled with what we had financially, but it bothered me to have more than other people our age. There were many jealous people that came and went out of our lives. During these years several comments were made about what we had, who we were, and rumors about how we acquired our money. (None of which were true!) There were also people who held their distance from us because of the money.

I wanted to be judged by *who* I was as a person, not by *what* we had. Dean and I weren't flashy; we had a nice house and went on great vacations. (And went out of our way *not* to tell people where we were going.) On one occasion, after a comment was made, I went and hid in my closet. After spending time there crying and complaining, I listened. God gently spoke to my spirit, He reminded me that it was His money, and that we were to use it for His glory. He also asked me who I was to question what He had given us. That day changed how I looked at what we had and how we used His resources.

In the late nineties, gardening shows were a big deal on HGTV and I was hooked. So were several of the people I was hanging around with. To say I had gardening fever is really an understatement. It was an obsession! We had a pool in our backyard, and had a lot of space to landscape. Gardening became my hobby. It was something I could do while watching my children swim. Since my photography studio was in the lower part of our home, I used the yard for outside portraits with people so I could justify the time and finances spent on the landscaping.

Our pastor's wife at the time was big into gardening. She asked if I would put my garden and house on the tour with the church. I was excited to be asked by *the pastor's wife.* The tour was supposed to be an outreach, a way to get non-church people to come to a church function. This was a new *adult* way to serve God.

After the fact, I decided that the garden tour didn't really work that well. It ended up being a social gathering with not much of God in the middle of it. They had a great turnout, but it was mostly church people hanging out together. I know that getting believers together and making new friendships is a good thing, but church people already hang out. Why not introduce your friends outside of church to your friends inside the church, and have a bigger party! If you don't have any friends outside the church, you need to get some! There is an abundance of unchurched friends, waiting to become church friends!

The tours were also a discouragement to many of the ladies that saw my house. While they were touring, I heard a few murmurs. How did this young thirty year old have such a nice house? How could they afford it? It started a jealousy thing. (I told them the bigger the house is, the more you have to clean! Not sure if it helped.) Church people are human . . . just because we go to church doesn't mean that we don't still live in this world. We still struggle with jealousy and the same sins that people who don't go to church struggle with.

We should have only done the gardens and skipped the house tour. But the best thing that came about from that day was the pastor's wife opening up her own backyard and doing a very cute little garden party at the end. I thought this was a neat idea. A garden party would be fun, and it could be a *REAL* outreach. I put this in the back of my mind for a while and kept building my garden.

*The flowers of all our tomorrows are held in
the seeds of today. - Chinese Proverb*

It was a few years later, when God popped the garden party idea in my head again. If you haven't figured it out yet, if God thinks it's a good idea, I'm usually willing to put a plan into action providing it will reach those that don't know Jesus yet. I asked my friends who liked to garden and cook if they wanted to get together and reach out to the unchurched. They were excited to use their skills for God. We planned to have fun appetizers, a plant exchange, a self-guided garden tour and, of course, social time. But, if we were going to gather a lot of people, we needed to incorporate God.

During the first tour our backyard had many plants, but this time the yard was really landscaped; it had a pond, waterfall, firepit and the plants were bigger and more mature. Our house was what they wanted to see the first time, not my yard. But now, I knew my garden would be the focus – no house tour!

When I work on these outreaches, I can get side-tracked! Satan can make me think about things that are *not* that important. I become like Martha in Luke 10:38-42 where she runs around the house preparing for a party that Jesus is attending. Actually, Jesus is already there, and she's spending all her time in the kitchen getting mad that nobody is helping her. She is messing with things that are not all that important instead of spending time with her guest. I can be this way, too! I get so focused on insignificant stuff and think to myself, "If things are going to get finished, then I'm the one that is going to get it done!" Can you relate? After days of pruning, dead-heading, and so many other "important things," I was exhausted! But before everyone arrived, I needed to do one more thing! The sidewalks needed to be hosed off. (I was still immature as to what was really important – I should have been praying.) After spending an hour hosing off the sidewalk (I mean right after I turned off the hose), God decided that I missed a spot – the sky opened up and poured rain all over the yard while I stood there getting soaked! *Really,* I can't stress this enough. It was one of those nice days with just *one* cloud in the sky. The cloud wasn't even dark! It didn't even look like it could rain! The rain lasted only moments, and then it was clear the rest of the night. I guess you had to be there, but it was so funny! What took me over an hour to hose off, He washed in two minutes!

Before the guests arrived, we prayed, but it was brief. *Now,* I would have bathed the entire event in prayer. I may still have hosed it all down, but I would have prayed at the same time – for all who would be in attendance, the words the speaker would speak, the weather, ears to be open to hear the truth, hearts to be softened and so much more.

We encouraged the ladies to bring a plant out of their gardens to share for a plant exchange – so everyone could go home with a plant. We had appetizers (that were over the top fancy!) to enjoy while strolling through the garden. The weather was fabulous; it was a great evening to be outside enjoying God's beautiful creations! After everyone had time to chit-chat and look around, we gathered and had a speaker give a garden-themed speech with the gospel clearly presented. (It's amazing how much the Bible has to say about nature and gardens.) Before we ended the talk, we explained how to have a relationship with Jesus. We had several ladies in attendance that evening, including some of my relatives who were not believers yet.

We did these garden parties for about three years. Every year they continued to grow bigger and better. But I'm not sure how many unsaved people were invited. Again, it turned into a church social thing, even though it was not sponsored by a church. It seemed the church people who came brought other church people. But, Lord willing, it planted seeds.

I invited people from three cul-de-sacs to the garden party – only ten ladies from thirty houses came, but it wasn't from the lack of inviting. Again, what I find to be disappointing is how some won't even invite their unbelieving friends to outreaches like this. It was a fun opportunity with the gospel mixed in. We had invites printed to make the task as easy as saying, "Would you like to go to this garden party with me? It's something I want to go to, but not alone." Just ask.

> **Ripple:** Host a small garden party or a picnic and plan a way to introduce God into the event. Pray before the food and DON'T FORGET TO PRAY FOR THE EVENT!!!

Allow me to get a little preachy. When we get to Heaven and stand before God, He will show us how many opportunities we missed. (I will have plenty of my own things to answer for.) But I seriously, don't want God to show me the people I failed to invite to church or functions like this. I've read several books where unbelievers have said, "Nobody ever invited me to church or church function." That's a sad statement!

Every day I try to live my life in such a way that I accomplish at least one thing that will outlive me and last for eternity. - Vernon Brewer

If we believe we have a more abundant life than unbelievers and life after death, **why** do we keep it to ourselves? People in closed countries risk their lives to worship God. They may even go to prison for owning a Bible or even just one page of it. If they tell family members they've accepted Jesus Christ as their Lord and Savior, they risk being turned into the authorities! Some are excommunicated forever from their family, friends, and their communities. What's the worst thing that could happen to us here in the United States — our family members think we're strange. Sure, some may get mad at us for a while . . . why, I'm not sure. Maybe . . . some friends will stop hanging out with us, but I would rather lose a friend by telling them about Jesus than lose a friend for eternity by *NOT* telling them about Jesus! *THINK* about that last statement. Americans have become soft. Everything is supposed to be politically correct. Don't tell anyone that Jesus is the **only** way to God . . . that's offensive. Sometimes, we have to be offensive but with love! It's a matter of eternal life or eternal death! Think about it . . . who do you think planted the seed that Jesus is offensive? Satan . . . maybe? Okay, that's off my shoulders. Let's move on.

I mentioned earlier, we had a pool, landscaped yard, and a pool house. The same pastor's wife that asked me to do the garden tour asked us if we could host a couple of missionaries in our pool house. We were okay with that, but at the time there wasn't a bedroom. There was a bathroom, kitchen and an area to eat, but we said yes anyway. Dean bought a blow up bed and hung makeshift curtains for their privacy. It was not perfect . . . it might not have even been comfortable . . . but, they did stay for a few days.

After they left, my husband became excited about another project. He decided we needed to add on to the pool house with a entertainment and guest room. This began a new adventure of hosting missionary families. (My parents often hosted salespeople and out-of-town family in our home when I was a child, so this was not a new concept for me.) We hosted missionaries from different churches and other Christian organizations as well. Hebrews 13:2 says, "Don't forget to show hospitality to strangers, for some who have done this have entertained angels without realizing it!"

This is where you get to see the bad side of me. Dean can be very generous "a spender" and I am known to be very frugal or "cheap." Dean wanted to provide food for the guests that stayed in the poolhouse. I thought we were being generous with free lodging. Why take it to the extreme? (I was pretty stingy back then!!) We ended up providing some fruit and snacks, but I didn't have a good attitude about it.

I was young and immature and we had several expenses; the big house, pool house, pool, and three children attending a private school. These were not inexpensive expenses. I wanted to save all the money we could in case our businesses failed. I feared that as easily as it was to reach our financial position – it was that easy to lose it too. I forgot what Hebrews 13:16 says, "And don't forget to do good and to share with those in need. These are the sacrifices that please God." I also forgot that these were God's possessions to use how He wanted — not mine. I had a trust issue and a selfish attitude!

Give God what's right, not what's left. - Adrian Rogers

We met a lot of lovely people and have many stories from those who stayed with us. Here's a couple: We had one family that arrived late in the evening, we quickly got them settled in and said good night. It rained a lot that evening! The next morning, I was working in the yard and the father came out of the pool house and said, "I didn't know that you had a lake in your backyard." I said, "We don't, but when it rains that hard, the creek in the back of our property floods the lower part of the yard for a few hours and then goes back down." He must not have noticed that the playset was in the middle of the "lake". He was amazed later when the backyard was green again. A missionary from Brazil, kind of a rough looking dude, stayed in our pool house for a few weeks while he worked on his book. One day he went to the bank – remember he looked a bit out of character for our town. He looked around but realized it was not the right bank, so he left. Then he drove down the road and walked into another bank. When he finished his banking, he walked outside to lights flashing and police officers demanding him to lie down on the ground with his arms and legs spread apart. While laying on the ground, he explained his story. (The police in our town could be a bit overzealous since we don't have much action.) They thought he was casing banks to rob them. Fortunately that only happened to one of our guests – but it did make a memorable story.

I won't exaggerate, hosting people took a lot of effort, and it wasn't always convenient. We used the pool house as an extension of our home. So even though the people weren't in our living quarters it was a bit inconvenience. When they left, I cleaned – this was like cleaning a whole house after someone moves out. Sometimes I did this with a good Godly attitude, and sometimes I really complained!

As I sit here and type this some twenty years later, I have so many fond memories from that time, they more than make up for all the expense, inconvenience, and energy of hosting.

Since we've talked about the poolhouse, we might as well talk about the pool too! In our minds, our pool was built for having lots of people in it. As a matter of fact, the pool salesperson became snippy because we kept asking for prices for the next size larger. We did this three times but went with the pool three times larger than the first pool quoted.

We glorified God with our pool also. Besides hosting all of our kids' sports teams, school, family, and others, we also used it for baptisms for our church and late night youth groups even after our kids were too old for it. What is the sense of keeping things all to yourselves? Remember, it's not really ours anyway, it's God's. With that being said, sometimes God wanted me to share it with people that I didn't really want to share with. There were times we would be out of town, and God would lay it on my heart to call someone to let them use it and this verse would pop in my head. (James 4:17) "Remember it is a sin to know what you ought to do and then not do it." I know that the Holy Spirit lives in me because eventually . . . I would call and offer the pool to them.

Happiness is not so much in having as sharing. We make a living by what we get, but we make a life by what we give. - Norman MacEwan

Ripple: Let your church know if you can host missionaries when they come to town. If that's too big, host a dinner party or make up gift baskets for them.

QUESTIONS

1. What was the most unconventional way you've served the Lord?

2. Has satan ever attacked you while you were trying to do something good for God?

3. What is the most unusual question you have ever been asked about God? Or asked?

4. Have you ever used your yard or home for God? BBQs, dinners, book studies?

5. What was the lowest attended church event that you attended? Did you still give God the glory?

6. Have you ever offered your skills or resources to the church? How?

7. Have you ever spent time listening to a missionary? From where? Or read a about one?

8. Do you pray for your church service, small group, or an event the church is doing?

9. Do you have any moments of regret for being stingy to God and His people? How?

10. What was your biggest sacrifice to the Lord so far? What did it cost you? (Time, money, convenience.)

5

—◦◦◦—

Back to the Pebbles

LEARNING AGAIN

Dean and I had been going to Sunday School (small group) since we had joined the new church. The lessons had started to become very repetitive. So, I thought maybe the time had come to learn more Bible basics. (Just so you know, Dean and I had both discussed this situation for months.)

Our two younger kids were still in Children's Church, and they didn't mind if mom and dad were around them. Again, I said to Dean that I was going to move on and would love for him to come and help me with the kid's Sunday School classes. (I don't know what goes through his head when I say these things.) I asked if he would be the crowd control. I would lead our son's fourth grade class. Zack was thrilled with the idea, so Dad agreed to help. Bless his heart.

The church provided all the materials to teach for an hour every Sunday. These Bible stories had more details than what we talked about in Awana. Plus, having the teacher's materials gave me even more information to digest than what the kids were getting. I enjoyed sharing Bible lessons with the kids and Dean didn't mind sitting in the small chairs, while he kept the kids focused.

Several of the kids in the class were my son's friends, and had been to our house to play. Most of their parents were strong Christians, but kids will be kids, and sometimes they couldn't sit still. But it didn't hurt that I knew their parents, and these children knew that if I were pushed too far with their "naughtiness," I would have a talk with their parents. Dean might have had the more difficult task in the classroom than me. We had a couple of children who were a little more ornery than the others.

Dean was not the disciplinarian in our home; I was the bad guy, and he was *always* the good guy. So, I enjoyed the reversal in the roles for a change. I was able to keep talking while he handled the kids. The nine months that we were with these children went by very fast, and I learned a lot.

When the kids started fifth grade, they moved up to junior church. The leaders teaching that class had been doing it for years and were great. So, we decided to do our younger daughter's class. Katie is almost two years younger than her brother, but only one grade below in school. We were going to be fourth grade teachers again. I really wasn't thrilled about repeating the class, but our daughter was so excited, and I would really benefit from the repetition.

I wasn't too nervous to lead Sunday School for children – I am not a teacher, but I trusted the Lord to equip me. Many people are afraid to step out of their comfort zone or give up their time to serve others. People want to be with their friends in adult groups. But, what a great way to serve the Lord and spend extra time with your children. I know that our children loved having us as their Sunday School teachers. We all have great memories of us learning together.

Experience is something you don't get until just after you need it. - Steven Wright

Maybe you think you can't speak in front of a crowd or you think you're not teacher material. If you pray and ask God for help, He will help! If you're worried about the time commitment, let the church know that you only want to teach for a year, which is not really a year! – You are only teaching one day a week. Really, how many days is it? What's the worst thing that can happen to you? You enjoy the kids so much, you might end up in Children's Church for years.

> **Ripple:** Volunteer for crowd control for a Sunday School teacher or be a substitute teacher once in a while. Volunteers get sick and want to go on vacations. What a blessing you would be to the leaders. Even the thought that someone was willing to help will bless them.
>
> **Ripple:** Ask Sunday School teachers if you could donate some incentive or Christmas gifts for the class. (The teachers usually pay for the gifts.) or maybe help throw the class party!
>
> **Ripple:** Have your child write a thank you to the Sunday School teachers . . . you could add a note of thanks too.

MORE CHANGES

When our oldest daughter finished fifth grade, we started thinking about what the next year would hold for her. Abby would be in a building with all the sixth and seventh graders in our town. Her graduating class size at that point was about six hundred kids.

Dean and I had gone to the same small-town high school. (We met in typing class. He kept unplugging my machine so I would have to crawl under the desk to plug it in.) Both of our graduating classes had about one hundred kids. Dean felt that the school our children attended was too big and was concerned that they wouldn't have the opportunities we had in high school. He felt we needed to enroll them in the small Christian school in our town. (When I say small, I mean Abby's *entire sixth grade class had six students in it!!!* Our other two children had about ten students each. *Really small!*) I wanted our children to stay in the public school and be the Christian example to their friends. I guess I wanted to evangelize through them, but I lost that battle.

Christian schools, here we come! Wow, was I on a learning curve. I learned that you don't drop off your kids at a small Christian school and pick them up. *Oh no* – this is a ministry!! In order to keep the school going, besides paying a large tuition, you were required to help out because tuition did not cover all the expenses. Did I mention . . . I still had a job at this time? One way the school earned money was by distributing phone books because the phone company would pay volunteers to do this. We also worked a snow cone stand in the summer. All the other fundraisers, I have blocked from my memory!

Plus, there was other work. My husband was the contractor who helped build the high school gym. Somehow, I was elected to do the landscaping. Yes, I picked up the bushes and planted them all. Fortunately, I didn't have to plant the trees or do the landscape rock. There's one more area Dean volunteered for – school board. If you ever mention to my husband the years he spent on the school board, it makes his blood pressure go up. The kids bring it up every year just to see their father react. LOL! It was work . . . when you dropped off your kids you hoped nobody would see you so you didn't get volunteered to do something else. I will admit this bothered me! But, it wasn't all bad. I did learn a lot of things at this school!

I learned the differences between denominations. I was under the assumption that the people in our church's denomination were the only ones going to Heaven. The others may not make it to Heaven due to their doctrine, until one basketball game. I started a conversation with the mother of a child from the school, and I found out she was Pentecostal. I had to know – so I asked – what do Pentecostals believe? When she gave me the whole gospel, I was *shocked* 😊 I had to rethink things again. So, I continued asking other ladies what their beliefs were, and lo and behold, it seemed to me they understood the gospel message. Yes, we did have some different opinions on things that made our denominations different from each other – losing your salvation once you are saved, being sprinkled or submersed during baptisms, and speaking in tongues; but we had the same basics. If we confessed our sins and believed that Jesus died on the cross for our sins, was buried, and rose from the grave on the third day, through faith in Him, we will be in Heaven some day. If we believed these truths, not in our minds but with our hearts, we could know that Jesus was our Savior, and we would spend our eternity with Him. The Bible says, "That if you confess with your mouth that Jesus is Lord and believe in your heart that God has raised Him from the dead, you will be saved" (Romans 10:9)

> *You should never have to tell someone you are a Christian. They should know by the way you treat them. - Tom Krause*

To me, the other stuff seemed not as important! I still feel this way. I'm not here to judge if a person is saved or not, but you should see some fruit. *No*, not bananas or apples – the fruit of the Spirit in Galatians 5:22-23 Love, joy, peace, patience, kindness, goodness, faithfulness, gentleness, and self-control. There should be evidence of these character traits in the people who claim to be Christian.

> **Ripple:** Think about any misconceptions you've had in your spiritual upbringing. Write them down and share them with others. I've told all of my children how misguided I was about these issues and have set the record straight in our family and with you!

Here is some of what I learned from our children attending a Christian school and being around Christians from other denominations. I will start with some of the bad things. Christians can be poor sports!! As I watched our children play sports at this school, I saw some ugly sportsmanship! Another misconception: *Christians are not perfect!* The sports teams would run up the score during a game. No team needs to win by forty points or more, especially against a non-Christian school. No mercy or embarrassing the other team is not ok. It's okay to win, but to shamefully run up the score is not worth the stats. They should have thought about the big picture. Putting Christ and Christians in a poor light is disrespectful and doesn't build up the kingdom. A couple of the coaches threw temper tantrums – and other inappropriate behaviors happened at all the different sporting events that included coaches, parents, and students. The real problem was that most of the misconduct happened with the adults. So not only was the other team watching, but so were our students. Now, in all fairness, not all of the adults were necessarily Christians at the Christian school.

We also had parents who tried to bend the rules for their children with the dress code. What does that teach your kids? That if you don't like the rules – complain or break them? Not cool. You get my point. Leadership was also sometimes not Biblical either, but remember we're not perfect and we all have lessons to learn.

The positive side of a Christian school, our children and I made lifetime friends. Another friend, Joan, (okay I can't stand it, her name is Joanne but her dad spelled her name wrong on the birth certificate and spelled it Joan.) demonstrated immediate prayer. During many conversations with her, we would stop and pray about something. Ordinary things like if at a game someone was hurt, we would stop what we were doing and say an out-loud short prayer. "Dear Jesus, please let everything be alright with that player." Or if someone was sick, instead of saying, "That's too bad, I hope they get better," she would say, " Let's pray." If I was struggling with something, she would start praying for me right there. These were simple prayers, but they were immediate. You never doubted if she would pray for you. She did it immediately! Many people will say, "Oh I will pray for you." I'm sure many people mean to pray for the things that they hear and voice concerns about. But we get busy and forget to pray about it. Can you relate?

I have tried to model this to my children, believers and unbelievers, especially when people are hurting! I will grab their hands, even strangers, and say a quick prayer right there out-loud so they can hear it. It lets people know that praying is just simply talking to God. ***No appointment needed!*** I've never had someone say, "Don't pray for me!!!!" It might even open up a God conversation with someone and it lets them know you care.

> **Ripple:** Try to make this a practice. If someone is struggling this week for some reason, stop the conversation and pray. This takes practice, – but if you forget you can call the person when you remember and pray with them on the phone.

I had several good role models at this school and learned how to be a better Christian by watching others live their lives. When I saw a good example, I would apply it to my own life. I hope that's why you're reading this book, to learn and copy some of the things I've learned. One example was the time I received a thank-you card that really wasn't necessary! My son's friend was invited to come over to our house and swim. This young man had two younger brothers who would be jealous that their older brother would get to go swimming while they were stuck at home. So, I invited the mom and the two brothers to come also. It's never fun to be the ones left at home. (I always think the more the merrier!) Karen and her three boys came over, swam, and hung out with us for a few hours of fun in the sun. When they left, they all said thank you. A few days later, I received a thank you card in the mail. This mom thanked me when she left and so did all the boys, but she took it a step further. It seemed over the top to me at the time, but it made me feel really good. It was a simple thing, but it took time and effort to pull out a thank you card and a pen to write a little note. Then to buy a stamp and put it in the mail. I was so impressed with this act of kindness I copied her.

This was not modeled for me in my home, but that is not an excuse. If such a little note in the mail could have such an impact on me, why not adopt the idea and keep it going? I've been doing it ever since. My mother-in-law, Mary, always wrote thank you cards to us at Christmas and other holidays. I don't know why this idea didn't click with me until Karen sent her thank you, but both were great examples!

You don't have to be a 'person of influence' to be influential. In fact, the most influential people in my life are probably not even aware of the things they've taught me. - Scott Adams

When our children were little, after Christmas was over, I would have them write thank you notes to their grandparents and everyone else they received gifts from. They would tear off the fronts of the Christmas cards we received for Christmas and would write on the back of them – recycling at its best. We received a lot of Christmas cards from businesses and some were funny: like elves packing gifts on a construction truck. Those were the first cards the kids would pick out for my father since he's a bit goofy. They thought he would think it was funny. Next, they would pick out the religious ones for the other grandparents. With time, they even started thinking about which card went to which person. Our children didn't always care for this activity, so when they complained I told them that we could return the gifts and request that they never buy us gifts again. They would immediately start to write! The thing that I liked about the kids writing thank you notes was that they had to stop and think about what people had bought them. Children get so many gifts for Christmas that it's one big pile in the living room the following week. They don't always remember who gave them that special toy they love playing with, plus it reminds them to be thankful.

Every year, they put more thought into their cards. Our kids are grown now, and Abby and Katie have continued writing thank-you cards. The youngest daughter spent so much time writing *long* thank you cards after her wedding, that they took her two months to finish. (She also had her new husband write some!) I had at least three friends of mine tell me that they cried after they read their cards and how special they felt with what she said in them. Even our adult son bought thank-you cards and sent them out after Christmas last year. (Without being told he should.)

It feels good to receive a handwritten note expressing how thankful someone felt with the kindness they received. It sticks with you. It reminds me of the story in the Bible that makes my blood boil! In Luke 17:11-19 As Jesus continued on toward Jerusalem, He reached the border between Galilee and Samaria. As he entered a village there, ten men with leprosy stood at a distance, crying out, "Jesus, Master, have mercy on us!" He looked at them and said, "Go show yourselves to the priests." And as they went, they were cleansed of their leprosy. One of them, when he saw that he was healed, came back to Jesus, shouting, "Praise God!" He fell to the ground at Jesus's feet, thanking him for what he had done. This man was a Samaritan. Jesus asked, "Didn't I heal ten men? Where are the other nine? Has no one returned to give glory to God except this foreigner?" And Jesus said to the man, 'Stand up and go. Your faith has healed you.'" Glad I wasn't the mom of the other nine lepers! They may have gotten their leprosy back! Jesus likes to be thanked! Even though the one leper didn't write a thank you note and mail it to Jesus, he did walk all the way back to find Him. He fell on his knees and thanked him for being healed! He put action into his thankfulness! That's what we need to do – put action into being thankful. As a matter of fact, as I wrote about people in this book that had had a positive influence in my life, I wrote them notes and thanked them for the impact they had on my life.

> *The really great man is the man who makes*
> *every man feel great. - G.K. Chesterton*

I didn't learn this from the school, but while we are on the subject of cards, I will mention this – Birthday cards! After the kids started writing thank you cards, we had to talk about why we didn't write thank you and sign our names. Because there is not much effort in that! So each time one of them received a card, they started noticing what people wrote in them. Yes, it's good to pick out a card with nice things written in it. However, as the kids and I discussed throughout the years, it would be even nicer to get an ordinary piece of paper with a handwritten note saying what that person likes about you instead of what Hallmark thinks you need to say to that person.

When Zack would receive a card for something, the first thing he would do was flip the card over and say, "They spent this much on a card??? I wish they would have just sent me that money and written a note saying Happy Birthday." Our daughters used to save the cards they received, but only the ones that had a personal hand written note. The others were recycled. Take time and write a special message about the person in the cards you send. These will be the cards that don't end up being recycled! Birthday cards are a great way to tell people you thought about them and to express your love. When I was little I had an aunt that would send a birthday card every year with a stick of gum in it and forty plus years later I still smile when I think about that. She made a huge impact with just a stick of gum!

> **Ripple:** Always be prepared! Buy a package of thank you cards and get some stamps. In the next month try to write one thank you each week. There is always someone to write a thank you note to, even if it's your hairstylist or your boss. Write a few thank you's to people who have influenced your life. While your at it buy a few birthday cards too.

Back to what I learned at the school; I was made aware that there are evil spirits all around us. The churches I had attended did not talk about them or had not explained them very well if they did. I understand, you can only fit so much into sermons and if they did explain them, I missed it. (This is why you need to read the Bible yourself.) They also didn't talk much about the power of the Holy Spirit. It was like the Holy Spirit was mystical, and we shouldn't talk about something we didn't know much about.

I was at my son's basketball game, when my friend, Joan told me about a fictional book she had read, about demons that harassed a town. She said it was very interesting and recommended I read it. I told her I was not interested at all and would *NOT* want to read it. At the time I was having occasional nightmares that were evil demonic type dreams. So I sure didn't want to read something that could make it worse. I was afraid to tell people about these dreams because I didn't think Christians should even have creepy evil dreams like these. When I did finally tell someone, they told me to pray out loud and tell satan to stop invading my dreams in the name of Jesus. And you know what??? I took that advice! I prayed about it, and may have only had one or two of those kinds of dreams since then. When satan bothers me, I start praying, which I hope he really dislikes!

A few months had passed and Joan gave me a book to read and said it was good. I didn't think much about it because several people who I hung around with, had been reading the *Chronicles of Narnia* and the *Left Behind* series. I thought, "Great! Another series to read." I started reading and got sucked in and *sure enough* . . . it was the book that had the demons in it. She was so sneaky! (I am not a gullible type of person. I thought I could trust my Christian friends.) It's called *This Present Darkness*, by Frank Peretti. It's a good, and no, it didn't give me nightmares. It is a fictional with some truth mixed in, and it made me think about how aware of the spiritual world we should be. I'm not saying that every bad thing around us is caused by demons or satan, but we should not be so naive about the fact that there are battles being fought in the spiritual realm all around us. The Bible is very clear about this. In the book of Ephesians 6:12 it says, "For we are not fighting against flesh-and-blood enemies, but against evil rulers and authorities of the unseen world, against mighty powers in this dark world, and against evil spirits in the heavenly places."

If you read it, it will encourage you to pray for Washington DC and Hollywood. There are definitely spiritual battles going on in both of those places. Plus, it may make you more aware of the protection you should be wearing. The Bible talks about spiritual armor. Ephesians 6:13-18 says, "Therefore, put on every piece of God's armor so you will be able to resist the enemy in the time of evil. Then after the battle you will still be standing firm. Stand your ground, putting on the belt of truth and the body armor of God's righteousness. For shoes, put on the peace that comes from the Good News so that you will be fully prepared. In addition to all of these, hold up the shield of faith to stop the fiery arrows of the devil. Put on salvation as your helmet, and take the sword of the Spirit, which is the word of God. Pray in the Spirit at all times and on every occasion. Stay alert and be persistent in your prayers for all believers everywhere." *Not only should we pray for protection for ourselves but for believers everywhere.*

> **Ripple:** Look up spiritual armor (Ephesians 6:13-18) and put them into practice! Make yourself aware about the spiritual battles that are going on around us and share them with co-workers, family, or friends. Pray for God to protect you and other believers.

FIELDTRIP OF DOUBT

I love field trips! I went on ALL my children's field trips! I'm proud of that fact . . . my children . . . not so much. Our oldest daughter's field trip was scheduled to happen toward the end of the school year. Abby was a sophomore at the time and really didn't want me to go, but how could I resist? Since this was a small Christian school, volunteers were limited. My husband was even talked into getting a bus license – another thing to add to the list of ways to volunteer for at Christian school! Since Dean was going to be the bus driver for the field trip, Abby didn't have a choice of whether or not I was going. Of course I went!

This would be unlike the other field trips I had been on. This time we were doing a trip that the Bible teacher planned where we were going to four different places of worship in Des Moines, Iowa: an Islamic worship center, a Buddhist worship center, a Hindu Temple, and a Jewish Synagogue. The purpose of this trip was to learn about these different religions and their worship styles so we would know how to witness and build bridges with people of other beliefs, as well as strengthen our own. I didn't know at the time that Iowa was such a diverse community. I had never noticed these places of worship because they were smaller and placed into small neighborhoods. A few were built on the outskirts of town.

The students were instructed before we left the school on the bus to ask nice polite questions so we would not sit in silence after the worship leader finished talking to us. I'm sure they were instructed in the classroom about some of the questions they should ask. I was glad that we ALL received the announcement . . . so I wouldn't be my typical inquisitive self.

The four stops were a lot to pack into a day!! I don't remember all the details from each of these places, but I will tell you what is still stuck in my brain. The first stop on this field trip was a Buddhist Temple. I remember that they had a little garden in the back with a small Buddha statue. This was where their attendees could leave little food sacrifices, flowers, beaded necklaces, and other kinds of tokens. What struck me most about this were all the flies that covered the orange that was sliced in half on a plate in front of Buddha. Sorry for the disrespect, but it looked like a mess to me. I wanted to know who the person was that cleaned up all this stuff, and what did they do with it? Did they just dump it in the garbage? How long did they leave it sitting there? And when they took it away, did that interfere with the prayer of the person that left the stuff for Buddha? (I know people leave a lot of adornments on tombstones, but this is not the same as leaving all these things for a god.) *QUESTIONS??? I had a lot of them!* All these things seemed to bother me, but I did not ask the questions that were rolling around in my mind that day. Since they were not very polite, or at least not how I would have asked them. I do have a way of being very blunt. Plus, my nose has a way of scrunching up when I think things are not quite right. So my questions didn't get asked or answered.

The next stop was an Islamic worship center (this was post 9/11) and honestly, at the time I did not know a lot about Islam. Mostly what I had heard was that they were extreme, and that only came from what the news said. I do remember that we sat in a large open room with ladies who wore scarves on their heads. These ladies did not smile, talk, or make eye contact with us; they sat with their backs up against the wall and listened while the leader told us about their mosque. What I found strange with this group of ladies was, when surrounded by young people, they didn't smile or make small talk with the children.

I did ask the leader if they reached out to people about their religion and how they went about doing that. He said that they don't really do evangelism like the Christians do and didn't go much further in his explanation. Question asked, but not answered!

Next, we drove a distance out of town to a Hindu temple. This was elaborate! They had a room of about sixteen life size statues (gods); eight on each side. The statues were each in cubicle-like spaces. The room was kind of dark, and it felt a little eerie. The thing that struck me most was all the flowers, food, and tokens left by people who prayed to each statue. They would pick out the god (statue) that they felt could answer their prayer, and they would leave a sacrifice at the altar of that god after praying. Again, who cleans all this up? Do they feel strange talking to a painted wood statue? I was concerned about the statues that didn't have any sacrifices in front of them. Did these statues feel lonely? Did they want to get revenge on the other statues since they were getting all the attention? How do you not make one god angry or jealous while talking to the other ones? Was it like having two parents? If you don't like the answer you get from one, you go and ask the other one until you get the answer to the prayer you want? I was confused! I know these are simple-minded questions, and again not really worth asking. I had a very disrespectful attitude about the whole thing. (While writing this section of my book, I asked Abby and her friend Jeremiah, who ended up being a pastor, what they remembered about this field trip. The Hindu temple was the place where both of them felt heavy darkness and maybe evil.

Our final stop was a Jewish temple, similar to a large church with stained glass windows. This was the religion I could relate the most since I had read and heard more about what Jewish people believed. They at least believe in the same God as Christians. They believe the Old Testament of the Bible. So as far as I'm concerned, they are halfway there. They just need to believe that God has already sent our Redeemer, and that's Jesus Christ!

This is where more questions were asked because I'm sure the students had heard more about Jewish customs than any of the other religions. Of course, I had a question. I wanted to know how they receive forgiveness for their sins since they don't make animal sacrifices anymore? In the Old Testament the Jewish people had to make a blood sacrifice (animals) to cover their sins and to be in right standing with God. Christians believe that Jesus is our blood sacrifice and that He is the one who atoned for sins and continually covers our sins if we confess them to Him. But Jewish people don't believe in Jesus, so they don't have a way to cover their sins and appeal to a perfect God. But I kept silent. (So unlike me!) One question asked was, if the Jewish people were worried that maybe Jesus was the Messiah they were looking for. The Rabbi said that *if* the Jewish people were wrong and Jesus *was* the Messiah, then God would forgive them since they were God's chosen people. I didn't quite agree with his answer, or that the Bible would agree, but I listened and soaked in the whole experience.

Each of these stops took about forty minutes listening to what the leader had to say, the students asking a few polite questions and a tour around their facility. On the bus ride, between the different places of worship, the Bible teacher would talk about what we saw at the last stop. He would answer a few questions, and tell us what to expect at the next stop. He also mentioned that in each of these religions you, the person, had to appease the god. In some cases you had to figure out what god you wanted to worship. It was getting to be a bit confusing to me as to how all these religions still existed. How do we know what religion is the right religion? This was the question that was running through my mind. Each leader believed that their religion would get them to Heaven. But they couldn't all be right!

People who don't have a religion will try to tell you that all religions lead to God. *But,* I'm certain that not one of those religious leaders would agree with that statement! We each have a firm belief in what is believed to be true. But again, *not* everyone can be right! I was unprepared for this field trip!! I know the students probably talked about what to expect as they had studied the beliefs of other religions, and I'm sure they prayed before they went. All of these things would have been so helpful to me! *Especially the prayer part!* I remember for days after this field trip, asking myself how all of these people could believe what they believed to be true. Are they believing in their religion because that is what they had been exposed to while they were growing up? Did their families expect them to follow in their steps? Or is their religion the only religion that they knew anything about? Questions? *I had a LOT of them!*

That summer we took a rare vacation to Wyoming. I remember going horseback riding and feeling this uneasy pressure in my heart to know *what I really believed!* I started thinking through my religion. Did Christianity make any more sense than their religions? I even remember going out for my morning walk along wooded trails, and while I was walking I was talking to God. I remember saying to Him, "I'm not sure if I believe this whole gospel thing that I've been told. I'm not sure if I believe in You." I also started thinking I was a bit odd to keep talking to a God that I wasn't sure was real. And if He was real, what did He think about the fact I just told Him, that I didn't think that He was real? That made me a little nervous, but something kept me praying or "talking." At this point I wasn't sure what I believed. I usually pray for my family and other things going on, but this was a different kind of prayer.

I told God I would keep praying to Him, but He would have to somehow show me how to believe again. It was so strange, but I remember I didn't feel alone on that path. As the week went on, the whole Christian religion started sounding like a science fiction movie. The "Almighty God" up in Heaven sends down His Son as a baby to save the planet. The Son grows up, heals a few people, does some miracles, and then He dies on a cross. The Son is buried and then three days later He comes back to life. If we believe that to be true, that is what makes it possible for us to go to Heaven. At the same time, I also did not believe in worshiping a statue that was brought in with a two-wheeled dolly by some delivery person. Then set it up in a cubicle in a building in Iowa, a statue that some man designed and painted. Statues don't eat food, so why do they put food in front of a statue?

And, while we are on the subject of statues and idols, why do some Catholics put so much emphasis on Jesus's mother, Mary? I was talking to a Catholic woman that prayed to Mary instead of Jesus because she felt a woman understood her more than Jesus, a man. Mary was another person that God used to further His kingdom. She is not to be worshiped. So why did she think that was acceptable? Why is there so much emphasis on asking the priest to forgive you of your sins? Only Jesus can forgive your sins that you commit against God. In 1 Timothy 2:5 it says, *"There is one God and one Mediator who can reconcile God and humanity – the man Christ Jesus."* And Exodus 20:4 says, *"You must not make for yourself an idol of any kind or an image of anying in the heavens or on the earth or in the sea."*

Hinduism is a religion that believes a person is made into different things until you're good enough to be nothing, and that doesn't sound real either. Nor do I have the desire to keep being reincarnated until I reach nirvana only to become nothing! Nor do I believe that we live, die, get buried, and then turn into dirt. I don't believe that is all there is. (For some reason my dad still believes the dirt one.) I knew there was truth somewhere. I just needed to figure out the truth.

I was unsettled. I did keep praying, thinking, and asking the God in Heaven, who I wasn't sure about, to make Himself real to me. I kept thinking back to when I accepted Him as my Lord and Savior. There was such a transformation. I felt like I was never alone, that He was there, that my life had a bigger purpose. I thought back to how my life radically changed overnight after asking Him into my life. I no longer had the desire to do bad things. After salvation, I thought of other people more than myself. I had no fear of death anymore, and I knew death led to a better place. Of course these were all feelings. I didn't have proof that my religion was the right one, just the feeling of it.

With so many questions, I decided that when I returned home, I had to have a conversation with Pastor John. *WOW,* I finally got to the point in my life where I was willing to ask questions, even though I felt like a really *bad* Christian. How can one be a Christian when you aren't sure you believe in Christ anymore? I don't know? When I told Pastor John how I felt, he shocked me with his answer. He told me that he has felt this way before, that he sometimes has doubts, and that a lot of strong Christians have doubts sometimes. (I didn't know this until years later, that Billy Graham had a crisis of faith just like I did! If he can have a crisis, anyone can!) God doesn't want us to blindly go along with our faith. God wants us to search and believe with facts. My pastor also said that this was satan trying to manipulate me so I wouldn't be an effective Christian anymore. He also said that if you take a look at other religions, you will see that Christianity is completely different. Christianity is the only religion where God does something for you and not the other way around. In all the other major religions you have to earn your way to Heaven or to reach nirvana (who wants to go to all the trouble of being reincarnated over and over to only become nothing?). In Christianity, God has done the work for you. Christ died on the cross for your sins so you can be made right with God. Plus, there would be no reason for Jesus to die if there were multiple ways to get into Heaven!

I thought about several reasons why I believed in God. People have given their fortunes and lives to tell other people about Jesus. Yes, other religions do this too, but they are not trying to convert people; they tend to force their religions. I thought of the way my life changed when I accepted Christ into my heart. I didn't know how to fake the conversion that I had or the peace that I received that night. I know that all those years before I accepted Him, I felt He was pursuing me. I also knew that Christianity was the only religion where you were loved by God. I'm not sure if people from other religions feel loved by their god.

Religion is spelled DO. The gospel is spelled DONE! -- Bill Hybels

Psalms 115:3-9 sums up what I was thinking, "Our God is in the heavens, and He does as He wishes. Their idols are merely things of silver and gold, shaped by human hands. They have mouths but cannot speak, and eyes but cannot see. They have ears but cannot hear, and noses but cannot smell. They have hands but cannot feel, and feet but cannot walk, and throats but cannot make a sound. And those who make idols are just like them, as are all who trust in them."

Christianity started making sense to me again. I still had doubts, but knowing that other Christians have doubts too was comforting to me. It's not always easy being the only one that thinks so much differently than other people. All summer I kept praying, and eventually, I sensed that I was starting to believe again. I'm not sure if I found all my answers during that time, but I decided Christianity made the most sense to me. I needed to believe the advice that I had been telling my father over the years. My dad believes you're going to be dirt when you die. (Yes! I received permission from my father to write this.) I believe in accepting Christ's work on the cross and having Him as my personal Savior. *What do I have to lose??!!!!* If I'm wrong and I turn into dirt when it's all over, I lived a good life! If my dad is wrong and he doesn't turn into dirt when he dies, he spends an eternity away from loved ones, especially God. My dad has *a lot t*o lose. I choose to believe in God!

The faith which saves is not one single act done
on a certain day: it is an act continued and persevered in
throughout the life of man. - Charles Spurgeon

Over the years, I have read several books on Chirstianity, and there are so many arguments and proofs that the Bible is real. One of the facts that convinced me to believe again was the multiple number of copies of the Bible that have survived over the years. They have found 5,000 Greek copies of the New Testament, 10,000 copies of Latin ones and 9,300 copies in other languages. There are more historical copies of the New Testament than all other historical documents combined. Also, the fact that *IF* the Bible was a made-up story, the writers would have done a better job of writing the story line. They would *NOT* have had women as the first witnesses to Jesus resurrection. (John 20:11-16) Or have so many women in important parts in the Bible. Women were pretty much second-class citizens, even the courts would not use them as witnesses in Bible times. Jesus was known as being a friend to women and talking with them in public. (John 4:4-30) Protecting a woman caught in adultery. (John 8:1-11) And having them as part of His ministry team. This would not be the way religious people would try to start a religion! (Luke 8:1-3) But that was what Jesus did. The Bible also has two women that aren't of Jewish faith in the lineage of Jesus which is too scandalous not to be true. There is so much evidence, that it doesn't take much faith to believe. For further study I recommend you read *The Case for Christ* by Lee Strobel.

There are also so many people that have died to further the kingdom of God, and when these people die they are not promised riches and virgins; they get to go to Heaven the same as anyone else that believes in the gospel. It's worth saying one more time. When everything is over and *IF* it is not true, *what have I lost?* The time I prayed for the people I love. Being a loving person, having patience with people, and having self control over the things I say and do. (*Not* always being blunt! That is proof enough that the Holy Spirit is within me!!!) Having peace and joy that I am not in control of this world. Money spent to help people in need. Caring for the environment. Listening to uplifting music, and not watching TV or movies that don't have moral values. Caring for the sick and hurting people I know. Being respectful to my husband, which does create a better marriage. Reading books that helped me to live a better life. Writing this book! Well . . . if that's what I have to lose. It's not a bad option. If I chose *NOT* to ever have faith and believe in God and what Jesus did to give me a good and an eternal life with Him and I was *wrong* . . . that's not a risk I'm willing to take! I do not want to spend an eternity in Hell thinking I should have had faith to believe. I decided that taking a risk to have faith to believe in something I could not prove or see, is the definition of faith. Hebrews 11:1 says, *"Now faith is confidence in what we hope for and assurance about what we do not see."*

I also decided that if I was truly going to have faith in God, then I was going to be all in. Since that summer, I have been 100% sold out to God. As difficult as it was to go through that time of doubt and searching, it has made me a stronger Christian. When people ask me why I believe, I have answers. Ask yourself, why do I believe in God? I've asked many Christians this question and most cannot give me a good answer. How are you going to convince anyone else to believe in God if you don't know why you believe in Him?

Side note - during this time of doubt, Kameo, my would-be step-sister who came to my book study, chose to accept Christ as her Savior. She told me how she had a dream and knew that it was true and how after accepting Him she felt forgiveness and a peace that she had never felt before. At the time I felt kind of like a fraud, but I also think the timing was God reminding me of how I felt when I first believed in Him. Listening to her tell me about the peace she felt and the things she felt forgiven for was another reason I believed. No book or counselor can give you the kind of peace God gives! I praise the Lord that He made Himself real to me and Kameo!

Ripple: Read a book about different religions on how to build bridges to witness to people of different faiths, or at least learn what they believe. Talk to someone about their faith that is different from yours. It may open a conversation so you can share your faith. Maybe they have questions about Christianity. (BEFORE DOING THIS: Pray before reading these books and before you open up conversations about other religions. It may save you from going through a spiritual battle as I did.)

Ripple: Have conversations with believers and those searching. Ask questions: Why do you believe God is real or that Christianity is the one true religion? Better yet ask yourself and take time to write them down!!!

Here are a couple of other small things I learned at the Christian school. Zack was assigned to read *The Lion, the Witch and the Wardrobe.* I told him I wasn't sure he should read a about a witch. This was before the movie, *Chronicles of Narnia* came out. I told him that we would read it together. (The book was so amazing that I also read all the others in the series.) All were good and had several truths that I have kept in my life. I've learned not to judge a book by the cover or title which is so true.

I have read many good books with really bad titles, and really bad ones with really good titles.

Another valuable story or in this case a poem that came from school was one Abby shared with me. It has become a symbol of how making a difference in someone's life for eternity is what I wake up thinking about in the morning. Maybe the reason I am so passionate about sharing the gospel is because I was older (ripe age of 14 ½) when I accepted Christ as my Savior. I remember the direction my life was taking (not a good direction). Or if it's the gratitude I feel that someone told me, and therefore I need to pass on that favor. The poem is similar to the footprints story, but this one fits me to a T. When I share this poem, I put myself into it.

I was walking down the beach and there were thousands of starfishes scattered along the beach from the storm the night before. They were still alive but they could not make it back to the water. So I started picking them up one by one and tossing them back into the ocean. In the distance I saw another person walking towards me on the beach. As the person approached me they asked, "What are you doing?" I told them I was trying to save the starfish by getting them back in the ocean. The person said, "There are thousands of them. You can't possibly make a difference!" I stooped down, picked up a starfish, and tossed it into the ocean, and said, "I just made a difference to that one!!"

Since then, I have worn a starfish necklace as a reminder of how we can all make a difference in someone's life. When my necklace is mentioned, I tell the story. You and I can't tell everyone about Christ, but we can make a difference in people's lives every day either negatively or positively. Make an effort to have a positive attitude towards others and life in general. Even if it's a compliment, a smile, or just saying "good morning".

We can't help everyone, but everyone can help someone. - Ronald Reagan

QUESTIONS

1. Have you ever served in the youth department? In what capacity? Was it a good experience?

2. Do you have your children write thank you notes? Do you?

3. Have you ever questioned what other denominations believe?

4. Have you ever had a misconception about a religion or denomination?

5. When there is a crisis do you pray immediately in front of the person?

6. Do you have a Christian role model? What is the best spiritual idea you have copied from someone?

7. Have you ever received an unexpected thank you card? Have you ever been thanked for a thank you card? How did it make you feel?

8. Have you ever had evil dreams?

9. Have you ever doubted Christianity? Why do you believe? What are your answers to a skeptic?

10. Do you know what other religions believe? What is the major difference between Christianity and others?

6

—◊◊◊—

Some Stones Skip Better Than Others

FAMILY ADVENTURES

When our children were in elementary and middle school, we would schedule family adventure days. The kids were perfect ages to get them away from the TV and out of the house. During these adventures we would get in the van and go with no plan. We would stop wherever and whenever someone wanted. There were no rules except that Abby, Zack, and Katie had to go. Sometimes they would bring a friend or have a cousin join us.

Before we left the driveway, we would choose a direction – north, south, east, or west. (Eventually we found a spinner to set the direction we would travel.) Next we would stop at our local convenience store and each of them would pick a snack, candy, and a drink! Nothing healthy here. That was part of the fun! Once we were loaded again, we drove in the direction that the spinner told us to go. No rules, remember? So we would stop and explore anywhere they wanted. At every small roadside park or playground, I would make the kids get out and swing, or go down the slide before they could get back into the van. I love minivans!! The kids could get in and out of their seatbelts all by themselves, so when the doors opened they were free.

The kids loved these adventures because they had the authority to make decisions. Sometimes they wanted to go to a place we would drive by all the time but never went in. This kept them looking out the window so they wouldn't miss anything. Typically, when we are in the car, we're in a hurry to get to our destination and there is no time to stop except for the errand we went for.

Here's an example: There was a mattress store in our town that advertised *all the time* on TV. They had a catchy little tune on their commercial that you couldn't get out of your mind once you heard it! (A song that I had to sing before typing this sentence.) You know, the annoying jingle that sticks in your head for a *really long time!* One day as we were driving along, Abby saw that store and yelled, "STOP! I want to go in there." I'm sure she didn't know it was a mattress place, but we stopped and went in and I'm sure the sales people wondered why this mother with three kids walked into their store and back out so quickly. Abby was curious about what the ad was singing about. It was a weird stop. But again, *NO RULES!.*

> *Why not learn to enjoy the little things-there are so many of them. - Saint John Chrysostom*

We never used our map or GPS (because it wasn't available yet!). We just drove. Often we were gone all day long. We would drive until we found a road heading back in the direction we needed to go. Occasionally we were in the city, but mostly rural gravel roads and really small towns. These were carefree days of time spent together exploring. We walked through creeks, picked wildflowers, and even went through the Matchstick Marvel Museum. (It was a place where they displayed different projects made with matchsticks: the White House, a battleship, and other items.)

One time on a gravel road in the middle of nowhere, one of our visiting passengers in the backseat had really bad gas. So every time there was a smell I would stop the car and everyone would get out and make a big deal about it; "Oh man, that stinks so bad!" "Wow, can't you hold that in?" "We will never let you eat that again." We really let him have it. It was all in fun, and it didn't bother the kid. (As a matter of fact, we still tease him about this as an adult and he was glad I could put the story in this book.)

Twenty years later we still talk about the adventures we had. I have even had the kids' adult friends ask me about the trips they were told about.

I would like to tell you something spiritual about these little adventures, but I can't. They are fun, happy memories that the kids and I share. But, I am *excited* to do these with my grandchildren as soon as they are old enough.

We will still keep the general ideas, but I have a lot of ideas of how we can incorporate God into the middle of these adventures. Make homeless packets for the kids to hand out through their own windows, or buy bouquets of flowers or pick wildflowers along the ditches to hand out to people we meet along the way. Write happy notes with a scripture and a picture that the kids drew to hand out to people. Taking Christian books (bought at a thrift store) or gospel tracts to pass out or leave in places where people will find them is always a good option. Bring a cooler with bottled waters to hand out to workers on hot summer days. Take rubber gloves along to pick up garbage in the park for fifteen minutes. Use sidewalk chalk to write messages on sidewalks like "Jesus loves you." I'm still working on this list, but these adventures will be *more* about blessing people while having fun!

I believe this is something that my kids will do with their children. How do I know this? Because they have been doing these adventures with their friends since they could drive! Side note: we did not have to deal with cell phones at the time. Now, I would put everyone's cell phones in the trunk so everyone was focused on each other.

SEVERAL YEARS LATER: I "adopted" my neighbor kids. (I was sick of waiting for grandchildren.) I decided the two boys up the road didn't have any grandparents in town, so I made me their Grandma Jen. I text them, write cards, play cards, buy them gifts and love on them like any grandma would! I decided to take Tommy and Johnny to do one of these adventures, a practice run for when my biological grandkids come along. We did the snacks and dropped off books and tracts. We ran into different businesses and went to the neighborhoods where Dean and I grew up and live in when we married. We also visited the church where we served for all those years in the children's ministry. It was fun to take them inside to look at the church and tell them of my adventures. One of the boys ate ice cream twice! No rules!

The day was fun until the last half hour when we were heading home. The younger brother had been riding in the backseat for a while and wanted to get up front. So, we made a quick pit stop and switched seats. Then . . . all of a sudden we needed to make a detour. We headed to the emergency room! (Make sure all hands and feet are in the van before the door gets slammed!) One of the boy's hands was in the door jam when the other brother accidentally slammed the door on it. (Glenda, their mom, couldn't stand that she was going to miss out on the memories of this adventure, so she was in the car, too.) All ended well with a splint and no broken bones and memories that won't soon be forgotten! Good thing this was a practice run for my grandkids! I suggest that you skip the emergency room.

> **Ripple:** Plan an adventure with family or a friend. Get snacks, turn on the Christian radio station, sing and drive without a plan! Add some good deeds along the way and the memories will last a lifetime! Maybe for an eternity!!!

GROWING UP

At this point our kids had all moved up to their next level of church programs and didn't really want mom and dad to follow them anymore. It was time to serve God without the kids. By this time, I had been going to church with services that I understood for years, had been in adult and children's Sunday School classes, went to church camp, and surrendered my life to Jesus!!! I was also reading my Bible and had started reading Christian books on growing your faith. I was ready for the next step. Or so I thought.

I had started hanging out with the other mothers from our children's school, and was *asked* to attend a book study. (It's thrilling to be asked!) We would all read separately the week before and then would come together at a gal's house to discuss a chapter each week. This was great, I met a lot of ladies I didn't know and we discussed God without children. It was a bit overwhelming since I had been hanging out with kids for so long. I had forgotten what it was like to have an adult conversation, let alone discuss topics that the other participants may know more about than me.

This was way out of my comfort zone. I am an independent, secure woman, not emotional, and don't have to be told repeatedly that I am loved by God. I get it. But I have met really shallow women who are appearance driven and try to be the best of everyone around them, always judging. I've also been around women that love to hug, too much. I *know* I am being judgemental myself. This was how I felt, justified or not, and this was a stretch for me! Maybe . . . more of a stretch than church camp! But it all worked out! I loved it! We didn't have to hug, we did not discuss shallow topics, and I learned a lot. I did this for a couple years, and then circumstances changed and I had to stop going.

I should have known God was up to something, but I didn't catch on until He nudged me in my sleep. (It must have been the only time I was quiet or still long enough for Him to speak to me.) He said I should lead a Bible study for adults. – Women adults! Was this one of my hair-brained ideas? Was it God's? Did He think I was ready for the next step? I wasn't sure. Sure, I was smarter than the fourth graders I had taught, a proud moment for me, but was I smart and brave enough to lead a Bible study with adults? I negotiated with God, "Please let me do Christian book studies like the one I attended and do not make me do the Bible." I was not ready for that, and I know that teaching from the Bible is a very serious thing. It's mentioned in the Bible. James 3:1 says, "Not many of you should become teachers, my brothers, for you know that we who teach will be judged with greater strictness." I reasoned with myself that this verse must mean teaching from the Bible and didn't include books. God seemed to be okay with this idea. . . I would *not* be the teacher, just the facilitator. The person who picked the book we discussed, set the time and place, and had the coffee ready. I was really nervous, but I knew God had told me to do it, and it wasn't going to kill me. Plus, He woke me up several nights in a row until I agreed. I wanted to sleep and knew He would get His way, so I gave up. I should learn to be obedient right away . . . God has proven to me enough times that when I step out in faith, He will be there to accomplish what He has planned. I just needed to be willing.

Faith is not something you fall back on, faith is
something you step into. - Liz Curtis Higgs

This all came about because I was "flusterated" that all the Awana workers and the choir people couldn't go to Bible studies since *someone* decided that all church functions should be on Wednesday nights. It was hard to find volunteers for Awana when choir practice and the men's and women's Bible studies were all on the same evening schedule! (Note to pastors: If you want awesome children's groups, don't have all the adult activities the same night!!)

I've found that if you have a problem with something, God usually let's you be the solution to it!

When I had finally agreed to God's idea, I approached the pastor about leading a study in my home. The pastor told me that he wanted to do all the Bible/book studies at the church. I'm not sure what his reasoning was, but I explained to him that God had told me to do this. He suggested I maybe do it some other time. I knew that wasn't what God had told me to do, so I again explained to him that God had laid this on my heart to do, and by now I knew God had the *final* say! The pastor said it would be fine putting this off for a while. I replied, "When I get to Heaven and God asks me why I didn't lead the study, you will not be there to tell God that you said, I shouldn't do it now. I will be representing myself before the Lord, and I am going to follow God's leading." I wasn't disrespectful, but when you know that God has told you to do something, you do it. Plus, by that point I already had the courage to do it! I didn't want to chicken out and use the pastor as an excuse. (Now, in all fairness I'm sure not everyone should lead a study. But the pastor could have had someone from the church come listen and coach me on leading one. When you have people that want to volunteer time leading a study, the effort should be made to help encourage them.)

At the time, I was a little disappointed with the direction of this church, but didn't want to leave. Our oldest daughter was having trouble in the youth group. Some of the girls were being mean to her, and things were not being handled the way I would have liked. In a year Zack would also be in the same high school classroom. So this time, Dean and I both decided it was time to find another church. I'm not a church hopper. We were at the first church for fourteen years and the second for about ten. It was not an easy decision because I loved this church and the people in it, but this was the right decision. (Sometimes you do need to move on.)

Have I mentioned that God has a sense of humor? I knew that He had led me to do the studies, but I was still nervous about leading one. So, I bargained with Him again. Lord, I need someone to be my backup. My friend Jenni said she would come to the study: I could talk her into everything! (She did Awana, church camp, children's Sunday School, and so much more.) I invited several others from church, family members, and some of the ladies at the Christian school my children attended. I invited Zack's soccer moms, and my mom's boyfriend's daughter, Kameo, who was my age and an unbeliever at the time. As I mentioned earlier, she accepted Christ as her Savior because of these studies. When I invited Kameo, my mother told her that she didn't have to go because it would be about Bible stuff. Kameo said she came because someone actually thought about her enough to *ASK*! Again, all I did was ask her to come, nothing more than an invitation, which changed her eternity!

> **Ripple:** Ask someone to do a book study. It could be just the two of you during lunch. Or start a small group to discuss a Christian book you love. It's really as easy as inviting others to join you, read a chapter a week and then discuss it the next week.

I ended up with a class of about fifteen ladies. That's why you have to keep asking. I won't lie, you will get so many more no's than yes's. Actually, they will tell you "maybe" most of the time, and then won't come!!! (Our study was on a Friday morning, so that made it harder for working people to say yes.) I thought about the ladies that had committed to coming and I didn't think I could lean on any of them for Bible knowledge. I needed someone whom I could use as my Bible support system like Moses. He reasoned with God for someone else to go talk to Pharaoh about all the plagues that God was going to send to Egypt, more than once in Exodus 4:13, "But Moses again pleaded, 'Lord, please! Send anyone else.'" In verse 14, God agreed and Moses ended up with his brother. (I love my brother but he wouldn't work in this case.) I needed a sister, I needed a wing-woman. Someone who had gone to church all their life. I asked a gal my husband had known all of his life and I had said, "hi" to for at least ten years on Sundays. I figured she was older than me by fifteen years, had gone to church all her life, plus, she was in choir and couldn't go to studies either. In reality, I really didn't know this woman, and if I had, I would have been shaking in my shoes!!! God has a sense of humor! He had her agree to come – I thought for support! But she was more of a listener, not much of a conversationalist. Not very helpful for book *discussions!!* The people who came to that first study were very quiet people. Good thing I love to talk!

Throughout the years, God has led me to almost every kind of Christian book there is, by many different authors. I don't care to just study one author. There was a period of time that women's groups thought they could only do Beth Moore studies. I like to mix it up and get different perspectives. I prefer men authors, they tend to deal with facts and not a bunch of feelings. But lately, I have found women writers who have moved away from mushiness and feelings. Women that have courageously stepped out of their comfort zones to serve God in phenomenal ways.

We also did a novel. I had read it years ago, and many of the points stuck in my head: *The Edge of Eternity* by Randy Alcorn. It had so many good analogies that I really wanted to discuss it. The book reminds me of *Pilgrim's Progress,* with a modern twist. The characters are on a spiritual journey through life when they run across different people and situations along their path. Here's an example: they come across a few people in a small jail along the side of the road. The doors to their cell are unlocked. They have been set free, but the prisoners are convinced that they are still locked up. Similar to people who think there is no way out of their situations, they remain trapped by fear, anger, shame, and anything else that holds them captive. They are not walking in the freedom of Christ. Another path leads them to a beautiful mansion where they stay much longer than planned because life is so comfortable; they don't want to leave. It's like people today that surround themselves with everything they could ever want . . . the latest gadgets, waffle makers they use once a year or top-of-the-line TVs in every room of their homes. They forget the main mission in life is about glorifying the Lord, growing more Christlike and helping those in need. The trappings of material things make us think life should be comfortable, but we forget that our real home is in Heaven with Christ. If you take time to examine your own life, you can see where you are in this journey, and if there are adjustments you need to make. When preparing to discuss it, I asked the ladies to find Bible verses that went with the different scenes the travelers approached, like when the people were in the prison. One of the verses that was chosen was John 8:36, which says, "So if the Son sets you free, you are truly free." We need to shine the light of God's Word in our situations.

Our group has met over fifteen years now and this was the only book over the years that had mixed reviews. But, guess which one we have referred to several times since doing it?? It was one of the hardest to discuss since it was a fictional, but well worth the read as far as making you think about the different sins in our lives. If I was to ever do this book again with a different group, I would assign each person a chapter that they could pick apart and then let them lead the meeting. Listening to different points of view and seeing how they pull things from their own lives and situations would change it up.

Books on growing your faith and how others share the gospel are some of my favorites to discuss. That is another reason this book is structured the way it is. Again, I'm so thankful Rhonda wasn't afraid to share her faith with me, I've never understood why Christians say they are private about their faith. To me that is like saying, "I don't care about other people." I'm also puzzled why Christians want to spend years building a relationship with a person before they share their faith in Jesus with them. Let me remind you that I had absolutely no relationship with Rhonda. We met for thirty seconds before she asked if I wanted to know how to get to Heaven. She probably spent less than an hour sharing with me about how to have a relationship with Christ. And since that night I have never talked to her again. (Except I did go to her husband's funeral to let her know what kind of impact she had made in my life. Okay, add another five minutes of time of knowing Rhonda.) We are also not guaranteed a tomorrow, today is the day to share.

DEVASTATING, DEBILITATING, DISEASE

During this time in my life I was also dealing with a secret! *I had something going on!* It all started around Christmas,1998. Our youngest daughter caught the flu and of course, it had to be on Christmas Eve!! Try telling a four year old that she is not going to her grandparents' house to get gifts with all the other ten grandchildren that are about her age. I had two options – tell her that we are staying home and listen to her have a meltdown, or go to the grandparents' house and try to explain to my sisters-in-law why I brought her and exposed their kids to it. You guessed it! We stayed home! Not all of us, just Katie and me. Dean took the other two kids and went with the promise he would bring her gifts when he came home.

The decision to stay home was the right one because she ended up being very sick. She didn't even cry or throw a fit, but curled up, watched some television, and fell asleep. All five of us ended up with a virus that made us very worn out. It wasn't the stomach flu, but you didn't want to eat and you couldn't stay awake! Everyone was healthy enough to return to school after the Christmas break, (which was *not* much of a vacation with everyone being sick). I, on the other hand, was still worn out. My business was slow during January – everyone is photographed before Christmas, and spring pictures would not start up until March. I rested during the day, but by evening I was still drained. I would start to feel better, and then would relapse again. This dragged on into spring.

Then the weird symptoms began, like not having peripheral vision – I felt like an owl who had to turn its head in the direction it wanted to see. Odd! Then colors that were vibrant were dull to me – most people might not notice, but remember at the time I was a photographer. I really noticed it when the crossing signs for children, you know the really bright yellow ones that indicate where pedestrians cross the road, were a dull yellow instead.

Side note: At the time, Dean and I were not getting along very well. Children, work, stress, and I felt not as loved as our kids were. Maybe I felt like no one was helping me out while I was under the weather. Dean was the kind of father all kids want – fun and let them get by with a lot and he spent more money on them than I did. I was the cheap one that always said "'no." I resented being the grouchy parent – the one who reminded them that it was bedtime. Dad would read and play with them before bed, and there was always a lot of giggling going on. I felt left out even though I was the one that sent him up to put them in bed. Dean didn't get as much quality time with the kids as I did, so that was their time together.

Really, I don't know why we weren't getting along. – We just weren't! So when I told him I was having all these different symptoms, he thought

I was doing it for attention. They were weird to me also. He told me to go to a doctor. I went, and the doctor told me he didn't know what was causing these symptoms and recommended that I see a neurologist. You would think I would get a little sympathy because it was serious enough to see a specialist. *NOPE!* Maybe . . . this was why I was a little annoyed. He went with me to the appointment – I think he was waiting for them to tell me that my symptoms were in my head and that I was imagining all these things.

Sitting in the neurologist's office, Dean sat on one side of the room, and I sat on the other in silence. The nurse came in and gave me the usual routine - temperature and blood pressure. Then the doctor came in looked at the notes and asked if I had any out-of-the-ordinary stress and asked what had led me to his office. I told him about the flu, the weird symptoms, and anything else I could come up with that seemed out of the ordinary. I wasn't trying to fabricate something, I wanted to make sure he had all the facts so he could figure it out what was wrong. He jotted some notes and then told us he had seen a patient that week that couldn't walk due to the flu. I didn't have a clue as to how bad the flu could be. Look it up! It can cause all sorts of weird problems and death! It made sense. I *had* been really sick with the flu recently. Then he said the most shocking thing after that. Very bluntly he told us that this could all be left-over effects of the flu OR this could be multiple sclerosis or MS for short.

He grouped the flu with MS! I had a neighbor with MS so I was not clueless as to what he was saying. *I was just shocked!* I then asked him to clarify what he said since he said it so nonchalantly. I said, "Are you talking about multiple sclerosis?" He said it could be, but he was assuming it was the flu. *WHAT???* Who puts both of those diagnoses in the same sentence? Then he said, "Go home and give it a couple more weeks, rest, and if it all goes away, it was the flu." I looked across the room at my husband to see what he was thinking. I couldn't tell. He just sat there looking like I felt. As we got up, the doctor said to call him if there were any more symptoms. Then he said, "The check-out counter is out to the right and around the corner. Bye." What do you say to that??? . . . Bye

I checked out while Dean went to get the car to pick me up. Once we were in the car, I found out what he thought. *"That doctor is insane!"* Then he said, "What were you thinking he was going to say, after you added all those symptoms. You were asking for him to come up with something." . . . I don't know how I was to blame for what that doctor said. I just wanted him to figure out what was wrong with me. The lack of energy and weird symptoms had been going on for a couple of months, and I was ready to start feeling good again. After the initial shock went away, Dean calmed down. We agreed that we wouldn't say anything to anyone since we really didn't know what was going on. Time passed, and the symptoms seemed to go away. Of course in the back of my mind, there were those lingering letters, *MS*. I'm pretty sure they were in my husband's mind too. But when thoughts entered my mind, it reminded me to pray.

About a month later, things seemed to return to normal and what the doctor had said had been blown off and dismissed. Until . . . a year later. It was the end of the next summer and I had been working on a small decorative pond in our backyard. In one afternoon I was bit by at least twenty mosquitoes. I had bites all over my body. No big deal, but at the time, the West Nile Virus was prevalent in our state. That evening I was tired and my muscles hurt so I thought I had West Nile. There was no reason to confirm it with a doctor, since there wasn't anything they could have done for me. The only groups that needed to seek medical attention were the very young or older people. I fell in the middle.

But, after a few weeks of these symptoms, I also developed some vision problems and weird headaches. The top of my head would tingle like when a foot goes to sleep. It didn't hurt but it was a weird sensation. Being a photographer and having vision problems doesn't work well for business. And of course those letters came back to my mind . . . MS. After the headaches started, we didn't waste any time. We went back to the neurologist again. This time he started ordering tests. First he wanted to rule out lyme disease. When that was ruled out, they ran tests to figure out if it was multiple sclerosis. At the time, there was *no* test you could take that says 'Yep, you have MS.' It is a process of elimination of other diseases and a process of tests being positive that can *indicate* MS.

I later found out that MS is one of those diseases that fit you into a category. I was a caucasian woman, mid thirties, living in the midwest where there are long periods of time without the sun. (Lack of vitamin D which the sun provides is what scientists were leaning towards for what causes MS, but not all of them agree on that). And of course you have multiple symptoms of something. Before the doctor made his diagnosis, he wanted to run more medical tests. *A lot more!*

This happened during my busy season. While the kids were at school, I would take medical tests, pick them up from school, and go to work in my studio. I had multiple eye exams with an optometrist at the hospital, blood tests, pet scans, MRIs, and several tests that I honestly don't even know what they were for. The last big test he ordered since everything else up to that point was inconclusive at best, was to test my spinal fluid. This involves a large, long needle being inserted into your spinal cord to suck some spinal fluid out. This was not the worst test, but maybe the *most dangerous* one. The fluid I had to drink before the pet scan was the *WORST!!*

The spinal fluid test caused the biggest problem though. After it was performed, the doctor said, "You need to go home and lay still for several hours." The hole where the needle went through needed to seal up. He said that if I developed a headache to call the office. Days later, I didn't really have a headache, but when I walked, my head kind of throbbed. It was a headache that I couldn't describe and only occurred every once in a while. We went to church that weekend; and while I was standing in the gym of our church, someone slammed the door on the other end of the room. It caused my head to hurt and throb. Again, my husband thought I was exaggerating. He asked how slamming a door across the room could cause my head to hurt. *I didn't know, but it did!* None of this made any sense to him OR me either. I knew what I felt. Dean said he didn't remember the doctor talking about a headache. *I DID!* So I called the office on Monday, and they told me to come in immediately! Dean drove me back to where they did the spinal tap. As soon as I walked in the door, two nurses grabbed under both of my arms to help walk me to the back room while Dean checked me in.

This bit of drama gave me some satisfaction! Dean now knew something was wrong!! I wasn't acting, which is funny since I don't remember ever acting like something was wrong when it wasn't. (At least not as an adult. I did go to the school nurse several times in elementary school. She was nice and we would sit and talk, and then she would send me home even when she knew I was faking.)

Turns out, my spinal fluid had been leaking. My brain was not floating in the spinal fluid in my head . . . it was gone. My brain was banging against the walls of my head – imagine a funnel with a tube, the tube and funnel are filled with a liquid and a floating ball is in the cone part of the funnel. If you drain the fluid, the ball is no longer floating. It is bouncing up against the funnel walls. That was my brain without spinal fluid. The fluid drained out of the puncture at the bottom of my back, on the inside. It was *not* draining out of the puncture wound on my skin. It was leaking into my body. So, back to the surgical room I went to have another plug inserted in my back. Fortunately, this time it sealed.

All this testing didn't happen overnight. We would do a test and then wait two or three days. When that test didn't result in any answers, we would schedule another test. This was a very long and very inconvenient process – it took a period of about four months. Dean and I were still not getting along that well, and the testing added extra stress to our relationship. I'm not a worrier, which probably made him more confused; I am the kind of person that is not afraid of what a doctor may say. It is what it is. There was nothing I could do about my health until we found out what I had, so there was no reason to worry. Even then, who knew what I could do? It was in God's hands. I needed to keep praying like the verse says in Philippians 4:6-7, "Don't worry about anything; instead, pray about everything. Tell God what you need, and thank Him for all He has done. Then you will experience God's peace, which exceeds anything we can understand. His peace will guard your hearts and minds as you live in Christ Jesus."

The doctor ruled out things I *didn't* have, but I didn't feel any closer to knowing what I *did* have. Let me stop right here and say, I was getting *very impatient!* My husband didn't really have much to say about the situation. He's the type of person, if we don't talk about it, nothing is wrong. We weren't telling anyone. I had nobody to talk or vent to about what was going on. I would usually at least tell my mom, but since it had to do with my health, there was no way I would tell her. She would fall apart, and *I didn't want to deal with that* on top of everything else. Then the symptoms all kind of went away again. *NOW WHAT???*

Side note; the doctor sent me to the optometrist I went to in our town (I knew him personally). He asked me what the doctors were looking for. I hoped he wouldn't say anything to his wife, but I told him they thought

I may have MS. He looked me in the eyes and said, "I have several patients with that disease, I don't think that you have any signs of it." That sounded good to me. Of course what did he know? He's just an optometrist. (But it did give me hope!)

> *We have no right to ask when sorrow comes our way,*
> *why did this happen to me, unless we ask the same question*
> *for every joy that comes our way. - E Joseph Cossman*

Here we go again! Another symptom! Really, I can't even remember what it was. I went to the neurologist again, and he bluntly said, "I'm making my diagnosis! You have MS!". Well, I wasn't quite expecting that! I don't know why, since we were trying to rule it out. All the tests I had taken had come back negative for MS with the exception of the MRI. The MRI was the only test that gave any indication of something. It showed some *little* white spots on my brain that he said could be from MS, or they could have been there all my life. So why all of a sudden jump to that conclusion? Maybe my husband was right. Maybe I was sending vibes with my impatience. Maybe the doctor wanted to stop testing and start doing. I didn't know. After the doctor announced his diagnosis, he said, "I'm going to hook you up to an IV and start giving you some steroids to stop the attacks on your body." He told me it would take about an hour. So Dean said he was going to take off and run some errands and would be back to pick me up. (I need to stick in a disclosure here . . . Dean's mother passed away when he was only sixteen years old. He still to this day does not like going to hospitals or seeing someone sick. I guess that's how he deals with it.) Of course, this may be another reason why we weren't getting along! I kind of felt abandoned, but I also didn't want him to stay either because he would sit in silence or blame me that I was in this situation.

The doctor escorted me to a sterile room and a nurse started prepping me. First they put in a PICC line. This was a needle with a thin tube that was inserted into a vein that would stay in my arm for a week. A nurse would use this line to give me an IV of medicine instead of poking my veins every time.

As I lay in this room *all by myself* with an IV hooked up to my arm, I had time to think, pray, and do business. I made a few calls – the first call was to Sara, the babysitter; she needed to pick the kids up from school. Then I called Pastor Bill, and told him I wouldn't be at Awana that night. Then I prayed, and peace flooded my soul.

When the doctor finally came back, I asked a few questions or chit-chatted (not sure now) but this part I remember. Something triggered a response from the doctor that he didn't think I understood what was happening to me. Maybe I was too calm. I don't know? In a very blunt and forceful way he said, "You have a *DEVASTATING, DEBILITATING, DISEASE!*" I think he was mad that I wasn't falling apart. Or maybe he thought I was in shock. I looked at him matter of factly, and said, "Yes I understand, but do you understand that I could die in a car wreck on the way home?" My point was . . . it's out of my hands, I'm doing all I know I can do on my part . . . I've prayed. It's all in the Lord's hands. I didn't think falling apart was going to do me a bit of good!

I won't go into all the details of this part of my life. I did the IV drips for a week and then they put me on a medication that required me to inject a needle into my stomach, bottom, thigh, or upper arm three times a week. Here is what I do remember about those first few weeks. I tried to have pity parties, I would ask myself, why me? I then asked, why not me? Who would I want it to be? I actually reviewed in my mind the people closest to me and came up with the probability that I was mentally stronger than most of them, and didn't get to choose anyway. Every time I tried to go down the pity party road, in my mind I would remember someone else I knew that had something much worse than me to deal with. I finally gave up because God wasn't letting me get by with it. And besides parties are more fun with people and nobody knew but Dean.

Your problems don't define you, they refine you. - Carlos A Rodriguez

One thing I vividly remember during this time, I went to the mall shortly after being diagnosed. My thoughts were I would never be *NORMAL* again. (I had to work through this for only about a day or so . . . because is anyone really normal??) I walked into a store, there was nobody but the clerk and me. She asked how I was doing. How do you answer that question when you feel like your world will never be the same and you will never be normal again? I know it's something most people say when they're greeting people. I notice that sometimes people don't even wait for an answer. I've learned to look at people when I ask that question, to see if their answer matches their facial expression. I told the woman I was fine, but I felt anything but fine that day!! If she would have even looked me in the eye and appeared interested, I would have poured out my feelings to her. Which makes me think that others would, too.

> **Ripple:** Ask someone how they are doing today. Take time to really listen, it's a hurting world!

I was *very active* during this period of my life. I ran a business, cleaned my own house weekly, took care of a large landscaped yard, raised the kids, and on and on. The dumb thing the doctor said that really upset me was that I was going to need to take naps. That is the one thing that really bothered me. Seriously, this sent me in a downwards spiral (funny thing, now that I'm in my fifties, if I can take a fifteen minute power nap, I'm thrilled!). We only told a very small number of people about my condition after the diagnosis. I mean small! Maybe twenty people. I don't know what Dean's reasons were that he didn't want to tell anyone. But I didn't want to be known as Jennifer, you know, the one with MS. That is how people would describe my neighbor who had this disease. That is NOT how I wanted to be described. There are better adjectives to describe myself than that woman with MS. But, I finally had it with all the secrecy! I needed to tell someone my secret, someone to share with what I was going through. I went looking for support at my good friend, Jenni's house. I needed to know someone cared.

I was one of those kinds of women that did not like to hug! I have never been a real mushy kind of woman or a girly girl. At women's social gatherings, they always need to hug you for no reason. Well not me! I would always take a step or two backwards when they came towards me with open arms. That was about to change.

Jenni is a really sweet, soft spoken woman who is 6'1" tall and is really good at listening. I sat down, told her I had MS and that the doctor told me I was going to have to take naps! Seriously!!! I was really upset that my life was going to have to slow down so much that I needed to take naps. I knew I was being a baby! I don't know what was going through her mind, but she could tell it wasn't the disease that I was upset about. It was the fact that my high energy lifestyle might need to slow down. *She's really good at listening!* If I were listening to someone tell the story, I would have had to stop that person when she mentioned MS. But not Jenni! She sat and listened until I said what was really bothering me. (WOW! After typing that sentence, I had to reflect on how I really don't listen to people! When a friend tells you they have a disease and the friend is more worried about something other than the disease, and you pick up on that fact, that's really listening to what the person is saying.) I told you she was a good friend and a *good listener!*

> *I cannot even imagine where I would be today were it not for that handful of friends who have given me a heart full of joy. Let's face it, friends make life a lot more fun. - Chuck Swindoll*

When I finally stopped talking, she said, "You will only have to take a nap if you feel tired, and I don't see that happening any time soon." I don't know why, but what she said made me feel so much better, and *then* she caught me off guard! She grabbed me in the biggest bear hug I've ever had. I really think God was using her arms at that moment! I felt like a stick of butter in between two really warm hands. *I just melted!* Remember she's 6'1" tall and I'm on the vertically challenged side of 5'1" so it was like a big bear hug. Seriously, I melted into her arms. I was limp with a warm surge running through my body – God was telling me that everything was going to be alright in my situation. I also felt like the Grinch's heart had just grown inside of me. *I hope you understand!* I mean God was hugging me! When that hug was over, I was a changed woman. *No lie!* I wasn't grouchy like the grinch, but that hug was the best medicine that I had ever received in my life! I can't explain it other than it was a *hug from Heaven!*

Now any time someone needs a hug, my arms open wide. I hope someday I can be God's arms for someone else.

> **Ripple:** I know not everyone has a problem giving hugs like I used to. Give someone a hug today! You never know who may need to feel God's love!

Skip ahead seven years. I faithfully took my medicine like I was supposed to; injections three times a week. I continued working, gardening, cleaning the house, and raising our kids. In those seven years, I never had another symptom while taking the medication which to me says, the medicine is working OR maybe I don't have MS. I found out that taking a 10-15 minute nap is like drinking a can of coke without the calories, they aren't that bad. After reading and talking to many people with MS, it didn't seem to me that I had the symptoms that others had. Heat is a big symptom, it wears out people who have MS. I prefer eighty-five degree weather, sunny, and eighty percent humidity. Sweat dripping down my back is so much better than my shoulders hunched up to my ears because I'm cold! I also kept up my high energy lifestyle – running at full speed from sun up to sun down! I began having doubts about my diagnosis and the effects the medications would have on my body.

It was at a summer gathering in that seventh year that Carey, my sister-in-law, who is a nurse, said to me, "I don't think you have MS. You don't seem to have any of the symptoms that are typical with it. Have you given any thought about going off the medicine?" This was *not* something we had even talked about; she was just making an observation. I told her that I had been thinking the same thing, but I had made a promise to Dean, to continue taking the injections until the doctor said otherwise. She said she thought I needed to have a conversation about it with him, but that it was just her opinion. I had been thinking the same thoughts, and here she was confirming it. Our oldest daughter who had overheard the conversation with her aunt told me she didn't want me to go off the medicine. Abby felt it was working and didn't want me to have problems. I understood her concerns, but I knew something had been stirring inside me before Carey had even said anything.

I was leaning away from taking the medicine, but I knew I had two people that had to agree with the decision. I had talked with God about it and was sure He was the one that put the doubts in my mind and the words in my sisters-in-law's mouth. But it was time to confirm this was God's idea and not mine. I gave God two fleeces like Gideon did in the Bible. Remember Gideon? He wanted to make sure that God had really told him that he was going to save Israel. He asked God to confirm it was true. He gave God two tests; first he would put a piece of lamb's fleece on the ground and if there was dew on the fleece and the ground was dry the next morning, Gideon would be convinced. After the first test, he asked

God to reverse the test the next night and make the ground wet and the fleece dry. (Personally, I think he forgot which item he told the Lord to be wet, the fleece or the ground.) So he had to do the test twice to make sure. Or maybe that's something I would do. ☺ You can read about it in Judges 6:36-40.

I was going to conduct my own fleece test to make sure this was God's idea and not mine. I wanted Him to confirm it before I moved forward. Fleece number one, make my husband agree that I should go off the medicine. I knew this would be a big decision, and if you knew Dean, this would take a good week for him to think it all the way through.

In a conversation one night, I told him what Carey had said to me and he quickly agreed that we should try it. *I was shocked!* He rarely makes a big decision that quickly. I think he may have been waiting on me. I really thought he would have had more reservations about going off the medication. But I knew if this was God, it would be that easy. Fleece number two would be harder!! I had to ask the doctor.

If going off the medicine was really what I was supposed to do, he would have to agree. It's hard to get a doctor to change his opinion about a diagnosis and take you off the expensive medication that you have been taking for the last seven years, especially if it seems to be working. If this was God prompting me, I needed Him to confirm this decision. I made an appointment and went to the doctor. He looked me over, made me walk in a line toe to heel. He had me stretch out my arms, close my eyes, and made me bring my fingers to my nose. These were the standard tests. Then he asked me a few questions. Then I asked him what he thought about me discontinuing the medicine. He thought we should stop the medication but wanted to be the first to know if things changed or if I had any symptoms. I told him he could be the third person to know. I would know first, my husband second, and then I would call him. He agreed. *Seriously . . . this was a miracle and made the decision really easy.*

Ripple: If you are in a situation that you are unsure what to do, keep praying and give God a fleece test. But be prepared to do what He confirms for you to do!!!

Now that God had confirmed the decision, I had to step out in faith and stop taking the medicine. I know that sounds easy, but I had to ponder if this medicine was what was keeping me healthy. Did I really want to risk getting sick again? No! But after the two fleece tests, I stepped out in faith. But, every time something strange happened to me that first year, I did consider the possibility of it being symptoms of MS. It made me hyper sensitive to every little thing that was going on in my body. Oh, I tripped, could this be because of a dragging foot? I'm tired. My arm is tingling – that's how it was with every little thing.

It's been over ten years now and I have yet to call that doctor.

WHY? Why did I need to go through this? Why was I healed and not so many other people? Did I even have MS? I have pondered those questions on so many levels. Those are some of the questions that I won't have answered until I get to Heaven. My life changed in many ways through that experience. Here are a few of the ways God showed His love to me and changed the person I was. I felt a *strong* presence of God when I went through all the testing and the administering of the medication. I'm better at empathizing with people who are going through illnesses. I can discuss many medical tests someone might be going through and give them comfort and pointers. I learned how to *hug!!!* But, one of the best things about going through this whole ordeal was getting to see how I responded in this life changing situation. Most people can only talk about how they would react to bad news. That is a gift that has bolstered my faith and my walk with the Lord. I cherish every day and look to the brighter side of things. It made me a stronger, more compassionate Christian!!! (DISCLOSURE: I'm sorry to all my family and friends that are just finding out that I went through this. We really only told less than thirty people in all those years.)

Faith does not eliminate questions. But faith knows where to take them. - Elisabeth Elliot

TIME TO CHANGE AGAIN

I mentioned earlier that after our daughter's problems in youth group and the pastor not wanting me to lead a Bible/book study, our family searched for a new church. This time I knew what I was looking for in a church. I interviewed the next pastor myself. Amazingly, it only took one time again! I was looking for an outreach pastor who really practiced what he preached. Pastor John Colyer agreed to meet with me, and I asked him several questions about sharing the gospel with others. (Yes, there are pastors that only preach to the "choir" and don't reach out to people that don't believe in God. Strange, but true!) I asked him how he felt about a person that was led by God to hold a Christian book study in their home. He asked if the church could promote it and send people to it. (I had already been leading the study at our home.)

An immediate relationship was formed!! This pastor was a male version of me. He talked to everyone. People that didn't know Christ as their Savior were his passion. He even witnessed to another pastor in the town where we live. His church didn't just preach about a relationship with Christ, he wanted to make sure everyone had a relationship with Christ.

The first time we attended his church, Emily, a young teenage girl, introduced herself to Abby, our daughter that didn't have friends at the former church. Before their conversation ended, Abby was invited to youth group. All was good at church again.

We weren't in this church long when the pastor's wife *ASKED* me to come to a luncheon she was having. It was a God-orchestrated luncheon! Judy invited five or six ladies over the age of sixty and myself. I was in my late thirties. The luncheon was to introduce Judy's seventy-year-old mother, who had just moved to the area, to the older ladies of the church. *Why was I there?* I will never know. It was so random!

I enjoyed the luncheon because I like older people, even as a young child. I would hang with my parents and their friends while my brother and the other parents' children played. I loved hanging out with my grandma and my aunts when they would gather around my grandma's kitchen table (even when they tried to shoo me away). During my junior and senior year of high school, I had an Avon route (you know, ding-dong, the Avon lady is here) in my neighborhood. Actually, I had three routes. God gave me the talents of talk and sales. I was seventeen at the time and the people on my routes were twenty to sixty years older than me. Several would buy something each week so a week later I would return. I would bring their purchases, have another long conversation, and sell them more. I *loved* being with the older customers, plus the money I made was a bonus.

God doesn't call the equipped, He equips the called. - Toby Mac

About a week after this luncheon, God started waking me up in the middle of the night, *AGAIN!* My thought was, what does God want me to do now? He seemed to want me to do a book study with the senior ladies of this church. *WHAT???* Honestly, this seemed even more ludicrous than His first request, plus I was still meeting with the other group. I had only been at this church for maybe a month. But, I knew if I wanted to sleep again, I would need to follow God's calling.

I wasn't sure about leading another study at the same time, but I wanted to be obedient to the Lord. I met with Judy and told her what God had been saying to me while trying to sleep. The next week, the church put a notice in the bulletin to set up a meeting for any ladies over sixty who would like to be part of a new group. She took it as a sign from God that I should add another group.

I wish I had a video of that first meeting with those older ladies, most of whom I didn't know and who didn't know me. I was a young, full of energy woman about half their age. About ten ladies who were at least seventy years old or older attended. (The 55-70 year olds must have thought they were too young!) I explained that I was interested in starting a book study group for the older ladies of the church. I told you that God has a sense of humor. I am laughing while I write this. I asked them if they liked to read. One of the ten said yes. This was not my idea; it was God's, so I knew it would work out. ☺ Keep in mind, I didn't feel led to teach them anything because they were older and wiser than me. I'm not fearless, but when I have a challenge, my theory is,"What's the worst thing that can happen?" They think I'm weird? That might happen, but I have been known as weird by several people, so that's nothing really new. I have marched to my own drum all my life.

That day, the best study group was started! Seriously, I knew I loved older people, but they loved me too! I wish I knew what the first book was that we did that day and who the ten ladies were. I remember half of them, but that's why people should journal, which I have tried to do about a dozen times. I still don't have that skill down yet. (Does this book count?)

I have so many fond memories of the ten years that I led the JOY group

(Jesus's Older Youth), a name the oldest member, Mable, came up with. I loved these ladies; they were honest, loving, and had such a good sense of humor. I remember at some point, one of the ladies telling a new person that Jennifer didn't progress much in her ministry service. She went from diapers in the nursery to diapers in the geriatric group. (Their words, not mine.)

We did the studies once a week and extra activities during the month. Here I was, being a cruise director again. We made cards for missionaries, went on field trips to the apple orchard, (Did I mention that I went on all field trips with my kids until the day my oldest cried because she didn't want me to go anymore. Seriously, children cry because their parents won't go on field trips, *NOT* because they go!) and we made and delivered May Day baskets to business owners. Etc., etc., etc.

The best outing we did had to be the day we spent fishing at our pond. I'm not sure my dad would agree! I roped him into doing all the worms and taking all the fish off the hooks. It was a bit chaotic, like having a bunch of elementary age girls with fishing poles, hooks, fishing lines, nets, worms, giggles, and screams. I'm surprised nobody got a hook in their eye or fell in the pond. They squealed every time a fish was on their line. The pond is full of many kinds of fish, but it has a lot of bluegills and bullheads (We did not put the bullheads in our pond, they came on their own!). It was a day of catching, not fishing. Kay—seventy-five years old, had never caught a fish. She had tried on several outings, but had never pulled a fish to shore. (That's a very sad fish tale to tell.) We all decided not to leave until we had seen her catch a fish. When her bobber went under the water, the squealing really began. She pulled a four-inch bluegill out, but you would have thought she had caught a fifteen-pound bass. She was so overjoyed!

Most of the ladies had fished only a couple of times in their lives, so not much fishing skills, which was very evident in their techniques. But, we had a great time and memories to last a lifetime.

Ripple: Invite a few older ladies from your church and host a tea party AND invite a few from your neighborhood so they can see church ladies are fun too. Or better yet, plan a day of fishing!! Older folks like to feel they are still appreciated. We all do!! Or really make a ripple and host a Bible or book study for older people in your home or a nursing home!

When our last child graduated from high school, Dean wanted to travel more. We wanted to be able to visit our oldest daughter, Abby at Judson College in Elgin, Illinois and the youngest daughter Katie at Bethel University in St Paul. He said that it was too hard to schedule time away when I had groups on Wednesdays and Fridays. I chose to stay with the Friday group since they were all from different churches and the church took over the Joy group with over twenty-five in regular attendance.

Another thing I loved about this church was their discipleship of new Christians. They took time and personally helped teach and train young Christians. It wasn't, "Great, you're saved, come to church, and we will all go to Heaven together someday." They became friends and accompanied them to different functions within the church. They spent one-on-one time in the Bible and would answer their questions. Every church should have a plan on how to help baby Christians to grow. I know how important that is! What a difference it would have made if just one Christian would have taken me under their wing, guided me along, answered my questions, and pointed me in the right direction. My spiritual journey would have been so much different. If someone had *ASKED* me if I needed help, I would have jumped on the invitation!!! I know I could have asked, but honestly, I didn't want to appear dumb! Sidenote: Now churches offer programs like Alpha and new discipleship classes.

Ripple: Ask a leader if there is someone in the church that would like a mentor. Don't worry about what you know . . . you can search for the answers together.

Ripple: If your church doesn't offer new believer classes; suggest it to the pastor.

This church also held informal prayer meetings with the staff and anyone who wanted to come. They took requests from the people who attended, and prayed through an updated request sheet that had ongoing prayers from the congregation: homes for sale, people's health, pregnancies, salvation for friends or families, and other current requests. They also shared praises of answered prayers.

Read, *Fresh Wind, Fresh Fire* by Jim Cymbala. It's about a struggling church located in a poor neighborhood of Brooklyn that made prayer the most important part of the church. Now they are more than surviving, it's thriving!

Also, Pastor John preached on prayer during the services. He explained how important prayer was during Bible times and how it still is. When he finished the month long series, he wanted thirty-one people to sign up for one day per month to pray for the church and the requests of its people. He hung up a calendar page and people signed up for the day they wanted. By the time I signed up, only the thirty-first day of the month was left, which only happens seven times a year. Pastor John asked you to spend several hours in prayer for the church, staff, and the requests on the prayer sheet.

I committed for several years, but the enthusiasm of the project wore off, because there wasn't any follow-up with the people who signed up and they never offered sign-up sheets for new people. I felt trapped doing this forever. Don't get me wrong! I was honored to pray for my church but, it became something I had to do instead of something that I got to do. When you start to have that type of an attitude, it's time to step back and re-examine why you're doing it.

Here are some ideas on how I would execute this idea. I would gather these prayer warriors together a few times during the year to share their successes, failures, and how they prayed or broke their prayers down. I would also offer a sign-up sheet every year to give new people the opportunity to join in. I wouldn't limit the number of people that wanted to pray; there could be multiple people per day. Maybe, the people that had the same day could pray together. This way the church would be bathed in prayer each month.

> **Ripple:** Suggest a prayer calendar to your pastor, small group, or any group of friends and cover your church in prayer! Break down the week or month by how many people are in your group or committee.

This church also hosted Homes of Light events in December. These events were held in different homes decorated for the season. Refreshments were served, and there was time for socializing. Then the ladies were gathered into a room where everyone sat comfortably. The hostess thanked everyone for coming and introduced the lady who shared a small presentation about the meaning of Christmas. Next someone shared their testimony of how she came to have a personal relationship with Jesus and the difference it made in her life. When the talk was over she thanked the ladies for coming and offered them small goody bags to take home. (Here is a list of some of the things we included: small devotionals, bumper stickers or pens from Christian radio stations, gospel tracts, Christian books, chocolate, candy canes, a small Christmas ornament – we didn't use all of those items in one bag.) The evening usually lasted about an hour. (Try to keep it moving along so people don't feel trapped.) If they wanted to stay and socialize after the program that was great.

We encouraged the women to pick up their invited friends, neighbors, or co-workers to eliminate parking problems and for quality time with them. The follow-up happened on the way home with their invitees: discussions on the decorations, people, desserts, and the messages that were given and their thoughts on about them. Hopefully they also invited them to the Christmas service at their church. These events were held in multiple homes and neighborhoods in the same week (but if your church is large enough they could be held throught the month of December) which made it easier for people to invite people to something in a home rather than a church building.

The details: sign-up sheets for ladies of the church who would be willing to host an event in their homes and those willing to share their testimony at the event. There were also sign-up sheets for those who would bring desserts, a hostess helper, a person willing to give a short talk about the meaning of Christmas, and a person to introduce the speakers and keep the evening on schedule. There were volunteers that make small guest packets for the ladies that attended. This outreach offered many different opportunities to get people involved. Those who volunteered felt like they helped be a part of something bigger than themselves.

> *I have but one candle of life to burn, and I would rather burn it out where people are dying in darkness that in a land that is flooded with light. - Hudson Taylor*

Invitations were printed so the ladies could easily invite people. The homes and dates were posted in the bulletin so everyone knew where the closest home was hosting an event. Make sure women have a phone number to RSVP so everyone can be prepared for the number of attendees in each home. Keep numbers low to have space enough to create a cozy feeling.

These evenings typically had a great turn-out of new people. I know of two ladies that, as a result of our home being opened up to these events, accepted Christ as their Savior. One of them prayed the prayer of salvation on my bench in the women's restroom. Another gal informed me that her sister-in-law invited her to an event in our home, and that is where her journey of becoming a Christian began. Think about this. I didn't do anything but offer our home for the event. But, what a blessing! I was willing to use what God had entrusted to me to further His kingdom, and to have a small part in both of their spiritual journeys.

> **Ripple:** Have a get-together at Christmas, talk about your favorite Christmas memories, and tell them why Christmas is important to you. This does not have to be awkward. Ladies love to see people's homes decorated for the season! They love to have a reason to get out of the house.
>
> **Ripple:** Keep an eye out at the consignment stores for Rick Warren's book, *The Purpose of Christmas*, it is a good one to give at the end of the night for a giveaway or as a door prize!
>
> **Ripple:** You can also give *The Purpose of Christmas* to teachers, hair stylists, or whoever you see in December.

QUESTIONS

1. Have you ever gone on an adventure? One with no agenda?

2. Do you go to a Bible/book study? How were you invited?

3. Have you ever asked someone how they are doing and received an unexpected answer?

4. How do you feel about hugs? Have you ever had a hug that felt like it was from God?

5. Have you ever given God a fleece test? What was it?

6. Have you ever been awakened by God about serving Him?

7. Do you journal? What do you journal about?

8. Have you ever mentored someone?

9. Have you ever been on a prayer chain? What was your experience?

10. Do you have Christian Christmas parties? Do you invite unbelievers?

7

—◦◦◦—

Making Lots of Ripples

ANOTHER CHANGE

Time to change again. If there's anything that is certain in life, it is that it changes. I know change can be scary and disruptive. You start to figure out your schedule and what you're supposed to do each day and *BAM*, everything is different! If you need more changes in your life, have kids. They have a way of pushing you out of your comfort zone! As our oldest daughter was finishing up her sophomore year, we started to think about college. We wondered if the small Christian school our children attended was preparing Abby for the next phase.

So we had a conversation with the kids about switching schools. We received mixed reactions, emotions and Abby was not in favor of it. The two younger kids who were in middle school wanted to make the switch. They wanted to have more than twelve kids in their class. (They would have over forty kids per class in the new school.) We left it up to them, but proceeded with the process of school interviews, tours, and meeting the teachers. Abby came along but was still not ready to make the switch. (We did tell her that she could stay at the old school.) As summer was coming to an end, she did not want to be the only hold out, plus her friend was making the switch also. Decision made.

Bigger school, more lessons, and of course more people. I will admit that the thing I liked the best about the new school was *NOT* the twenty mile drive across town both ways, but the fact that you could drop off and pick up the kids. You weren't stopped to volunteer for something everytime you were in the parking lot. It was more established! The fact that I didn't have to volunteer as much made up for the longer drive.

No Christian school is perfect because the people attending aren't perfect. So of course, there were some bumps along the way. One day, while Abby was walking down the hallway, a boy knocked the books out of her hands and nothing was done about it. Several years later, out of the blue, we had a knock on our door. Our daughter looked out the window and said that it was the boy who was mean and knocked the books out of her hands. She refused to answer the door. So I did. I asked what he wanted, and he said that he needed to speak with Abby. He was polite, so I made her go outside and talk to him. I watched from the door in case anything happened, plus, I was really curious. This young man had taken the time to seek her out so he could apologize for his behavior towards her. Keep in mind, this was years later.

How impressive . . . I cried! Abby was able to let go of whatever bad thoughts she still held onto about the matter. I thought about the great spiritual growth this young man must have gone through! Christian schools instil Christian values and teach the kids what the Bible said, but until they grow up, you don't know if it is sinking in. Proverbs 22:6 says "Direct your children onto the right path and when they are older they will not leave it." God's Word had penetrated his heart as he matured, and then he made it right with those he wronged!

Many times I wished I could go back and apologize to a girl to whom I had redirected all of the bullying toward me. To take the harrassment off of myself, I started teasing this girl for her looks, and I must say it was very effective. All the negativity I was receiving was now being directed toward her. I still feel shame and guilt over the immature way I handled that situation. I have been forgiven from the Lord, but to have an opportunity to make it right, would be great. "Sorry, Penny." Is anyone perfect that goes to a Christian school? No! Are any of us perfect? No! We are all just a work in progress.

Ripple: Think about the missed opportunities in your life . . . is there a way to correct any? Talk about them with your children and grandchildren. Let them learn from your mistakes. Discuss how you could have done things differently and ask them how they would have handled the situation.

A HANDFUL OF SEEDS

What could I learn from this new school? During an assembly, author Mark Cahill talked to the students about the two books that he had written: *One Thing You Can't Do in Heaven* and *One Heartbeat Away,* that he gave the kids for free. Our kids said I should read them, and of course . . . I did. Mark was *all* about sharing the gospel! I remember several ideas I picked up, but the one that really struck me was something like this, "God has given us a pocket full of tickets, and it is our job to hand out ticket after ticket to a place called Heaven."

Think about this . . . if there was a free concert, and you could have as many tickets you wanted to hand out, you would hand out all the tickets you could. You wouldn't question whether or not the people you were handing tickets to could attend the concert or not, or if they really wanted your tickets. They had the opportunity to go if they wanted, because you had given them a ticket. The person doing the concert had done all the work for them to attend. The only thing the people with the tickets had to do was show up at the concert. Heaven is so much better than a concert, and it's for an eternity! Why would you not pass out all the tickets to Heaven you can? Or, in this case, be willing to tell everyone the best and greatest news there has ever been!!!

The tickets he talked about passing out, were gospel tracts (These are small pamphlets that have a story that grabs your attention and then explains how to have a relationship with Jesus and spend eternity in Heaven with Him. They come in many versions but have the same gospel message). He handed out tracts or left them where people would find them.

For those of you that don't believe gospel tracts work, let me tell you about Jeff. Before becoming our children's junior high youth pastor, he was a young man working at our Iowa State Fair. While on his lunch break, he walked through a building where people show their wares in booths: anything from metal buildings, pots and pans, hot tubs, colleges, and churches. Many church booths would hand out gospel tracts, and he accepted several different ones from them. While eating his lunch, he read them ALL and accepted Christ, right there at the Iowa State Fair. After serving as a youth pastor, he became a missionary to Africa. *So, don't get me started that gospel tracts don't work!* God can use anything to lead someone to Himself. (Fun fact: Hudson Taylor, the famous missionary to China, also accepted Christ as his Savior after reading a gospel tract that his mom had lying around their house.)

I had never seen or heard of gospel tracts before. I loved the idea and take them everywhere I go. I feel like I am planting seeds or passing out "Heaven tickets." I pray someday I will meet many people that come up to me in Heaven and say, "You know that gospel tract you handed me or that one you left in the women's bathroom? I found it and prayed to accept Christ. You started my journey." The Bible says in 1 Corinthians 3:6-8, "I planted the seed, Apollos watered it, but God has been making it grow. So neither the one who plants nor the one who waters is anything, but only God, who makes things grow. The one who plants and the one who waters have one purpose, and they will each be rewarded according to their own labor." Together we help someone's eternity!!! I leave tracts everywhere: women's restrooms, dressing rooms, in the books I leave places. I hand them to the waiters and waitresses, valet parkers, under windshield wipers on cars, in the seat back pocket of airplanes (these I put inside the air magazine). I have even been known to fold them up and stick them inside beer cartons at grocery stores. That little opening on the side is perfect! (I really would like to talk to the people that found them in their beer cartons.) I also hand them out to trick or treaters on Halloween, put them in May Day baskets, and if I know someone is an unbeliever, I put them in their Christmas cards. Sometimes I stick them in the mail with my bills that I am paying. I carry them everywhere I go.

Only one life, 'twill soon be past, only what's done
for Christ will last. - Charles Studd

If we believe the truth about God, Jesus, Heaven and Hell. Why?? would we not share this good news! My brother Jay has a lawn care and snow removal business. That profession has a lot of turnover with employees. A *lot!!* When they come to our home, I am quick to hand them cold water, a snack or hot chocolate, some hand warmers, and a gospel tract. I do this as soon as I see a new employee because I may never get the chance again. If they continue to stick around, I continue to be kind to them. One, I get better service! And two, I hope I'm planting seeds that someone can water . . . oh yeah, I watered, too (bottled water, lol). Someone needs to harvest!

I also hand out tracts to anyone that does work at our house: the cable guy or a worker that needs to do a repair. I've had many great conversations about God while they work. Usually I offer them something to drink, so they can see that I'm nice. Then start the conversations about small stuff, the weather, how busy their day is, if they like their job. People like to talk about their families, and then I try to bring God into the conversation along the way. A few, have told me their problems, I listen and tell them how God has helped me through some hard things. Sometimes they have questions about God that they have never asked anyone about.

Yearly, we have our furnace serviced, and I had a gentleman who must have been to our home before because when I handed him a gospel tract. He said, "You gave me one of these before." So, I asked him if he read it and he said, "I did and I gave it to my wife to read." He told me it was interesting. I keep a supply of books on hand and pulled out *The Purpose Driven Life* and asked if he had read it. He said he hadn't, so I asked him if I gave him a copy, would he attempt to read it? He said, "Yes," so I gave it to him.

I also sell a lot of things on Craigslist and have met many nice people over the years. Whether they buy or not, I hand them a gospel tract before they leave and tell them that having a relationship with Jesus Christ is the most important thing they could ever do! I tell them to take time and read the tract I'm handing them. You never know who God will send your way, to get the gospel in their hands.

Most people will tell me they are Christians – because they go to church, their parents are Christians, or because they grew up in America. That usually leads me to another conversation about their "Christianity." If

I think they have a firm grip on their relationship with God, I sometimes ask why they didn't hand me a tract. It used to make me sad when I handed a Christian a tract because I wanted to get them in the hands of unbelievers. But, God knows who needs to get these seeds or who needs to be encouraged. I hope receiving a tract encourages them to be bolder in their faith and they share it with someone else.

I once met a man who lives a state away but traveled to Iowa for business. He purchased a Craigslist item from me and a month later came back and purchased another item. The second time he came he mentioned the tract that I gave him before and told me he knew God had sent him to my place. I showed him how to put the Bible app on his phone and encouraged him to listen to it while driving. Since he had contacted me, I had his phone number and sent him encouraging text messages occasionally, asking and prompting him to read his Bible. Believe it or not, this has happened with several people. I had many items for sale and sometimes had repeat customers.

Stretch yourself by passing tracts out, not all conversations end up with God in the middle of them, so don't be discouraged if they don't. It's more about the effort in sharing God with others.

There are several places you can purchase different kinds of tracts. You can also get free tracts from the Fellowship Tract League. I usually make a donation, so they can keep their ministry going. This is an easy way to spread the gospel and keeps me hopeful that I'm making a difference. Isaiah 55:11 says," It is the same with my word. I send it out, and it always produces fruit. It will accomplish all I want it to, and it will prosper everywhere I send it. "

> **Ripple:** Order 50 tracts and put them in your purse, billfold, back pocket, or car. Pray in the morning, and ask God to show you someone that you can hand it to. Or put a few in beer cartons!

BOOKS BOOKS BOOKS

When kids are in the junior high years routines seem to make it less noticeable that things are changing. Even when the first child goes to college, because you still have two in high school. But you tend to notice when they all go off to college or out into the world. Another change!! During our oldest's senior year, I wanted to spend more time with our kids since they soon would all be gone. It's hard to go to all the school activities and sports games when you work in the evenings and Saturdays. I had slowed my business down quite a bit when I had been diagnosed with MS, but now I decided to shut down my business entirely, which was a huge decision!!

I had been a portrait photographer for twenty-four years. I have never really regretted the decision, but I do miss the creativity of the business and the people for sure!! Half of my business was repeat customers. Over the years they had become my extended family, so not taking some of their senior portraits after I had photographed them from infancy, was really hard!

Over the years I would tell people with children, you will always be chasing them. The older they get, the more you have to chase, IF you want to see them. I finally took my own advice, and chased our children to all her games and school functions, and never regretted that decision!!

Ripple: Be involved in the lives of your children and grandchildren. Try to make it to at least one activity per week. I know that sports games when kids are little tend to drag out, but they will remember it. Try to strike up a God conversation with the people next to you while you watch!

With my business shut down, one child graduated from college and married, one in college, and one starting college, we were now empty nesters! I had more time to read!

Unless a book is untruthful, I finish it to the end . . . even if it's boring. If I start one that is hard to get through I will start another one as an incentive. I will read one chapter of the hard one and then read the better book after as a reward. I do this because I don't want to miss that one thing they say that changes me for the better.

I can't tell you how many times that I counted down the pages before I was done, to have that last chapter be the best one of the whole book. Of course it happens the other way too!! The first chapter is the best one, and then it goes downhill from there. I hope mine is one that is good all the way through!

During our son-in-law Jon's graduation for his master's degree, I was read while we waited for it to begin. (College graduations are really boring! You don't know anyone except that one person who is graduating. At least at high school graduations you know several of the kids.) Before the ceremony started, a friend of our daughter's asked me how many books I read in a year. I took a wild guess, but didn't really know. Our Abby answered for me, "A lot." . . . How many do I read in a year? I was really curious and wanted to know, so the next year I kept track. I wrote them down in my phone's note app and gave them a rating of one through five thumbs.

This has turned out to be good plan! I've used it to tell someone if I liked the book they are asking about, it helps me to pick out one for someone who is going through a difficult situation, and it helps me remember which book I want to use for our study group. This is hard to admit, but the list has saved me time from reading a chapter or two and then saying to myself, "I think I have read this before."

The first year that I kept track, I read eighty books. – These are all different sizes. The following year, I set a goal to read one hundred in a year. I met that goal!! You will read later, it was a bit tricky because that year ended up being a bit chaotic. The last few nights of that year I had to stay up late. *I was NOT going to miss the goal by just one book!*

The best thing about this challenge . . . I found out that I could do life with a lot less television. I would start watching the evening news at 6:00 pm and kept the TV on until the late news was over at 10:30 pm. Looking back now, that was a lot of television!!! I now use that time to read or spend with others.

It's hard to read a book while cooking, but instead of watching TV, I started listening to church sermons or podcasts. It's about the right amount of time and much more uplifting! I now skip the news and read the headlines on my phone. Life has a lot less stress and depression without it. (Which was even more true during Covid.)

Ripple: Give up one hour of TV a day and read a Christian book. Listen to a sermon or a Christian podcast while doing different activities like cooking.

Ripple: Share with others the ones you think they would find interesting or would apply to their circumstances.

Let's dive more into the subject of books. I've learned just about everything I know from them! Seriously, I was *NOT* an academic person in school. I use the creative side of my brain, which worked out for me since I was a photographer by trade.

When I was pregnant with our first child, every doctor's visit resulted in an arm load of pamphlets to read. I thought that you were supposed to read them – I'm not sure how many people actually do, but I did. My mom and mother-in-law both worked, our baby was coming in nine months, and Dean didn't know any more than I did about being a parent, I needed all the help I could get. I'm not a nervous kind of person, so I wasn't worried about parenting . . . I just wanted to be a great one. So I read! (This is the sad part! I didn't know there were books that talked about how to raise Godly children! ☺ I didn't know what I didn't know. This is even sadder! The church ladies gave me a baby shower, and *I DID NOT* receive one book on raising Godly children, nor did I receive a children's Bible! That's sad! Nor did I get one on how to have a Godly marriage!)

I recently read *The Family Blessing* by Rolf Garborg. It was about praying blessings over your children. It's great to give as a baby gift. I wish I would have read it while my children were little. I would have prayed blessings over them while they were growing up. Most of my prayers were, "Lord, please keep them safe and healthy," or "May they pass this class." Maybe . . . if I would have prayed blessings over them at the beginning, school would have been easier for them. I prayed our children would have a lot of common sense, which they do! But, they all told me I should have prayed for book smarts, too. When I told my friend Marcia that, she said that what I prayed for was good, the kid with common sense should have prayed for their *own* book smarts – since they had common sense!

> **Ripple:** Give a book on how to raise Godly children to a mother-to-be or a new mother. Maybe that mother will raise the next Billy Graham.

If I had questions about anything I was interested in, I would read. This is sad but, most of what I read when my children were little was how to decorate your home and gardening books – alot of wasted time. (I did use my garden for His glory.) The first Christian book I was introduced to was *The Purpose Driven Life* by Rick Warren, our church asked everyone to read it because the pastor used it for a sermon series. (This was the fall after church camp.) That was another turning point in my spiritual growth.

When I decided to get serious about being a mature Christian, I started reading. To be honest, most of the people who speak truth into my life are the authors that I read. I have had a few friends that have helped my Christian walk along the way, but life is busy and I can always pick up a book. Don't misunderstand what I'm saying, I read my Bible every day, but for me, hearing how someone trains up a child for God is easier than trying to figure it out on my own. I find it interesting to hear how other Christians do things right and wrong. I read so much that I usually know how to deal with a problem when it appears because I have already read about it! I don't read how to have a better marriage when things are bad. I read books about how to have a good marriage when things are good. I read about what happens in your grief before I go through grief. What's good about this plan is that I'm ready before most problems come my way. Also, I have answers for people when they are going through their problems. I don't know if this makes sense to you, but it makes perfect sense to me.

I buy most of my books at thrift stores. Besides helping different charities while shopping at them, you can get them cheap. There will always be people that must have the newest and most talked about book when it first comes out. I choose to wait, since I have an entire bookshelf full that I still need to read. I'm not the fastest reader, but I find that if you really want to read and learn, you will find the time.

I read Christian books on how to grow my faith or how others are growing theirs. I don't read Christian novels very often, but you can learn from these also. I read Randy Alcorn's, *Safely Home* and learned so much about how the persecuted Christians in China live . . . I cried my eyes out. It made me ponder, how much time do I seriously spend praying for my Christian brothers and sisters who are being persecuted throughout the world? Anytime you read, it's good to reflect on how to apply what you've learned to your life. I hope if you've gotten this far in my book, you figured that one out already! I've prayed for persecuted Christians occasionally in the past, but since then, praying for them has become something I do every night. When you think about how some Christians suffer for their faith, isn't praying for them the least we can do? We get to climb in our warm beds at night instead of the floor of a jail somewhere, or being awaken at the slightest noise because someone may raid our house to arrest you for being a believer.

> **Ripple:** When you read a book, think about what you learned or were made aware of and figure out if you can apply it to your life. Before starting a novel, try to read one chapter first from the Bible or a book that will grow your faith.

I remember one book I almost didn't make it through, the author was whiny, and did *not* stick with her title theme *at all*. It was not life changing, but I finished it and learned how hard it was for her military husband to get a job when he finished with his deployment and the struggles her family endured while he served our country. Now I pray for military people as they adapt back to their lives at home and for God to provide jobs for them. If you take time to think about what you're reading and the author, you find ways to put God in the middle of it. I prayed for that author's writing and if you don't like my book, you can pray for me. Just don't pray that I will be a better writer since I still do not have that desire!

> **Ripple:** Pray for the people that help produce your entertainment : the authors of the books you read, song writers/ singers, artwork, chefs and actors. They are people too.

A BIG PRAYER

I hope I made my point . . . *I read!* I like ones that teach or give me so many ideas my head spins, and I realize at some point I will have to reread it. *The Circle Maker* by Mark Batterson was one of those books. The main point was how to pray big. We have a Big God, that says we can't fathom what He can do.

I put this into practice for an organization I volunteered for called Stonecroft Ministries. This is a national and international organization that is non-denominational. Stonecroft hosts breakfasts, luncheons, or dinners with speakers who have been coached to give their testimonies about how Jesus has changed their lives and how you can have a personal relationship with Jesus. This is an outreach where Christians invite their unsaved friends and neighbors. This organization then follows up with anyone who wants information after making a decision to accept Christ into their lives.

Let me sidetrack for a moment, when I first volunteered with this group, I ran into many obstacles. I went to churches, promoting the luncheons, but received a lot of push back! I wasn't asking for financial support, but wanted them to tell their members about the outreach program they could use to bring people to Christ. I explained repeatedly that if someone brought a friend to a luncheon, their guest would most likely end up attending their church. *Because, Stonecroft isn't a church! I can be argumentative at times, especially when I am passionate about something!* I want churches to remember that the church is *not* a church building. The church is you and me supporting others, spreading love and the gospel of Jesus Christ! Can we not support other organizations that are doing the Lord's work? Churches need to get behind other organizations that are trying to spread the gospel like they do. What a shame that they try to keep everything and everyone inside their buildings. If pastors would use these organizations a little more, then they could free up some of their own outreach money and use that for something else! Plus, they might have better finances by having a larger congregation. (Just my opinion!) Ok, back to how the *The Circle Maker* inspired me.

Annually, each Stonecroft group does a fundraiser to help with their expenses. Without knowing it, our little group in Ankeny, Iowa, ended up being in the top ten for fundraising in the nation!! (I believe you should give God 100% when you do anything for Him.) I bet you guessed my response. Yes, I was happy, *BUT . . . could we do more!?!* We weren't trying to be in the top ten, but since it happened and I read *The Circle Maker,* I decided that we were going to pray BIG!! We were going to have faith! We were going to see God at work! I think our silent auction raised around $4,000 the year we were in the top ten. So, I said to our local Stonecroft planning team that I was praying for a goal of being number one the next year. They thought that was a good idea until I said, "The goal should be $10,000." I love saying things that shock people. I knew what they were going to think of my goal. I relished their looks when I announced it, they were polite but you knew what was going through their heads. Did she say

$10,000? 😊 I wanted our goal to be one that we couldn't reach on our own! If I said let's raise our goal by $1,000, our team would have been excited, and they would have believed that *WE* could do it. They were on board, but I'm sure they thought I was out of my mind.

I was okay with that, I have really broad shoulders, *and they didn't read the book!* I also asked my Bible/book study group to pray for the $10,000 goal. A few of them are involved in the Stonecroft (I'm good at recruiting!!) so they already knew what I was going to pray for. I know if God wants to raise $10,000 for a Christian organization, He can do it!

(Disclosure!!! You have to know the people that attend these luncheons in our town. Most of them are older ladies on fixed incomes or widowed, so not big spenders.) I had to come up with some other buyers besides the ones who attend the luncheons.

> *People who say it cannot be done should not interrupt those who are doing it. - George Benard Shaw*

In the book, Mark talked about working like it depends on yourself, and praying like it depends on God. That's exactly what we did. – we started praying BIG in May with the fundraiser being held in October.

The first thing that started the ball rolling was Family Christian bookstores announced that they were closing all of their stores, which made me very sad. I think Christian book stores have such a ministry. We had two stores in our area, but I was out of town when they started discounting merchandise. As soon as I got home, I went straight to the store by my house. There wasn't much left and what remained was 90% off, so I bought what I thought we could use. Then Dean and I went to the store across town. They were closing that store less quickly and were only at a 40% mark down, so they had a lot more merchandise.

The store by our home happened to be a tenant in the retail building we own with a partner. I shopped in the store frequently and knew the store managers personally. I knew he was in charge of closing both stores. So, I did what I tell my kids to do. Ask!! What is the worst thing that they can say? No? I called and asked the manager if he would give me the 90% discount at the other store if I bought a lot of stuff. Remember, they were only at a 40% mark down. This was a *BIG* request. He took my number and called the owner. I had already been looking around the store for a while, when he called me back and agreed to give me 90% off. (I wish we would have had more time and a bigger truck. Dean's SUV does not fit as much stuff as my minivan, but I would make do.)

Dean had dropped me off and didn't know that I had wheeled and dealed with the manager. When I got the okay, I called and told him the shopping trip was going to take a little longer than expected. I explained I was going to buy a bunch of stuff and needed several boxes. He said, "What are you going to do with it all?" I said . . . I had a plan! Again, he knows if I set my mind to something, he might as well go along for the ride. He went across the street to the big box store and grabbed boxes. I shopped – *It was SO MUCH FUN!!!* The young gal that helped me had fun too – it was contagious. I bought all the gift sets, mugs, socks, and ect. My thoughts were on fundraising. We were holding a silent auction, and needed merchandise. Usually we get donations but when something that is normally $10 is now only $1, there is a lot of profit to be made. Plus, I knew I would find other uses for it. Needless to say, by the end of the shopping spree, I had an SUV full of merchandise. I spent approximately $400 for something that was worth $4,000. We now had a good start!

That summer I also went to the big Hwy 141 garage sales. This is a huge gathering of garage sales that runs one weekend each summer. It stretches over a hundred miles and goes into each of the towns that sit along this highway. People plan for this every year. Family members will open up their garages to family and friends that need to get rid of stuff too. At one garage you might be shopping from several households. It was an amazing summer of garage sales, not just the Hwy 141 sale, but all summer long. You wouldn't believe all the new stuff I picked up for next to nothing. I only bought when it was a good deal, and it didn't matter what it was. I bought a really nice set of Rachael Ray pots and pans, new and still in the box for $20! They were $70 in the store. I went to one garage sale where the woman must have been selling all her wedding gifts she didn't want. Everything was new in the box and only $1 per item. (And I'm talking about really nice items!) I could go on and on and tell you story after story of all the new merchandise that I bought for next to nothing!! Or for free! Yes, *FREE!* God was having people give stuff to me free so we could make this goal. I would ask the people selling their stuff if they would lower the price of certain items for a non-profit auction that I was working on. People not only discounted, they gave me the stuff!

At the end of summer, I assumed everything would come together to make awesome gift baskets. I would sort it all out later.

I also went to most of the businesses in town to get donations. While asking, I would tell them about the goal, the book I read and how I was praying BIG! Because I had so excitement to see how God would answer this prayer, they were excited about giving. A kid's Kindle was even donated from a Toyota Forklift Store. I could tell story after story of God being in the middle of all this . . . ok, two more stories. I asked our bank to donate. Dean said that there was *NO WAY* they were going to donate to our group. A week later they called and donated $500. (I didn't even know banks donated money.) I used it for the garage sale items and the purchased merchandise.

I also asked a local jewelry store about a donation. Dean said, "They are Jewish; they are *NOT* going to donate to a Christian organization!" *Guess what? They did!* They not only donated – they gave: shopping after hours for you and your invited friends. They would send a limo to pick up everyone and each person received $100 to spend for up to five people. The buyer of the package is given $500 to spend! The package is worth over $1,000. Wow . . . God put an exclamation point on it for my husband's doubts. Of course, Dean then said with a bit of an attitude, "Well now you have to get someone to bid on it." He was being a bit of a fun-sucker, but I didn't care because God gave us a BIG donation!

As merchandise filled our house, the team decided we needed more buyers. I asked friends if they were interested in buying some of the duplicate gift certificates. In years past, we had not always gotten full value of the gift certificates. But that would not be an option this year. In the spirit of getting everyone excited about the $10,000 goal. I came up with an idea to help push people to give the value of the certificate, plus something on top of it. God popped a slogan in my head, "Give me a high five or a big ten!" When someone bought a gift certificate, I asked them if they would pay $5 or $10 (the "High five" or "Big ten") over the value of the gift certificate.

Weeks before the silent auction at least 50% of the certificates were sold. Like I said earlier, we have done silent auctions in years past and the most we usually get for certificates is face value. People want a good deal, myself included! (This was a lesson learned while trying to reach our goal. You're giving to the Lord; you're not looking for a good deal when you're donating to His causes.)

By the end of summer, the donated and garage sale items filled up the corners of our garage, closets, and pantry! I'm not kidding, I had so many boxes and don't forget . . . the large SUV full of Family Christian stuff.

Dean and my mother continued to wonder who was going to buy all this stuff. I explained to them both that God provided all of it so He would get it sold, too. I was a *little* nervous, but I was running on adrenaline! I had witnessed all the little miracles while acquiring these items, so I trusted He would come through. Seriously, all I did was ask – God was the one who touched people to give and buy the certificates. The team decided we needed to host two auctions, one in the morning with the older ladies and one in the evening with younger people and spouses. I like having men at silent auctions because men don't like to be outbid – they keep the donations going up. I've seen women stop bidding on items just because their friend really wants the item. ☺ Having two auctions would double our chances to sell more!

Our oldest daughter came home to visit for a week, and my mother came over to see her. Both agreed to help me pull out all the items. They were amazed at the mounds of boxes that piled up in the garage. (Because I had stored stuff in every corner, closet, and garage, nobody knew how much there was . . . including me!) They thought the pile was big, but when all the items came out of the boxes, we were *all* overwhelmed!! It filled three bays of my four car garage. This pile wasn't even the donated items from businesses! This was just the stuff from the garage sales and the Family Christian Store. I began to think that I may have gathered too much. (As a matter of fact, the planning team told me it was time to stop gathering. I knew they were right, but it was a bit addicting!)

It was a bit like Christmas every time I opened a box. It was exciting because some of it had been in boxes for months, and I had forgotten what I had. There were so many *blessings* in each of these boxes and memories of how God had provided!

Everything was unpacked and I noticed that my mom and daughter were not nearly as excited as I was. They wanted to buy things or for me to give them some of the stuff. Then the questions started: "Who's going to buy all this stuff? How do you know what to put together in the baskets? Do you know how to arrange baskets?" After an hour of questions and negativity, I said, "I'm not sure, but God will help me! He's the one that provided all of this." Then I said, "Let's go in the house, and we can sit down and talk." That was my way of clearing out the room of some of the clutter. (*The clutter of my mind!*) Later, I would go do it myself *without* the commentary.

I looked at Pinterest for auction ideas and there were a lot of good ones. But, when you have a bunch of random stuff, you just have to start grouping it together. Kitchen, kids, spa stuff, etc., etc., etc.!!! I love being creative? I had so much fun!! The team wanted to help me, but I didn't know what to have them do. It was a lot of work and time and it probably would have been easier to just ask people for money. However, I was thinking about Ephesians 6:7-8 that says, "Work with enthusiasm, as though you were working for the Lord rather than for people. Remember that the Lord will reward each one of us for the good we do, whether we are slaves or free." What can I say? I was working for the Lord.

During our monthly staff meetings for Stonecroft and at my Bible/book study group, my prayer request was, I want to see God raise $10,000 for this fundraiser. I think by the beginning of September, they were sick of my request and thought I was in over my head. But things were about to change.

As each basket was assembled, I would put the completed baskets in the great room of my house. Each week the Planning Team members and Bible study groups saw more baskets and heard updates as to what God was doing. They may have even begun to believe that God might answer this BIG prayer. The garage was getting cleaner but the great room was getting more and more cluttered. (Did I mention that our house was for sale during this time? Fortunately, we only showed it once while all this was going on! But it did add a bit of stress.)

The people who were praying were excited to see God move in unusual ways. I began asking other friends to pray for the $10,000 goal. I knew if God decided to answer this request, we would all see the BIG prayer answered. I wanted people to see my faith in God, as over the top. We all need to have our faith stretched, and everyone loves to see a miracle!

Auction time was near, and I was more excited about the prayer request being answered than the auction itself! Most people, unless it's a life or death situation, don't ask for really big answers to prayer! And truth be told, I think the people who prayed were excited too. They wanted to be a part of something big that God was doing.

The invitations were sent and flyers announcing the luncheon were up all over town! Prayers were being prayed! We sat back and waited for the reservations to come in. I had been talking up this goal for months now. As days were crossed off the calendar, the RSVP's for the luncheon started trickling in. I was like a kid waiting for everyone to respond about a birthday party I was having. It was agonizing! Remember that feeling? At first you know everyone will be coming, and then you start realizing you are going to be at your party by yourself or with the same few friends that are always there. A week before the auction, I knew our numbers were low. I made calls to see why people were not RSVPing, and that's when I heard about the conflicts people had with that evening. I'm not proud of this, but I was getting angry! I had put a lot of effort into this auction plus a lot of time. I had everyone around town expecting us to reach this $10,000 goal! I was starting to feel let down by people and God. I didn't want God to look like He couldn't make this prayer happen. I had really stuck my neck out for God and besides, *I didn't want to look foolish.* I know this sounds really bad, but that's how I felt. I was defeated and taking it personally! But there was no turning back now.

Notice how many times I wrote "I" in that last paragraph. At some point I began to think it was up to me to pull this miracle off. Not intentionally, but it did creep in. All summer I put everything in God's hands and gave Him all the credit! But when the numbers for the luncheon and dinner looked bad, I started to take on all the responsibility of getting people to attend and the stuff sold. I wasn't relying on God anymore. It became all about what I had to do. I forgot all the times in the Bible that God made things seem *impossible,* like in the book of Judges. Here's Gideon again (Remember the two fleeces?). The Lord told Gideon that he was going to go fight the armies of Midian. Gideon was ready, the odds were stacked against him, but the Lord was on his side. He had a large army but was way outnumbered by his enemy. I'm sure after the fleece test, he was sure he would see a victory. And then God stepped in and said,

(Judges 7:2-3) "You have too many warriors with you. If I let all of you fight the Midianites, the Israelites will boast to me that they have saved themselves by their own strength. Therefore, tell the people, "Whoever is timid or afraid may leave this mountain and go home." Of course by the time God was done with Gideon's army, he went from 32,000 to 300 fighting men to win a war. I'm sure Gideon was not confident about going to war with only 300 men! Even 32,000 men did not compare to what the Midianites had, but God had told him to do it!!! I, on the other hand, did not have God telling me not to worry about a packed banquet room of stuff to sell. My attitude about the situation was bad! I whined and complained. Look at all this stuff! I spent all summer long gathering this stuff! Do you know how much time these baskets took to make? I can't believe people won't be coming to my function. Can you relate? Do you remember me telling you how much fun I had? I'm glad you did! Because all of a sudden it was nothing but work, and I had suffered doing it. Nobody appreciates me! Wow, this sounds pretty pitiful!!!

Somebody should have slapped me! Had it been one of my friends that acted like this, I would have slapped them. *Not really.* But I would have reminded them how God loves to do the impossible. I needed to hear the truth and not the lies of satan. God *NEVER* performs miracles the way we think He should! (Think about it. If it was easy, we wouldn't have needed a miracle.)

Failure is not falling down, it is not getting up again. - Mary Pickford

I felt a little better after the morning auction, but still pouted most of the day. When the first auction was over, I went home, packed the van bottom to top, unloaded and arranged it all again. This verse came to my mind, "Never be lazy, but work hard and serve the Lord enthusiastically (Romans 12:11). Everything was placed on the tables. People arrived and we started again! Only a few men were brave enough to show up to what is usually a women's function. I'm not sure if they were brave or if their wives told them they had to come.

We had a live auctioneer, auction off some events we had added to get the totals up. Horse riding lessons, a lake cruise with friends, two kayaks to use on a private lake, and a *fabulous jewelry package.* But our bidders were not very excited.

After the evening fundraiser, I heard several of the men, including my husband, talk about how great the speaker was and how moved they were by her talk. Duh!!! We had a speaker with a very powerful testimony speaking to lead people to Christ. That was the most important part of the evening. Somehow I "forgot" that. My priorities were out of whack! Like Martha in Luke 10:38-42. *Yes,* it was a fundraiser and *yes* we wanted to see this BIG prayer answered. But honestly, salvation of souls or even a deeper commitment to God should have been priority number one! After listening to the men go on and on about the speaker, my heart softened. They were shocked when they heard her life story. The speaker shared about how her parents were abusive to her and younger brother. Then the foster parents whom they were placed with were worse than their parents! She wanted to leave her home, but wouldn't leave her brother with the foster parents without her. (She should get the sibling of the year award!) Then she talked about being adopted into God's family and what a difference that it made to her life. (That's the short version!)

I take powerful testimonies (personal stories of how people's lives were before and after they accept Jesus into their lives) for granted, since I hear them at Stonecroft luncheons and at women's functions at church. How often do most men hear testimonies? Churches should make this a normal-every-month type of thing. It's good to hear a sermon every week, but to hear a person – like yourself talk about their journey to salvation and the struggles of their circumstances can be as powerful as any sermon. We've been to several churches on our travels, and have seen powerful life transformation testimonies. They are so powerful and easy to remember so they can be retold. (Honestly, as I sit here and type, I can recall several testimonies that I have heard over the years and the powerful impact God had on their lives and mine.)

Overall, we did have a good evening. People went home with some really nice stuff, a good meal, and a message that stirred their souls! The auction was over and my house and garage were a lot less cluttered, which was great!

The next day, Kim, the bookkeeper for our group, called me with the total; we were $500 short. She was excited – I should have been happy, especially with the low number of people that had attended and the weak bids. To say I was disappointed would be an understatement!!! I received two offers to make up the difference, one from Dean and the other from one of the ladies with Stonecroft, but I thought that was cheating! I wanted to see God make this happen and not me! I asked for a week longer before we closed out our sales for the auction. I needed to collect money from a few people that owed me for items they bid on without being at the auction, so I hoped that I had miscalculated the totals of the items I had sold before the auction.

I went to our garage where everything had been stored and prayed, "God, I'm worn out! . . . I know toward the end of this journey I thought I was the one making this prayer happen, and I'm sorry. There are so many people waiting to see a miracle happen. We are so close. We didn't pray for $9,500 . . . we prayed for $10,000 and I'm still praying that you make it happen."

> *"What do you mean, "If I can"?" Jesus asked. "Anything is possible if a person believes!" - Mark 9:23*

I bought the certificates that didn't go for face value, to hopefully sell a few more with larger offers. I took the certificates with me as I collected everyone's debts. As I gave them their items, I also showed them the remaining certificates. At the end of the week when the total was counted again, it was a little over $10,000! And I *did not* cheat or take anyone's pity money! Prayers of many people were answered in a BIG God way, and even my faith was strengthened. All those results came from praying and reading one book!

Ripple: Make it a goal to go to a Christian fundraiser once during the year and make an exceptional bid.

Ripple: If you are a woman, look up Stonecroft Ministries to see if they have a group in your area you could attend to hear a great testimony. And take a friend.

Ripple: Arrange a basket and donate it for a fundraiser.

Another book that impacted my life was *The Hole in Our Gospel* by Richard Sterns. I chuckled a few times, as I read about a grown man under his blankets trying to hide from God so he would not have to respond to what God wanted him to do in his life. Can anyone relate? Richard was a CEO in the Lenox dinnerware company when God asked him to be radically obedient and step out of his comfort zone. I love books on how God uses ordinary people to serve Him.

He quits his job and goes to work with World Vision, and God opens his eyes to the problems of third world countries. World Vision International is an evangelical Christian humanitarian aid, development, and advocacy organization. It's a child sponsorship program in third world countries to provide food and an education. The extra money goes to help dig community water wells for people to have clean water to drink. He explains what a difference having clean water, food, and an education can have on people around the world, how having these basic necessities can open people up to hearing the gospel.

I will never think of poverty the same way again. American poverty is different from third world poverty. In America, we have access to water at any time. We don't walk miles with a broken jug to gather dirty water full of bacteria from animals that defecate and clean themselves in it. We have government food stamps and churches that provide food if we are starving. Where do poor people in third world countries go to get food when everyone is as hungry and poor as they are? The governments in these countries don't offer many solutions. Richard asked the question in his book, *"Do we live to eat or do we eat to live?"* Reread that sentence one more time and really think about it! How much of a person's day in a third world country is about getting water or food just to survive? Think about your day and how it is planned around food. The questions we ask are: how long will the line be at our favorite coffee shop in the morning? Who am I having lunch with in the afternoon? What are we going to do for dinner tonight? Are we going out to dinner or staying in? And if we're staying in, what are we going to make? If you're eating out, where are we going? The only question people in third world countries are thinking about is *IF* they will even have food to feed their children before they put them to bed at night.

Always put yourself in others' shoes. If you feel that it hurts you, it probably hurts the other person, too. - Rachel Grady

When I finished the book, I went back to the Family Christian store, where I bought it and looked through the cards of children that needed to be sponsored. Each card had a child's name, age, where they live, and a picture of them. When you sponsor a child, you pay a monthly fee to provide for their needs. I looked for the one child I felt no one would pick. To make sure, I asked the manager of the store which child's card she remembered having been there the longest. She handed me Estavao's card. He was a twelve year old boy from Mozambique. He was not a child they would have put on a commercial or poster – he had epilepsy, trouble learning in school, and was an older child that looked like he needed help. I knew he was the one! I took his card home and have prayed for him ever since. He eventually moved out of the program which led me to sponsor two girls through Global Fingerprints, Sonal and Ruby, who were both from India. I had the two girls only nine months before relief efforts were told to pull out of their country. I wrote to the girls but never received any correspondence from either. Later, I adopted other children through Compassion International and World Vision. I have seven children (not all are financially sponsored) to pray for each day, for their water, food, clothing, shelter, for them and their families' salvation, and that they will be missionaries to their families and communities.

> **Ripple:** Look into organizations like Compassion International, Global Fingerprints, World Vision and many others. Sponsor a child in need.
>
> Read *The Hole in the Gospel*... see if it changes your attitude and the way you think about food. Or read another great book *Too Small to Ignore* by Dr. Wes Stafford, a former president of Compassion International. Same type of organization – totally different histories.

Not only do books change my life! I also use them to change other people's lives and to further the kingdom. My father, John, volunteered at the local jail for many years and distributed books to the prisoners to pass the time in their cells. While I'm at thrift stores or garage sales, I look for Christian paperbacks to purchase for the jail. (Prisoners can only have paperbacks because they can use hardbacks as weapons.) The jail had plenty of secular books, but not enough good Christian ones. The Bible is what will change their lives forever, but they won't always choose it. I want them to have several options that will lead them to Jesus.

While checking out at a Teen Challenge thrift store, the cashier, a young man, asked me why I was buying so many copies of the same book? I told him about donating them to a prison which started a God conversation. He told me he had done some time in jail, and read Christian books that had boosted his spirits while there. He also said the need for them was enormous, thanked and told me to keep up the good work.

> **Ripple:** Donate paperback Christian books to a local jail or prison to make a difference in someone's life.
>
> **Ripple:** Pray for the people in prison – for their hearts to be open to the truth and salvation – to learn and grow in God's ways – that they would share that truth with others.

Not everyone agrees I should give books to the jails. Someone once told me that it was a waste of my money to spend it on prisonors. That they need to do their time in misery with no entertainment. I don't agree. Prisoners are people that have made really bad choices. Many grew up in dysfunctional families and were not cared for or kicked out. Drugs and alcohol are another big reason why people end up in jail. Our society is falling apart due to the fact that our leaders want to take God out of our lives. Prisoners should do their time, but there needs to be a way to show grace and mercy to them while they are serving their sentences. God believes in second, third, and fourth chances, so while they serve, why not give them the hope of Jesus Christ? I have news for you . . . there are going to be a lot of people that have done really bad things in Heaven, including murderers! We are all sinners saved by grace.

Doctor and dentist offices are good places to leave books also. When I go to appointments, I take a book or maybe a child's Bible with me. I put a gospel tract in the back cover with a little sticky note on the cover that says, "Take and enjoy." So when people see the note, they know they can take it home and finish it.

At one doctor's appointment, I witnessed how well this worked. I went back with the nurse and left a book in the lobby. Thirty minutes later as I was leaving, I saw a woman reading the book I had left. They called her name and she tucked it under her arm and followed the nurse back for her appointment. If this woman is a believer, then I hope it encouraged her and she thinks about doing the same thing to bless someone else. If she is an unbeliever, I pray that a seed was planted, and that she will come to know Christ as her Savior. Either way, it's a win/win situation.

Keep shining through; you may be a lighthouse to someone trying to make it. -- Caroline Naoroji

The books I leave at these offices are about hope because, you never know what people are going through. Why not leave something that can be an encouragement to someone? Ones like *Fearless* and *You'll Get through This* by Max Lucado or *When God Doesn't Make Sense* by Dr. James Dobson are good ones.

Ripple: Take a Christian book to a doctor's appointment and leave it in the lobby on the coffee table with a note saying, "Take and enjoy it." (This may be the encouragement that someone needs to know that God is right there with them!)

Ripple: Take some gospel tracts and put them inside magazines in the waiting room. Or be bold and put one on the table.
(Pray that the right people would find them!)

Purpose Driven Life books are also good and cheap at thrift stores because Rick Warren sold so many of them. When we stay in hotels, before we check out I leave a gift for housekeeping: his book, a mug filled with a package of hot chocolate, a granola bar, a few small size candy bars and of course a gospel tract. I put this somewhere noticeable so when they walk in the room they see the gift. A note is attached saying God wanted them to receive this gift. I've also given these same ones to valet parkers, parking lot attendants, and other people who have some time on their hands. *The Purpose Driven Life* was given to Michael Phelps, the Olympic swimmer, that helped him with his journey to Christ, or so I read.

(While writing this book, I switched to leaving small devotionals instead for housekeepers since it's not as much reading.)

One time a parking valet remembered me when we came back to the same hotel where I had given him a book the year before. When I handed him a gospel tract, he said, "I remember you. You gave me a book the last time you were here." I asked him if he read it. He said, "I have started it but have not finished it yet." He also said he would start again.

Sometimes during conversations with hotel staff by God's mercy, I remember their names. This happened at a hotel in Parkland, Florida, where we had stayed the year before. I looked over at a young man behind the check-in counter and said, "Ben, is that you?" He had been a valet attendant the year before but had been promoted. He had gotten a new haircut so he didn't look quite the same, but as soon as he smiled, I knew it was him. We talked about his new job and if he had attended the church that we had discussed the year before. Dean looked at me and I told him this was the young man who parked our car that year. Not only did I remember his name, but also that his birthday was the same as Dean's, which impressed them both. (God gets all the credit that my mind was clicking on all cylinders)

We talked more about Calvary Chapel Church in Fort Lauderdale, the church we like to visit when in that area. I teased him that we come all the way from Iowa and have been to this church more than he has. That night Dean and I went to church and I grabbed a few invitations for their Easter services. I gave one to the gal at the Wendy's where we ate after church. I also gave one to Ben and the woman working with him. We talked about how good church had been and when the Easter services would be. The gal actually had been invited by her friend to go to Calvary, but she hadn't gone yet. I suggested that she and Ben should go together for Easter. I prayed. Only God knows if they went. I also left the Easter invitation for the housekeeper. Don't make handing out church invitations such a big deal!

The next year, Ben gave me a big hug as soon as he saw me. He admitted he didn't go to the Easter services, but mentioned his mom had just had a health scare, he said he was for sure going to Calvary Church the next day to say a prayer for her. (For now, only God knows if he went.)

Ripple: Next time the church has invitations to something that is happening, grab five and make it a point to give them all away! Even if you put them up on a bulletin board somewhere!

We travel by vehicle most of the time, so I keep extra copies of books in our car, which has come in handy on more than one occasion! We were at a cafe, and the gal that was running the place happened to be celebrating her birthday, so I grabbed a book from our car. (I also keep small gift bags and tissue paper in my car too! This can all be contained in a small rubbermaid tote). I gave her a *Purpose Driven Life* as a birthday gift. She asked if she could open the gift up in front of me. I said, "Of course." As soon as she read the cover she started to laugh and said, "I guess God really wants me to read this because I have been given it before," this started a nice God conversation.

Ripple: Buy five copies of *Purpose Driven Life* from thrift stores and give them away this week! Be creative as to who you give them to. If you have not read it, you should!

While waiting for our oldest daughter to give birth to our first grandchild, we spent the time going to thrift stores and looking around their city. I had picked up a couple NEW-looking books on marriage. One of them was, *For Women Only* by Shaunti Feldhahn. (I keep extra copies of these in a cabinet at home to give to engaged couples for gifts.)

Years ago while doing a study with this book, one section really spoke to me. Shaunti talks about how women want to feel loved. *Duh!* But the next part talked about how a man needs respect. Of course most of us think, well if he would show me more love, I would show him more respect. Except she really laid it on the wife to step up to the plate first. Ephesians 5:22-33 talks about a man loving his wife like Christ loves the church and how a woman submits to her husband. But in verse 33 it says, "So again I say, each man must love his wife as he loves himself, and the wife must RESPECT her husband." I had read that verse before, but had never picked up on the respect part. I had heard sermons about submitting to your husband, and if asked Dean, if I had the submiting part down, he said, "Yes, but not always the respect part!" Shaunti says, respect means love to a guy. Dean had the respect of his children and others, just not as much from me. I stepped up to the plate and our marriage got stronger. We are now four decades and counting, since that first prayer to have him in my life!!!

Everyone thinks of changing the world, but no one thinks of changing himself. - Leo Tolstoy

We were still waiting for our call to tell us that we were grandparents, so I went to stretch my legs and started a conversation with the hotel staff in the lobby. During the conversation I found out the young girl standing nearby was newly engaged. I decided to do a little more stretching. I went out to our car, grabbed a gift bag, tissue paper, and one of those *For Women Only* books. I wrote a little note on a piece of paper and gave it to her as a small gift.

(After this incident, I stuck little note cards in my box, too.) She opened it and was delighted and it started a God conversation there in the lobby. (In both of those situations, I also stuck a gospel tract in the back cover, just in case!!) SIDE NOTE: Since writing this book, I have come across another one that is equally as good and talks about the love and respect factor. It's called, *Love & Respect* by Dr. Emerson Eggerich.

Ripple: Get a small tote or a small diaper bag (they have many compartments). Put small gift bags, tissue paper, a package of blank note cards, and a few Christian books or small devotionals to bless people in those unexpected moments!

You read the Bible like any other book – one page at a time. Some of it made sense to me, and some of it didn't. Nobody encouraged me to read the Bible, except one eighteen-year-old young man. Nobody explained it to me, but I managed to get through the whole Bible. Also, nobody told me I could ask the Holy Spirit to help me understand the Bible. You can, and I would definitely encourage you to pray for the Holy Spirit's help when you do.

There are many Christian polls that say most Christians don't read the Bible. When I started reading mine, I was told by Christians that it was too complicated and too boring. I was also told to skip the Old Testament and just read the New Testament. (Maybe they said these things because they didn't want me to read it because then they would feel like they needed to.) It makes me sad that I was told these things, and I'm sure it makes

God sad, too. 1 Thessalonians 5:11 says, "So encourage each other and build each other up, just as you are already doing." Christians should be encouraging each other to grow in their spiritual walk with the Lord, and I take that literally!!!

Throughout the years I've encouraged my Bible/book study group to read their Bibles. I do this every few years since we have new people join and others that need to be reminded to continue. I also challenged my friend Scott to read his Bible, but he found it hard to find the time. I suggested that he listen to the Bible app on his way into work. He didn't know there was a way to listen to it, so I showed him how to use the app on his phone. (He listened to the whole Bible!) Glenda, my (adopted) neighbor, also reads through her Bible during her free time at work. At times she had questions or thought she might skip a section, but I cheered her on. Sometimes getting people to read does require extra nudging and encouragement along the way. During the week I will send a text to see if they have been reading their Bibles, or I will ask them what verses they read this week. It is exciting when they text that they read their Bible that day. Praise them along the way, take interest in where they are, and have conversations about what you learned while reading that same section of the Bible. People like to hear praise – even as adults and it's a privilege to praise others for reading their Bibles.

> **Ripple:** Pull out your Bible, call a friend and encourage or challenge them to start reading their Bible along with you. Even if it's only a chapter a day! Hold each other accountable.

Read or do studies on humanitarian books like *The Hole in Our Gospel* by Richard Stearns, about world poverty and child sponsorships like Kay Warren's book *Dangerously Surrendered* that dealt with the Aids disease, or *Born Again* by Charles W.Colson about prison ministry. *Undaunted*, by Christine Caine deals with human trafficking. Or a lighthearted book called *Miss Brenda and the Loveladies* about redemption and grace. These are sometimes tough but may inspire you to support these ministries or help you find your own cause to support. I leave these in places where people who have larger wallets will find them: nice hotels, airports, or cruise ships. Maybe the people that pick them up will be inspired to give to these organizations.

> **Ripple:** Read one humanitarian book per year.

I also leave books and gospel tracts in laundromats, where people have time to read while they wait. Don't assume that people won't read! I could tell you many stories about encounters that I have had with books and laundromats. Here are just two. There is a laundromat where I leave books regularly and had been there a couple days earlier but decided to drop off a few more off since I was in the neighborhood. As I walked in with the books, a big guy looked at me and said, "Hey!" It threw me off a bit because I thought he was going to say something about not leaving them. (This was during Covid, and I did have a few people say something about leaving books during a pandemic.) Instead he said, "Are you the person that leaves the books for people to take?" Remember, I put little notes on them that say, "TAKE & ENJOY." Then he said, " I really enjoyed the one on grace," which was *What's So Amazing about Grace* by Philllip Yancy. He asked if he could take a look at what I had and he took two. Then he told me that after he read those, he would leave them at the laundromat again. I said, "I hope you enjoy them." The other encounter was about a week later. It was during Christmastime at a different laundromat on the poorer side of town. I left a children's Bible and some kids' books at this one. I don't put a note on kids' ones so people can read them to their children while they are doing laundry. But, I know that people take them home, which is fine. This gentleman said to me, "Hey lady, can I take these books home to my kids?" I told him that would be fine. He then asked me if I was some kind of librarian. When I told him no, he said, "What church do you go to?" I replied I was doing this on my own. He said, "Hey, thanks lady." I can tell you that the $1 worth of books that I left there that day blessed me more than him. (Sidenote: I decided to *ASK* our Christian thrift stores if I could have the Christian books that they recycle, due to damage or other reasons. I now pick up boxes each month from three of the stores. *All I did was ask!*)

I also put Christian books in those little neighborhood libraries. These are mini enclosed bookcases that people build and put on a post by the sidewalk, so people can walk up and take one. When they are done with it they can return or replace it with another one. (I have been known to take a few nasty ones out of these libraries.)

For we are God's masterpiece. He has created us anew in Christ Jesus, so we can do the good things he planned for us long ago. - Ephesians 2:10

Besides paperbacks for jails, the hardcovers for random places like rest stops while traveling, and books for Christian friends to encourage their faith, you will also find in thrift stores little devotional type books. Some examples include: *Jesus is Calling* by Sarah Young, Max Lucado's, *Grace for the Moment,* and desk calendars that have devotions for every day. (Most of these look brand new, but sometimes someone has written on the first page, if you carefully remove that page, it looks new again.) I think a lot of Christian devotionals don't get read because Christians get them from acquaintances and from each other, like teachers that receive everything with apples on it – so they donate them. These are nice to keep on hand because devotionals are broken down to a page a day, so if people are not readers, this seems manageable to them. These books are great to use as gifts – birthdays, high school and college graduations, teachers (better than a mug), thank yous, Christmas, or sympathy/get well situations, ect. I also give these to – hairstylists (I go to various places, to have a different stylist each time), housekepers, massage therapists, healthcare workers, waiters and waitresses. (I have two ladies in my study group that give these to people facing hard situations.) Now you know why you can find these in the thrift stores. Just *DON'T* write in them so we can use them again for someone else!

Isaiah 55:11 says, "It is the same with my word. I send it out and it always produces fruit. It will accomplish all I want it to, and it will prosper everywhere I send it." This means God's Word will always accomplish what He desires, whether it is teaching, correcting, training, or leading us to Him. Think about the change that could happen by the end of the year if even some of these people start reading them!

(While writing this book, I gave a friend a devotional as a gift – she loved it so much, it resulted in her giving out five to her family, and they then gave to five other people. According to my friend, she knows of ten . . . that received a devotional because of her one!) To God be the Glory!!!

Ripple: If you have any devotional books, pull them out and give them away! Pick some up at a thrift store or buy several when they go on sale. Make a list of five people who you could give them to and start giving.

Books are a *very important* part of my life. If I had a bucket list, it would be to find mine in a thrift store some day!

QUESTIONS

1. Have you ever intentionally hurt someone's feelings? Were you able to apologize? Did you tell anyone how badly you felt about doing it?

2. Have you ever been handed a tract? Have you ever given one? How were those experiences?

3. Do you have any tracts you could hand out?

4. How much television do you watch per day? Per week? (Be honest!!!) Have you ever fasted from TV for a week?

5. Have you ever given a how-to- book (raise Godly children or how to have a better marriage) to anyone?

6. What is the best thing you've learned in a book (besides the Bible) ?

7. Do you pray for random things like the authors of books, Christian radio stations, singers of your favorite song?

8. What has been the biggest answered prayer you've had? (Oh, I so wish I could hear this one!!!)

9. Have you ever sponsored a child from another country? Do you pray for them often?

10. When your church is having an activity, do you hand out invitations?

8

---ɷ/ɷ---

Keeping the Ripples Going

THE HANDS & FEET OF JESUS

When our kids moved out, Dean said, "Now that the kids are out of the house, let's do some more traveling." God had decided to take me out of the cold, but guess what? I didn't necessarily want to leave my study groups, church, and volunteer jobs. I didn't want to stay in the cold, but I didn't want to leave either. I wondered how I would serve God while traveling. And who would I talk to? Where would I go to church? Plus, my older daughter asked me, "Are you sure this is how God wants you to spend your money and time?" Abby is good with guilt trips! She asked, "Is traveling to be warm really in God's plan for you?" I wasn't sure . . . if it was His plan or mine. That first year we were gone for seven long weeks – I was ready to go back home after two. We went to church in whatever town we were in, which solved one concen. It was fun to see how they did their services, and being with other believers made me feel closer to home! I was able to leave a lot of gospel tracts all over, but there had to be a better way to serve God than leaving tracts around town.

James is my favorite book in the Bible. James 2:18 says, "Some people have faith; others have good deeds. But I say, How can you show me your faith if you don't have good deeds? *I* will show you my faith by my good deeds." James understood that actions speak louder than words. It's all well and good if you read the Bible and know it cover to cover, but you better get the most important message out of it. The cover of the Bible should say *LOVE*. How do we love other by our deeds? You have to invest in people – *Time, effort and energy.* John 13:34-35 says, "So now I am giving you a new commandment: Love each other. Just as I have loved you, you should love each other. Your love for one another will prove to the world that you are my disciples."

My Bible/book study group had a four week period between books, so we decided to study the book of James. We discussed several of the hard verses such as James 4:17, which says, "So whoever knows the right thing to do and fails to do it, for him it is a sin." That's one of the hardest verses in the Bible for me! There have been several times that God has prompted me to be kind to someone that hasn't always been nice or even rude to me! And then do it with a good attitude . . . *that's hard*! We could've spent hours discussing that one verse, but it started to become a bit of a gripe session about how difficult people can make you sin, which isn't true, but sometimes it feels that way . . . we aren't a perfect group, just honest and working on becoming more Christlike.

We couldn't read James and ignore the fact that he said we should have good deeds. We decided to try doing two good deeds a day. The group had a hard time with that – excuses came out of the woodwork; some sounded like something a teenager would say . . . "I do this, and I do that. That doesn't count, or that counts extra. I do good things all the time. I do good things for my kids. I don't know what to do."

Some embraced the challenge and others didn't. We discussed what a good deed is – opening doors for people, letting people cut in line, being a respectful driver, cleaning off the counters before we leave public bathrooms, and smiling while saying hello. All of these are good, but good people that are *NOT* Christians do these things. Being an overachiever, I wanted to do good deeds that people knew were "God deeds" and give Him the credit. That's when the waiter and waitress idea popped in my head.

With a plan in my head and books in our SUV, we headed south. Maybe . . . I should have told Dean the plan, but I didn't want to be talked out of it. He was in for another surprise. (Side note: I reread Francis Chan's book *Forgotten God.* Francis talks about Spirit-filled Christians who give away extreme amounts of money, or talk to strangers about God or quit their jobs and go into ministry. He then talks about Christians, not in the Spirit, who want to be practical, and talk Spirit-filled Christians out of living radically for God.) I didn't want to be talked out of doing what God had popped in my head. Again, this is where journaling would have been helpful. I can't recall what state we were in or who the first waitress was when I put the plan into action, but I do remember the first two responses.

We eat out most nights and have interaction with our servers (who have a hard job trying to make people happy with their dinner experience.) We all know how crabby some people can be if the server forgets just one thing. I won't mention any names, but we have all seen them, customers that think they are royalty and everything should be perfect since they are paying $15 for their dinner.

The plan was to notice, converse with, and ask the servers for their prayer requests. Dean and I sat down at our table and the waitress came over, gave us the menus, took our drink order, and then I blurted out (read the next sentence as fast as you can). "We like to pray before we eat dinner, and I would love to pray for you. While you go get our drinks, will you think about something that we can pray for you about?" It was not graceful, and I'm sure I said it at record speed, *BUT . . . I did it!!!!* (I did not think up this idea – somebody along the way told me that they do this, I just copied a good idea.) The look on Dean's face was one of confusion! When the waitress walked away, he said, *"What made you do that?"* I said, "It was a good deed, and maybe it will get her thinking about God." He looked at me . . . with *THAT* look! The waitress returned and I asked her if she had thought about her prayer request. She asked, "Could you pray for my health?" I said, "Yes, but I forgot to ask you your name." (Health is a standard answer when they can't think of anything. But I have had many other responses.) She took our order and walked back to the kitchen. I then had time to talk with Dean, who by then had a small smile on his face. I said, "See, that went pretty well." He responded with, "She will probably spit in our food." He was just kidding, but he had to say something. Then we talked about what I thought I was doing.

I explained that I needed to have some sort of mission while we were out of town, and I thought servers could be my mission field. I was talking about God and letting these servers know that He cared for them enough to have someone ask them about their concerns. Then I told Dean, "If they spit in our food, God will protect us." – I'm not sure if that is true, but I haven't gotten sick yet.

The waitress returned with our food and chit-chatted for a minute or two. She asked us where we were from and thanked us for praying for her. She also thought it was a nice thing to do. Dean then relaxed about the idea but had a few suggestions on my approach. Then he said, "Are we going to do this for every dinner?" I, of course, said, *"YES!"* He said, "Let's just do it every once in a while." I smiled and said, "Okay." Of course, I was thinking every once in a while meant every time we went out to eat. Sometimes we get fast food or go to the grocery store, and I am not going to stop workers when they are in a hurry, so sure . . . every once in a while.

The next night we went to another restaurant. We sat down and Dean said, "Are we going to do that prayer thing again tonight?" "Yep!!!" I said. The waitress came out with the waters and the menus, and out came the pad, but she couldn't find a pen to take the drink order. The waitress then told us how many pens she goes through in a single night. She said she leaves her pen so the customer can sign the receipt, then they take her pens. I asked if the restaurant pays for the pens. She said they expect them to bring their own. And said that she used to buy good pens but it was costing her too much money. Bingo! . . . another God thought . . . maybe I could leave a few pens – with something about God or a church on them, after the dinner with a bow wrapped around them. I would have to look into this. Okay, back to the drink order. She found a pen. (A small side note here – I always order water, it's good for you and it's free – I use the money that would have been spent on a pop or lemonade for the gift.)

> **Ripple:** Order water at restaurants and pray for people in third world countries that would love to have that cup of water.
>
> **Ripple:** Start a collection of the money you save drinking water for organizations that build wells in third world countries. DENY YOURSELF OCCASSIONALLY!! It's good for your soul and for others.

I let Dean order first, and then I said, "Water please, and while you get our drink order, I would like to ask you if there is anything that we can pray for you about. We pray before dinner and would like to pray for you. You can tell me when you come back with our drinks." I said it calmly this time, and yes, Dean gave me that look, *"Are we doing this again tonight?"* And *YES,* he said those words when she walked away. I *knew* what he was thinking. When she came back with our drinks, she told us something other than her health. I can't remember what the request was, but she thought it was great that we talked and asked her for her prayer. (Again, a journal would be helpful to remember all the details.) She then took our dinner order and sat down at our table and talked to us for a while. Dean even started asking her questions – "Where do you go to college? What are you majoring in? We have two daughters that went to college". When she left to place our order, Dean commented on how nice that conversation was. We talked with her again when she brought the food out. Dean was warming up to this idea. God was doing His work in his heart, too. As we were putting on our coats to leave, she was still smiling, chatting and again mentioned how nice it was that we asked for her prayer requests. Then she hugged both of us! *BAM* . . . Dean's heart melted faster than the Grinch's! When we got in the car, Dean acknowledged that this was a good idea, and *WE* should keep doing this. And we do ☺

Since the first time I put this plan in action, some changes have been made. I now have a little bag that I bring in with me to the restaurants that has a gift bag, some tissue paper, and three different kinds of devotionals. I have a men's, women's, and one that is a smaller one, like a 30- or 40-day version. I give the smaller ones when there is not much interest from the server. These are never the same three since I pick these up secondhand. I build up my supply all year long. I stress this one thing: I give out devotionals that *look* new.

We still pray for our servers, but at the end of our meal when the server comes back to the table with our receipt, I hand them the bag with a devotional book, a gospel tract, and a business card size flyer for focus on the family. Usually, I write a short note thanking them for their service that night, that God chose them to receive the gift and that I hope they enjoy it. I have also made up business cards that have three really good websites on them that they can visit if they want to know more about getting to Heaven. (I'm in the process of changing this card to have the prayer of salvation on it.) I tuck this all down in the bag with tissue paper, and a few pieces of candy. In the past, when they asked why I was giving them a gift, I said that I appreciate the hard job that they have and wanted to encourage them. But I have changed my speech again. I decided it needed to be less about me and what I think, so I started saying that it is because I want them to know how much Jesus loves them and wanted them to have the gift. (I'm always looking for a better way!)

I have also started journaling . . . kind of. I started a journal with the prayer requests of the servers. When the servers tell me their requests, I write them down in my phone right away so I remember, and then transfer them into the journal. Once a week I pray through them for a year. Also, I pray that they will read their devotionals and accept Jesus Christ as their Lord and Savior! This helps me remember the restaurants that we liked and our time with the servers.

We have met so many, *SO MANY* nice people along the way. Yes . . . we've had a few odd encounters with servers. Even a few that didn't understand what a prayer request was. Some that can't come up with a request, but you can make a suggestion of health and they usually say, yes pray for my health. We have yet to have a rude encounter. We did have one server that never came back to our table – we walked to another restaurant down the road and had a great server that liked the prayers. We also had a gal that would not talk about God or prayer and wouldn't take the gift but she wasn't rude. (Both were in Key West.) ☺

Praying with our servers has led to many great conversations, hugs, and thankfulness. We've had several who cried; they thought it was so nice and others that wanted our names so they could pray for us. A couple of unexpected things we encountered along the way – I was prepared for mostly female servers, but found it's about equal. Guys like prayers more or as much as the ladies do. My only reasoning for this, is that women are talked to and asked about their feelings more than men are . . . just a thought.

On one occasion, we had a waiter named Michael. He was a young man about our son's age – upper twenties. We asked for his prayer request and told him to tell us when he came back with our drinks. He couldn't wait. (This happens often!! They want to tell you their request before getting the drinks.) He immediately told us that he was having a hard time in life right then, and he needed prayers to start hanging with the right people. He brought back the drinks, started tearing up and told us more. He added how special and timely it was that we would ask him that question. When dinner came, we had more conversation, and I told him that God knew who he was and that He had picked him to be our server that night . . . Oh my, more tears.

After we made it through the meal, (At this point, I had started giving the gift bags with the devotional book in them.) my first thought was that he was going to have a meltdown when I handed him the gift. *I was right!* I gave him the gift bag with the devotional in it and more tears started falling. He thanked us over and over and kept telling us how glad he was that we had come in that night. Dean went to the restroom and passed by Michael as he was showing all the other servers his gift. Next it was my turn, I told Dean I would meet him in the car. (We ate on the patio of Duffy's restaurant.) When I got to the car, Dean wasn't there. I looked over to the porch, and there was Dean and Michael in a deep conversation. So I waited. When Dean got in the vehicle, he had a few tears rolling down his cheeks. He had shared with Michael about how important it is to hang out with the right people, that he needed to find a good church, and that God was talking to him through us. Dean was really embracing this ministry. ☺

> *Good works do not make a good man, but a good man does good works. - Martin Luther*

The next year we had a sweet gal named Kaitlin at a different Duffy's on the other side of Florida. I asked the same question – How can we pray for you? She asked for prayers for her mom, Patricia who had tumors on her pancreas. Then she repeatedly told us how nice it was we did this and how glad she was that we came in. When we finished eating we asked for the bill – she said it had been taken care of. We asked why and who paid for it, she said that the restaurant provides her a few free dinners to do random acts of kindness and she wanted to give us a free dinner. *WOW!* We were trying to bless her, and we ended up being blessed, too! How's that for noticing someone and asking how we can pray for them? *FREE DINNER!!*

Here's how random life can be. We had to go back over to that side of Florida about a month later, and it was a different time, a different day of the week, and in a different area of the same restaurant. You guessed it. We ended up with Kaitlin again as our server! She recognized us right away and told us how she had been reading her devotional every day and underlining passages in it. *WOW!* This is fun! I love sharing Jesus with people, even with the ones who don't appreciate it, because the ones who do more than make up for the ones who don't! But really, you never know if those who don't just might appreciate it later! We had a nice conversation with Kaitlin again, and she had another urgent request for her brother and sister-in-law. She commented that we needed to come in more often . . . what a nice way to make a person feel really good. Not her . . . me!

A year later, at the same pizza place in Florida, we asked the waitress for her prayer request . . . she said, "I served you before." Yes, she had . . . *I even remembered her request!* It helps to actually be praying so you can remember them, especially if you do this when you're close to home. We eat out once a week in the summer, and tend to get the same servers several times during the season. I also occasionally see the servers around the town during the day. It's nice to be able to call them by name, say hi, and ask how things are going. (If you remember their prayer, you can ask them how that is going also.)

As I was in the process of finishing the edits of this book, I decided to get braver and seek out the servers I had been praying for, while out to dinner. I would ask the hostess for the server that had helped me the year before by name. Many times they did not know them – sometimes they could tell me where they had moved on to – but on those occasions that they happened to still be there, we had great conversations. Here's a few: CJ had asked for prayers about his girlfriend having a baby. When I told him I had been praying – he knew who we were and proceeded to show us several cute baby pictures of his daughter and said he was hoping he would see us again. Marrianna was a morning server at a hotel, which I saw for a week. She asked prayers for her newer used car to continue to run properly. (I gave her a devotional calendar at the end of the week.) When I saw her the next year, she excitedly told me she had been reading her devotional every morning and thanked me several times. But the best testimony by far was Donna. When we asked for her request the year before, she had been clean from drugs for two months and had wanted to remain that way. The next year we asked if she was still working at that restaurant. They said she was and was working that night, so we asked our waitress to have her come to our table. Usually, I will remember faces . . . this time I wasn't even sure if it was the same Donna we had the year before. (Remember I'm getting braver with each step!!) As she walked to our table confused as to who this couple was that had asked for her . . . I was getting nervous as to how to approach this conversation! How do you ask . . . were on drugs last year? I was committed at this point, and I didn't want all three of us to feel awkward any longer than possible! She bent over to hear me (I didn't want to speak loudly), and I said, "This is going to be a weird question, but did you happen to have a drug problem last year? She stood up, looked at me, and in an excited voice said, "You prayed for me last year!" Then she hugged me and thanked Dean and I over and over. Without asking her . . . she then told us that she reads her *Jesus Calling* book by Sarah Young that we had given her the year before, *every day*. Donna had remained clean and honestly looked like a new, healthier woman. Even though the situation could have been much different if it hadn't been her, I was so glad I asked the question. It was a highlight of our trip. (We also found out from CJ that the other waitress that worked at the same restaurant as he did – they were friends – had remained clean also from drugs.) It's fun to hear about answered prayers.

Faith is the willingness to look foolish. -- Mark Batterson

Another unexpected response that we have had occasionally were servers that have sat with us at our table or even in our booth while we prayed. The first time this happened we thought it was kind of weird, but we prayed right there with them. It's not a big deal, it just threw us off the first time it happened. Usually, it's Dean and me or the group we are with that pray for servers while they are getting our dinners.

One more disclosure. Asking people if you can pray for them should make you a *very patient and a more forgiving customer*. If a server goofs up your order, remember that you are representing the Lord! Grace and mercy may be called upon a lot. Sometimes, *a lot*. Another time, a server at a busy restaurant confused our entire order and our bill with the table that was right next to us. They were sitting so close, they were able to hear us ask the waiter for his prayer request and hear us pray for dinner. *They were close!* Dustin, our server, had to come back several times to confirm our order and the couple's next to us. When he brought our food, we ended up with one of their entrees and they ended up with one of ours – we just switched them. Next, our bills were mixed up. *Seriously,* for *thirty* minutes he tried to fix our bills! We had a lot of time to show the waiter *grace* while he worked on them. The couple next to us was getting very agitated with the waiter, so I started up a conversation with them. I pointed out the fact that not all people should be servers, but that he was trying and we should be patient. It worked! They were diffused, and we had a nice conversation with them. Bless Dustin. I prayed for him a lot; mostly that he would find a job that would best fit his skills. ☺ After we worked through the billing mistakes with the other couple (the bill was still not right!), the other couple left. On the way out of the restaurant, Dustin stopped and thanked us for not getting upset, having patience with him, and for the gift. Hopefully, Dustin reads about the grace of God in the devotional we gave him.

Sometimes servers are inattentive or don't know what they are doing, which makes me want to leave a small tip and no gift. But I'm reminded that those are the ones that might need it the most!

Getting hugs and thank-yous are fun, but more important to me are the servers that someday will come up to us in Heaven and say, "Hey I remember you. That devotional was just what I needed. It strengthened my walk with God," or, better yet, "It led me to the Lord. Thanks!" (And I bet I remember a few of their names!)

Ripple: Try asking your servers if they have a prayer request when they take your drink order. It will seem odd at first, but it gets easier. Then take it a step further and give them a devotional. If you live in the area, you could put some of your church pens in the bag also.

RESOURCES – GOOD DEEDS

By the time we get home from traveling we have a lot of hotel shampoo, conditioner, and soap. I finally figured out how to use these resources. Samaritan Purse has a ministry called Operation Christmas Child. This organization delivers gift-filled shoe boxes to churches in one hundred different countries in December, who then distribute them to impoverished children who may never receive gifts. These children then get involved with the churches that host small Bible classes, using the Christian storybooks, *The Greatest Journey* that are put in each box, to teach them about Jesus and how to have a relationship with Him.

Local churches that sponsor Operation Christmas Child provide boxes to take home and fill up with toys, trinkets, socks and many other useful things, including soap, toothbrushes and combs. After you pack your box (or boxes), you take them back to the church. They then send them on to Samaritan Purse. Each year I try to fill a few boxes or give the accumulated items (a lot of hotel soaps!) for other people to put in their boxes.

The children that receive the physical gifts also receive the most precious gift of all, the good news of Jesus. If you are not familiar with this organization, do a search and see what amazing things this group does. (There is a book about their ministry called *Operation Christmas Child: A Story of Simple Gifts*, that is filled with great stories and is a good read.)

> **Ripple:** Start looking for things throughout the year you can put in an Operation Shoe Box. If your church doesn't sponsor this program ask the pastor about starting it up.

Liquids cannot be put in the boxes, so I needed to figure out what to do with the shampoo and conditioners. Kim, a friend of mine, told me about making packets for homeless people. These can be as simple as Ziploc bags filled with shampoo, conditioner, and other toiletries. I bought a lot of socks when Family Christian store closed – these were good for Christmas gifts, but I had a lot of socks! I gave some to the local homeless shelter and the fundraiser for the Stonecroft ministries . . . and still had a lot of socks! So, I started putting a pair of socks in each homeless packet. I also put a personal note, a gospel tract, hand warmers, a granola bar and a mini New Testament Bible in them. (I now put packets in a reusable nylon bag like you get at a grocery store so they carry stuff in.) When I see someone in need, I give them a packet and a few dollars. I also pray for the one that receives the packet, that it will be a blessing to them.

I have often felt conflicted as a Christian driving away and ignoring people who were down and out. Yes . . . I've heard the arguments about enabling people who live like this. But, I worry about that one person who does need a hand-up – now I have a way to help that shows I see them as a person. 1 John 3:17 If someone has enough money to live well and sees a brother or sister in need but show no compassion – how can God's love be in that person?

Ripple: Make up a few packets for the homeless – stick them in a place you can reach in your car so you can hand them out your window.

I saw an idea of leaving Christmas stockings full of goodies at laundromats. I did something similar; instead I filled Christmas gift bags with candy, *a pair of socks,* a small box of detergent, and an ornament. I also added either the book, *The Purpose of Christmas* by Rick Warren, a small devotional, or a pocket New Testament.

Another random deed for laundromats – Put slightly used baby or children's clothes, in a box with a note saying, "Help yourself – God Bless!"

Ripple: Stop by a laundromat and leave a blessing for someone

Giving books to young children about God and the "true" Christmas or Easter stories is a great idea, too! Parents read them so you're really speaking into both of their hearts! *The Crippled Lamb* by Max Lucado (have a tissue handy). Is a great option!

Think of random people you can bless at Christmas – mail carriers, hairdressers, your favorite store owner, your manicurist, cleaning person, neighbors, foster parents, people that work at non-profits and pastors and church workers, etc. Christmas is a great time to bless people with a small gift that reminds them of Christ – an ornament that depicts Christ, a devotional, or homemade goodies with a note about how special they are and something about Jesus.

Ripple: Make up five random gift bags at Christmas – pray and ask God who should receive them – DELIVER

Another way to plant a seed is with my chalkboard by the central bathroom in our home. I write Christian wisdom or scripture on it. As people walk by, they take time to read what is written. I have had many good conversations about what is written on my chalkboard. As a matter of fact, several who have read my chalkboard are my son's twenty-something friends. I wondered if this age group would even take time to read what was written. (The message is short). I usually change the message every week. One morning I was pondering what to write, and I asked Zack's friend what he thought. Without any hesitation, he told me he really liked the quote by Dr. Seuss,"To the world you might be one person, but to one person you might be the world." He didn't say it exactly in those words, but he got the message. It had made an impression on him that stuck. A seed planted! When I see thought-provoking quotes, I jot them down in the notes of my phone. I use them for greeting cards, or a quick thought for someone special in a text to encourage them.

> **Ripple:** Get a memo board or cute cards; write a scripture or inspirational message and stick it on your fridge or where someone will see it. Or purchase artwork that has scripture or inspirational messages on them and place a few around your house.

Proverbs 11:30 says, "The seeds of good deeds become a tree of life; a wise person wins friends." If I see or hear of a great way to plant a seed, I adapt it to what I'm doing. Here are a few more ideas that show the love of Jesus to others. I bake chocolate chip cookies and give them to my adoptive grandsons and several others. People enjoy food, and you can make a lot of friends with cookies.

People who wonder weather the glass is half empty or half full miss the point. The glass is refillable. - Simon Sinek

Thrift stores – if you haven't figured out these are great yet . . . you've never been to a good one! Find one that sells children's Christian books cheap! Buy several and put them in the little "free libraries" in your town or laundromat.

Since we are talking about books again, what do you do with yours when you're done? I would donate your secular ones to a good Christian thrift store – so they can make some money for the Lord, and Christian ones you can leave in strategic places. I also have a little lending library of some of my favorite books that I love to loan out. People are not always good at returning them. . . so now, I write down what I'm missing and look for it at the thrift store. Why not try to get good books into the hands of other Christians, to help them grow. (I hope you give mine to someone.)

I got this great idea on vacation while watching out my window of a tour bus. There was a large field of flowers with a sign saying, "Pick your own bouquet $5.00." I adapted the idea on a much smaller scale and started growing zinnias – they make great cut flower arrangements. I buy vases at garage sales or thrift stores, and make up arrangements to encourage and bless people and give them away. Who doesn't like flowers?

Extra vegetables or fruit grown in your yard are great to share with neighbors or the local food pantry. Pumpkins in the fall are great too! These kinds of things build relationships with people, so later you can talk truth into their lives about Jesus. Handing out bottled water to people on bikes, construction workers, and sign twirlers could be a good deed, too. (Maybe add a gospel tract.) Of course, this does require advanced thought – a cooler with ice and water.

Be that neighbor that everyone wants in the neighborhood versus the one everybody complains about. If you are home during the day, why not help out those who work? Walk the neighborhood, pick up garbage that's floating around, take emptied garbage cans up to people's garages. Take the newspaper at the end of the driveway up to the door, do the little things that you see need to be done. Also be on the neighborhood watch program or watch people's homes while they are out of town. Maybe you can let workers in the door for neighbors, or be the designated house for delivered packages. Take time while you walk the neighborhood to think up helpful things you can do. Think back to when you worked outside the home. What did you need help with? Doing these things will give you an open door to talk to your neighbors and maybe that leads to a God conversation.

I hesitate to write this one because it may sound like I'm pawning off my garbage. Christian mail . . . I read most of my mail that comes from Christian organizations. (I do think they spend too much on color flyers, but that's just my opinion!) If there is something worth reading I will pass it along. I will put it in the books I leave places, I will leave the magazine types in laundromats, and I do put some in the magazines in the seat back pocket in the airplanes between their magazine pages. Who knows? Maybe someone will think about human trafficking, or about NOT having an abortion, or will read about keeping your family spiritually healthy. Hey, by donating to these organizations I paid for that mail, so I'm going to use it for God's glory!

> **Ripple:** Attempt to do one good deed a day. Try one of mine or come up with your own.

While I was finishing this book, our son became very ill, so much so that we moved in with him for several months. Besides taking care of him, I looked for ways to spread the gospel. He lived by several bike trails, so I continued to walk, bike, and pray. One morning, I walked by a message a child had written on the sidewalk with chalk. It said, "Have a nice day," with a smile. It made me grin, and gave me an idea. For the time we lived with him, I wrote *all* over the town with chalk. "Jesus Loves You." I tried not to get noticed – *BUT* . . . the messages ended up on the neighborhood Facebook page. (I don't have Facebook, but my son did.) One morning he said, "Mom, you're famous in the neighborhood." The comments were all positive, which was amazing considering at the time it was all about the Black Lives Matter slogans. I agree with their slogan but Jesus thinks ALL LIVES MATTER! (Nobody knew who wrote the messages except the few people that caught me!) The few that did catch me were very positive; they told me they loved the message. I then added this to things I do.

There are books written about good deeds, and you can even find great ideas on Pinterest. Anyone can do good deeds; Johnny the bagger is a prime example. I have read about Johnny in several books. If you haven't heard about him, here's a brief version – Johnny was born with Down syndrome. He writes encouraging notes, and while he's at work bagging groceries, he slips one into each person's bag. As time passed, people would stand in line (even while other lines were open) just to get an encouraging note from Johnny. He blesses people in his own way. I love his story!

Don't judge each day by the harvest you reap, but by the seeds that you plant. - Robert Louis Stevenson

Words can also be good deeds – like Johnny with his notes. We hear so many negative things all day long – from the shows we watch, to the negative comments made everyday by people we have contact with. Have you noticed that nobody points out the window at you and says, "Hey, your driving is great!" If they point, you know it's not because they like your driving. Have you noticed that people tend to make negative comments about service people? Why don't we say kind things when we get good service? How often do you hear someone go on a rant about something good? It's only when we're mad. You get my point . . . more negative words are spoken than positive ones!

Hebrews 10:25 says, But encourage one another, especially now that the day of his return is drawing near. Sending text messages to people asking how their day is going is a nice way for people to know that they're in your thoughts. Or, when you are reminded of someone and you have a positive thought about them, send a text, email, or a card telling them how thankful you are they're in your life. Write notes and cards and tell others what you appreciate about them. You can give out a lot of affirmation in your Christmas cards; but start earlier.

One year when our children were still in grade school, I made each of them and my husband a laminated heart for Valentine's Day with a list of the things I loved about each of them. While I wrote this, I took a moment to text each one to see if they still had their hearts. After fifteen years, all of them had kept the words of affirmation.

Sadly, people don't hear affirming words about themselves very often. Take a moment right now and think about the last positive comment you heard about yourself . . . still thinking? I know, they don't come very often. Why not change that? You don't have to wait until Valentine's Day to do this! Handwritten words make more of a statement and can be saved! Although, I do still have an email stored from a friend that sent me some *VERY* encouraging words years ago! I try to affirm, encourage, and tell people why I like them all the time. I also make it a point to check in on friends whom I haven't talked to for long periods of time, to let them know that I am still thinking about them.

> **Ripple:** Send out seven affirming messages – in whatever form and see the kind of responses you receive.

I am that kind of woman – the one who talks to anyone I'm around. (It used to bother my children when they were teenagers. – Now they expect it!) I have conversations with people in the elevator and with convenience store workers. I try to let people know I notice them. Sometimes it's talking about the weather or how busy they are. While I'm at it, I try to make a positive comment to them. Notice if a store clerk is efficient – if they are . . . say so. I was a brief owner of a coffee shop! Don't ask. I was thrown into the situation! I had employees, and one of the things I would try to encourage them to do was ask people if they wanted something else with their coffee – a cookie, a scone, anything. It's called upselling! So if an employee tries to suggest something else for me to buy at any store, I say, "No thank you, but you're doing a great job on upselling!" They usually smile *big*. If someone has a nice outfit on, say so. If a person has a nice smile, say so. This is not that hard to do, and it may make someone's day! This happened to me recently! I was having a very hard, stressful day!!! An older gentleman with his wife next to him said something so nice to me. It made me smile, and honestly it made my whole day! I passed by him on my way out of the store. I told him he made my day and told his wife that he seemed like a keeper to me.

Encourage mothers with small children – especially when the children are not cooperating. Make small talk with her. Remind her that "this soon shall pass." Or, compliment her on keeping her patience. Talk to the children, distract them – this could be considered a good deed! Offering to babysit for others is another great way to help out mothers with young children also.

If someone holds the door open for you, make sure you thank them. (I know this should be obvious but people don't always say thanks. Maybe they think it's an automatic door opener shaped like a person, holding the door.) You could always say more than thank you. You could say thanks, that was really polite or very helpful or tell them thanks and have a blessed day. I wouldn't write all this if this was a common thing to do. It used to be, but somewhere along the way – common courtesy disappeared. Have you noticed people don't even look at people anymore? This was especially noticeable during the Covid pandemic. Greeting people has become a good deed. Have you noticed that people don't even communicate anymore? When I go out for my morning bike ride or walk, it amazes me how many people will try to avoid eye contact. Plus, they wear those earbuds and can't hear anyone. I think people want to be noticed even if it is by a stranger. Don't give up, keep greeting and smiling! It's like Galatians 6:9 says, "Let us not become weary in doing good, for at the proper time we will reap a harvest if we do not give up."

Ripple: Hold the door for people and tell them to have a blessed day. (This is an easy one.)

For those pet lovers . . . offer to walk or watch your neighbor's pets. One year I purchased a bone-shaped cookie cutter and made dog treats for my friends and tied the cookie cutter on the baggie of treats with a bow. It's all about the extra effort. (It was a Pinetrest idea.)

Great opportunities to help others seldom come, but small ones surround us every day. -- Sally Koch

If your church doesn't host baby or weddings showers anymore, you could do this on your own or suggest to your church leaders the church could give one "BIG" gift, – it would be a blessing they could tell others about.

The church we attended hosted a shower for my wedding and for my first baby. Plus, I received a week's worth of meals after our first child was born. (All the women were invited – good way to meet people.) It was such a blessing to me

Ripple: Organize a baby or wedding shower for the church.

I have always been intrigued with asking questions!! (This is why there are discussion questions.) Ask anyone! If I don't know, I will ask. Why not? I have asked some goofy questions over the years. Usually the answers start nice conversations. For example, my husband dropped me off at a thrift store and a couple of older men were sitting in the parking lot on the tailgate of their truck. Dean, of course, came up with a dorky explanation as to why they were doing this in the parking lot. When I finished shopping, I asked the guys what they were doing. I loved their answer! They told me they were sitting in the parking lot waiting for pretty women to walk up and talk to them! (Hey, I will take a compliment any day!) After we joked awhile, they said they were waiting for their wives to buy everything in the store. They noticed we had Iowa license plates. So we talked about that, too. This conversation lasted about five minutes while I waited for Dean to pick me up. We all got a giggle out of the conversation, and everyone had smiles on their faces afterwards.

Ripple: There are many suggestions in this section to write on your index cards. (Have you been writing on your index cards???)

I'm not sure if this qualifies as a good deed, but it does make people feel good, engaged, and it's a way to get people thinking about God. Since I was in elementary school – I have always loved asking family and friends questions. My husband and son will only answer for so long before they get worn out, but the girls and I can do this for hours. Questions like . . . "What was the best vacation you've been on? Best Christmas gift? One person you would like to hang out with for a day?" What scene in the Bible would you like to see? Who in the Bible would you like to ask questions to? What would you ask Jesus?" One question I get excited about asking is, "What impresses you more, the *big* things that God created or the *small* things He created?" – My answer would be the small things. God is big!! It is not hard for Him to design galaxies, grand canyons, and mountains. But try putting spots on the back of a ladybug, or the spiral tongue on a butterfly, or snowflakes that are all different. – look up snowflakes . . . I'm even impressed they can get pictures of a single snowflake without it melting. Think about this . . . God could have made all bugs black, all sea shells white, or all trees the same. He loves detail in the small things.

Questions work best when people are trapped in a car or all eating dinner – they can focus better – less distractions. You can buy questions or do a search for them if you can't think of enough. I've done this with my adoptive grandkids during a family adventure. They didn't even miss their phones, and the time flew by. I also did this with my daughters' adult friends by a campfire. They really enjoyed the conversation, and when I stopped, they asked for more questions. It's good because it gets everyone engaged in the same conversation instead of two or three conversations going on at the same time. Ok, one more question: If you had the option to know the day you were going to die, would you want to know? And why? I wish I was there to hear your answer. ☺

Questions and the answers given help you to get to know a person in a much deeper way and have a tendency to play over and over again after the conversation has moved on. So if there are good God questions people may think and look deeper as to why they or you answered a certain way.

I want to be clear, doing good deeds does *NOT* in any way get you to Heaven, *BUT it may get someone else there.* If planting a seed by doing these things gets just one person to accept Christ as their Savior, it will all be worth the effort to me. Demonstrating these acts of kindness in front of your children and others may inspire them to do their own good deeds in their circles of influence.

> *The difference between ordinary and extraordinary*
> *is that little extra. - Jimmy Johnson*

I've seen this with my own children – in each of their own ways, they are doing good deeds and planting seeds. It's not unusual at all to hear from each one of them at least once a month telling me about someone I need to pray for, or someone they have talked to about God. One daughter makes meals for people that happen to be going through some sort of crisis. The other daughter is good about inviting people to the Bible study she leads. My son has had me pray for several friends who are going through different struggles and has put offers on his Facebook that he is willing to answer questions about God. It makes this mom very proud!! Honestly, I don't think they could do anything that would make me more proud than loving other people enough to share Jesus with them. James 3:13 says, "So if you are wise and understand God's way, prove it by living an honorable life, doing good works with the humility that comes from wisdom."

Here's one more thought on the matter of doing good deeds and sending out ripples! One of my favorite movies is *It's a Wonderful Life.* I love, love, *love* this movie! It does drag in parts, and it would be nice if someone would make a modern day version of it, *BUT* . . . it has such a great message! One person's life can have such a ripple effect on so many others' lives. The main character in the movie, George Bailey, didn't know the kind of impact he had on others until he had the opportunity to see what everyone's life would be like if he had never been born. He was kind and always tried to do the right thing for others, which made each of the other characters' lives better in some profound way.

I have often pondered what my life would be like if certain people had not been a part of it. I also have thought about how I have impacted other people's lives. I hope and pray that my actions have had a positive effect in the lives of others. Think about it . . . don't you want to be a part of making a positive impact on someone else's life? That could be another question you could ask someone – "Who is the person that has had the greatest impact on your life?" Yes, you could answer that question like my husband and say, "Jesus Christ," but who besides Him?

> **Ripple:** Write out some questions or put them in the note section of your phone. Then the next time you are with a group of people, ask some questions and make sure you ask a few God questions too.
>
> **Ripple:** Watch *It's a Wonderful Life* and soak in how much one person's life can affect another's.

QUESTIONS

1. Has anyone ever tried to talk you out of radically serving God in some way? What did you do?

2. What is your most failed attempt to serve God? Did you give up or try it another way? (I hope you know if it was for God, it was not a failure!)

3. Have you ever given any thought about thanking God for your water? Have you ever noticed that the drinks at a restaurant can add up to be as much as your meal?

4. Have you ever asked a stranger if you can pray for them? What were the circumstances?

5. Have you ever filled a shoebox for Operation Christmas Child? Or have you ever received a gift from an organization?

6. Have you ever given something to a homeless person? Did you feel like you were enabling them? Why or why not?

7. If someone walked into your house, would they know you were a Christ follower? How? How far inside would they have to get in order to know?

8. What is a good deed that you like to do?

9. Have you ever received a card that really spoke to your heart? From whom? And why was it special?

10. Do you have a question that you like to ask people? What is it?

11. BONUS QUESTION: Have you been writing on index cards any ideas that you can put into practice? What's your favorite so far?

9

———⟡———

Using the Right Stone

PRAYER AND FASTING

I mentioned earlier the time our church pastor wanted to cover our congregation in prayer. I ended up with the thirty-first day of the month. I didn't mention this, but we were also asked to fast (which meant abstaining from food on your assigned day), so the effort was double. I eventually quit the monthly prayers and went to prayer meetings, that met at the church once a week in the afternoon.

Years later, I felt that God may be hinting to me about fasting again, but He was being very indirect about it. I talked earlier about the book *The Hole in Our Gospel* by Richard Sterns. Do you remember that one question he wrote about? **"Do we eat to live or do we live to eat?"** I *pondered* that question a lot! We are so blessed in the United States to be able to eat whenever we want. Most of my days are spent eating. I have breakfast, a mid morning snack, lunch, an afternoon snack and then dinner. I might even have a cookie or some chocolate after that.

After reading *The Circle Maker* by Mark Batterson, I knew He wanted me to up the level of my prayer life. I hoped that if I prayed big, the fasting feeling would go away!

Dean and I start traveling in January – This is when pastors have a tendency to start the new year getting their congregations excited about growing spiritually. Many churches spend about three weeks on a topic – but, for Dean and I that meant three different churches – all three had the same theme. I've had this experience a few times. Maybe God thinks I don't hear the message the first time so He keeps repeating Himself in multiple states until it sinks in with me.

January of 2018, God wasn't being subtle any longer. On our way south, the first three sermons we heard were about fasting and your prayer life. It seemed to be the theme at the multiple churches we attended during that winter! Even in the books I read.. – that were *NOT* about prayer! God was getting persistent!

The one I read on my trip back home threw me over the edge. It was *Fast Friends* by Suanne Niles and Wendy Simpson Little. I thought it was about making friends. A person can never have enough friends and making friends takes a while, so I thought, "*Great!* These people have a method on making friends faster!" Well . . . I told you God has a sense of humor. That book had *nothing* to do with making friends or making friends faster! It was about two friends who decided to fast and pray together. *Great title!* But, *NOT* what I was expecting. Halfway through, I read the back cover. It talked about how these two women became prayer partners. Great! I loved the idea but, I missed the part about fasting. My mistake!!! *Or . . . God had a plan!*

God thought fasting was a good idea for me. He pursued me – He left me hints, but this time He was kind of sneaky! After I finished the book, I knew it would be part of my routine. When I latch onto what God thinks I need to do, and it requires more effort than I sometimes think I have, I, of course, want others to join me. I like to share these ideas with my Bible/book study group and then they get to be an important part of my spiritual growth. Lucky them!

I started fasting in April of 2018 – Our group started discussing *Fast Friends,* a month later, by the time we finished the book, I had already begun to develop the habit. The last day of our discussions, I asked the ladies to give fasting a try – Eight of the nine ladies fasted at least once. I'm not trying to guilt people into fasting, but notice Jesus said in Matthew 6:16, "And **when** *you fast*" – He does not say **IF** you fast – He says when.

Fasting is a discipline that prepares us for when temptation and trouble come into our lives. Jesus fasted for forty days and forty nights, and while He was fasting, He was tempted in the wilderness by the devil. In Matthew 4:1-11 it says, "For forty days and forty nights He fasted and became very hungry. During that time the devil came and said to Him, "If you are the Son of God, tell these stones to become loaves of bread." But Jesus told him, "No! The Scriptures say, 'People do not live by bread alone, but by every word that comes from the mouth of God.'" Then the devil took him to the holy city, Jerusalem, to the highest point of the Temple, and said, "If you are the Son of God, jump off! For the Scriptures say, 'He will order His angels to protect you. And they will hold you up with their hands so you won't even hurt your foot on a stone.'" Jesus responded, "The Scriptures also say, 'You must not test the Lord your God." Next the devil took him to the peak of a very high mountain and showed him all the kingdoms of the world and their glory. "I will give it all to you," he said, "if you will kneel down and worship me." "Get out of here, Satan," Jesus told him, "For the Scriptures say, 'You must worship the Lord your God and serve only Him.' Then the devil went away, and angels came and took care of Jesus."

> **Ripple:** Try to fast and pray for one day! If that's too hard, try skipping just one meal and pray for the amount of time it would take to eat that meal you skipped.

When I first started to fast, I had some really ugly thoughts. "How many other Christians fast? I'm already mature in my spiritual growth, so why do I need to fast? I have plenty of food and I don't need to lose weight, so is fasting necessary? Why don't other Christians take the time to fast?" Truly, I was bombarded with these and many others. I couldn't believe how negative my thoughts were. I was looking down on other Christians and felt I had to do something I didn't want to do. But then, I remembered the sermon where the pastor mentioned that sometimes fasting brings out a pride issue . . . *Yep, that's what it was.* Pride that I was fasting, but others weren't. Pride that I was above needing to fast. Pride that I felt like I prayed more than most people. Pride that I didn't need to fast because I had money to buy food, and had plenty of it in my cabinets.

The last thought really made me sick to my stomach! Now, I understood exactly what that pastor had talked about. It was confusing – I wasn't forced to fast. I was disturbed after I pondered my thoughts – so I'm sure that you thought the same thing. Then, I went the other way and started to beat myself up. What kind of Christian are you for thinking these kinds of thoughts . . . *you are so low.* You might as well *stop* fasting because you aren't glorifying God.

I don't remember how long I wrestled with these thoughts. But, eventually I saw them for what they really were, attacks from satan. I confessed my thoughts as sin to God and asked for forgiveness. I then told satan that I knew what he was doing and every time I had a thought like this, I would confess and praise God! I have found when I praise God, satan doesn't stick around very long. (I do know that satan isn't everywhere but use his name for all the evil forces that attack.)

> *When you face the perils of weariness, carelessness, and confusion, don't pray for an easier life. Instead pray to be a stronger man or woman of God. - Luis Palau*

You may be asking . . . what on earth can you find to pray about for an entire day? I pray through a few different prayer calendars for Christian organizations, prompts for government entities, current events, my journal of servers, plus family, friends, and other requests I've received.

I plan certain chores for my fasting days, ones that require no thought at all. I do laundry that day because folding and steaming clothes are really easy to do while praying. Dusting and vacuuming are other good options. While we travel, I try to pick the days we will be in the car the longest. There are times you have to be creative. December, for example, is a hard month to fast. It's very busy with people staying in our home. It's easy not to eat when people are around, but hard to entertain people while praying! I had to get creative; I used every little bit of time I was alone throughout the day. At the end of those interrupted days, I think God is pleased with the effort made.

I've prayed and thanked God for my meals since I became a Christian. Now I try to remember to pray for the people that are not as blessed with a meal, before eating. Fasting has made me more thankful for my food and the freedom I have to eat when I want.

It's also made me realize how much time on my non-fasting days could be spent on prayer. I'm also more aware of the many things around me that can be prayed about. For example . . . if you pick up a book to read, look down at the author's name – Pray for that person and the ministry that they have in the world. When you consume food, say a prayer for the people that work to provide it. If we take the time to think about where our items come from, it gives us an opportunity to be thankful which is prayer. Watch the news . . . you could spend hours in prayer. Pray through your phone contacts and for the spiritual influence you could have on them. (Side note: Send a text message to a few – that you said a prayer for them.) Honestly, you have an endless supply of things to pray about everyday. Fasting is something God has laid on my heart and I will continue to fast until God tells otherwise.

Our spiritual growth is primarily for the sake of others and, thereby, glorifying to God. - Randy Frazee

My prayer life has not always been this intense! When I first started praying, it was before bed with the prayer – Now I lay me down to sleep. I pray the Lord my soul to keep. If I shall die before I wake, I pray the Lord my soul to take. Or before meals – Lord, thank you for this food, bless it to my body. It didn't take me long to feel that if I was bored at what I said over and over, maybe God was too! After our first child was born, I *had* to start exercising. – You know, all that extra weight that was not birthed out!. I started by walking on a treadmill that was in our storage room with no TV. (This was before cell phones and iPods.) Just me and blank walls, I needed to find something to occupy my mind, so I prayed. I wasn't sure if it was okay to pray while on a treadmill, but I hated to waste all that time. So I prayed that God would understand why I was not kneeling by my bed.

Since I had several pounds to lose, there was a lot of time to pray. At least an hour every day. It started with the basics – family, friends, and anything else I thought of. As the hours with God added up, I felt that He was okay with the time spent with Him, *EVEN* while exercising.

I've read about how you should have a special place to say prayers, like a closet, a special chair, with a candle, a cup of coffee, and a journal. But, I'm not a prayer closet kind of gal or one that sits still very long. If I'm idle for too long, I start to think about all the things that should be getting done . . . Oh, I should go start a load of laundry . . . Oh, I should water the plants; that one looks a little thirsty . . . Oh, the phone is ringing, I should answer it. It's just my personality! Martha (Luke 10:38-42) and I are cut from the same cloth! Usually, I do two things at once. Listening to a podcast and brushing my teeth, or vacuuming and answering emails. Prayer is a little trickier. Talking to the God of the universe requires more attention! That's why I have continued to walk and bike while praying. Unlike other exercise partners, God is always ready, waiting, and keeps the same pace as I do. He also goes everywhere I go. (I remember all those vacations that I had to pack for my kids. I remember thanking God that He was easy to travel with!)

The first time my prayers became more focused was when our church did a series of talks about prayer. They taught that prayer is like five rooms in a home. When you walk in, there is a foyer in the space inside the door, before you are able to get comfortable. You take off your coat and shoes and unload your stuff – this is where you take time to **confess any known sins** in your life before you begin praying. The living room is the room that is still a little more formal – a pretty room – where you take **time to praise God** for who He is and what He's created. Then there is the trophy room – **thank Him** for all the wonderful things He's done in your life, answers to prayers, and all the things that He's blessed you with. Next is the guest room – this is where we **petition God for the needs of others.** And last is the family room – this is where you get comfortable – and **ask for your personal needs.**

For years, I did *not* pray much for myself – I thought it was selfish of me, so I prayed for everyone else first. At the end of my prayers I would pray for basic things – keep me healthy, help me to maintain my weight, and help me to be a good wife and mother, unless . . . I was interrupted or ran out of time.

I then read another book! It made a point that really struck home with me. If you don't pray for yourself, who is going to??? Think about it . . . when I pray for others, they receive less than thirty seconds each. My father doesn't pray. My mother prays occasionally. My in-laws have five children to pray for, plus spouses, grandchildren and great grandchildren. How much time am I being prayed for? How many people do I know that really spend time in prayer for me? If they do, how much time was devoted to me except the basics or an urgent prayer request that I send. So now, I'm at the beginning, I ask for good health, to maintain my weight, but I started adding things that no one would pray about.

I want to serve God and others the best that I can, so I ask God each day to fill me with His Holy Spirit, overflowing so that I can radiate Him to others. I pray to be filled with the fruit of the spirit: *Love, joy, peace, patience, kindness, goodness, faithfulness, gentleness and self-control* (Galatians 5:22-23). Who doesn't need all of those qualities in their lives? I find that as I say those words, I do think about whether I am displaying them in my life! It's powerful to say them out loud and to ask God to help me live out those attributes! Name one person you know who doesn't need more of those character traits in their lives. *EXACTLY!* That's why I pray for them. I also pray that He would help me to spread His gospel and divine appointments. To be a great wife who is loving, supportive, and submissive to my husband and a mother who sets a good example for my children. *Now* you know why I started praying for myself first. Who's going to pray all that for me – except myself?

Next, I move on to my family, sponsored kids, and extended families. My husband's family is currently at thirty plus people and keeps growing with all the weddings and babies. I have always felt guilty when I didn't pray for each of them and all the other categories of people in my life, organizations, missionaries, friends, etc. Needless to say, it was getting harder to get everyone prayed for. So, I changed it up again! Now I have more margin in my prayer time to mention current things going on. It also gives God time to speak to me during the day, instead of waking me up at night. I still confess my sins, praise God, and pray for myself and my immediate family members. But I don't pray for all the categories of people every day. I now have time to expand my thoughts and prayers for my immediate family now that each group has its own day.

Mondays – extended family
Tuesday – friends
Wednesdays – groups – Bible/book study and different groups that I am involved in.
Thursdays – the President, service people, military, pollice, fire fighters, emergency workers, teachers and ect.
Fridays – praise for God and all the wonderful things that I get to enjoy.
Saturdays – Christian organizations, missionaries, street ministries, and church services.
Sundays – contacts from the week – people that I have shared books or gospel tracts with and others that have requested prayers.

It's still a work in progress . . . always subject to change.

> **Ripple:** Reflect on your prayers. Have they changed over time? Maybe add more margin in your prayers, to hear from God. Use prayer as a way to start a conversation with your children, grandchildren or others. Ask how others approach their prayers.
>
> **Ripple:** Ask seven people what you can pray for them about.

Morning prayers . . . *in another book,* it talked about praying before your feet hit the floor. Greet the Lord, thank Him for your sleep, and say a quick prayer. Ask Him for wisdom for the day, help with what needs to get done, or just help to get out of bed. (I have only prayed that last one on really *COLD* mornings.) I'm a morning person . . . when I say quick prayer – *it's quick.* My son-in-law Jon says, I'm like a poptart. I pop up ready to start my day! (He needs coffee first!)

As I stated earlier, at the beginning of my spiritual journey, the time I prayed was before I went to bed. In my early childhood, I saw a painting of a child kneeling with folded hands beside their bed, and I assumed that's what I should do. As I got older, busier, and more exhausted at bedtime, I was less disciplined. I would get in bed, start my prayers, and seriously get only a sentence or two out before I was *sound asleep!* . . . Does this ever happen to you? When you run at full speed from the time your feet hit the ground, you are naturally tired at the end of the day. That's why I stopped doing evening prayers for a really *long* time . . . I would say goodnight to God, but that was about it!

When I added prayers before bed again, I decided I could do better. So, on my knees by my bed became my new plan. At first my prayers were for those that were being held captive, whether it was physically being held hostage, like human trafficking, or chains of addictions, drugs, alcohol, pain, lust, greed . . . that list can be long. Then I added prayer for my brothers and sisters in Christ that are being persecuted, for those that are sick, and for God to comfort anyone that lost a loved one that day.

*Prayer does not change God, but it changes
him who prays. - Soren Kierkegaard*

> **Ripple:** For one week, get on your knees before climbing into bed and thank God for all He has done for you that day!

Prayer is also a way to bring God into conversations. It might be telling others something I've been praying about, or telling someone about an answered prayer that I have received.

I was at a Christmas party, in a conversation with a gal I know and God become part of my conversation. I praised Him for an answered prayer that day – six green lights, a parking spot, and arriving at a meeting on time that I was running a late for. You would have to know the road – it has six stoplights that are not synced. The lights are tripped by cars coming off the busy side roads (If you make all green lights on this road you probably should buy a lotto ticket because it's your lucky day!). She started the conversation about how busy this road is at Christmas! I agreed, and told her I asked God to get me to my appointment on time and a parking spot by the door – since it was super cold! I told her, He answered it! She informed me that God does not want us to waste His time on such small matters, and that I should spend my time praying for starving children in Africa. ☺ *POLITELY* . . . I told her that I do pray for children in poverty and that God says to pray without ceasing, and started explaining that verse to her, but part way through my conversation we were interrupted by someone she wanted to talk to more. What she said really didn't bother me since I know what God thinks. God is okay with you praying about *everything!* 1 Thessalonians 5:16-18 says, "Always be joyful. Never stop praying. Be thankful in all circumstances, for this is God's will for you who belong to Christ Jesus." And Philippians 4:6 says, "Don't worry about anything; instead, pray about everything. Tell God what you need, and thank him for all He has done."

God is happy spending time with us – no matter where we pray – when we pray – or what we pray about! My prayers have evolved over the years, and I'm sure they are going to continue to evolve until the day I can talk to Him face to face.

Just keep on praying!

QUESTIONS

1. Have you ever fasted while praying? If yes, what is the longest you have fasted? If not, why?

2. Where do you pray? (Special place?)

3. What time of day do you pray most? (Morning or evening)

4. Do your prayers sound the same today as they did yesterday? Are they different from years ago? How do they differ?

5. Do you use special prompts? (Like when an ambulance drives by. Or while reading scripture?)

6. How much time do you spend praising God during prayer? Or do you?

7. Do you pray the same prayer everyday like the Lord's Prayer? Or the nighttime prayer?

8. Have you ever told someone you didn't know that you would pray for them?

9. Do you pray for yourself first or last? What is your reasoning?

10. Do you find prayer easy or difficult? Why?

(I just want to say again, there is no right or wrong way to pray.)

10

―∞―

An Overflowing Ripple

A FLOOD AND A WEDDING

The summer of 2018 was full of twists and turns and ups and downs. It was very unpredictable to say the least, and that may be an *understatement!* The summer started with our youngest daughter's boyfriend calling to ask if he could visit with Dean and me. (He texted me first and asked what Dean would say if he wanted to marry Katie.) Katie had dated her high school sweetheart Sean for eight years. We had been waiting for this day.

You would think that after Sean asked our permission, he would have asked Katie within the month. Nope . . . he kept putting it off. I finally started texting him pep talks – he was on his own timetable, not mine.

The first son-in-law did this too! Our oldest daughter went to Norway to visit her then boyfriend, Jon, and his family for a couple of weeks. (Jon's mom is from Norway, and the family moved there while Jon stayed in America to attend college.) He had called us before Abby left and asked for her hand in marriage. Of course . . . we gave him our blessings! Then we waited for Abby to call us from Norway to tell us that Jon had proposed – We never received that call from Norway. When she came home not engaged, we (I) got worried. It was hard to not say, "Hey, didn't he ask you to marry him?" When he finally proposed to her, we were told the rest of the story. The ring didn't come in on time, so he waited until summer was over and he was back in the States to ask her. I'm sure I kind of ruined the surprise by asking some weird questions. Did you and Jon fight? What did you do? Did he say anything about getting married? It all worked out, but it caused this mother to stress out a bit.

Sean finally decided on Memorial Day weekend, he knew Katie and her friends would be at our lake house. He told her he would stay in Minnesota to golf with his friends, because he had been in Iowa the week before. Sean's main mission was to make sure that she was surprised by the proposal.

The real plan was that he would golf part of the weekend and then drive to the lake and ask her. That was the plan, but Katie ended up sick and went to the hospital for a few hours due to dehydration. Sean got nervous that maybe this wouldn't be a good weekend, but I insisted that he come anyway! As far as I was concerned, he could ask her in the hospital. I was ready for them to get married! Plus, I thought it might take him another month to build up the courage to propose.

Katie, not feeling well, was disappointing, since her friends had come down to enjoy fun in the sun. I was disappointed because this was her big weekend.

Sean was on his way – The plan we had . . . needed to be modified. Her friends didn't know this was the weekend, but now I needed their help – to get her up and going, or at least showered. When I told them the secret, they were very excited and persuaded Katie to go to dinner with them . . . but she wouldn't shower. She looked fine, but *NOT* the way she would if she knew she was about to be proposed to. The girls tried, they told her they would help style her hair, but she didn't think it was necessary. This would bother her later when the plan came together.

Sean was down the road from our lake house setting up his proposal site and I needed to get Katie to the small beach area of the park looking out over the water.

I came up with a plan to get her to go on a little golf cart ride. I said there was a small emergency and needed her help to pick someone up at small dock located at the park down the road and take them back to our house.

Sean had framed pictures of his favorite memories for each year they had been together and set them up along the road to the destination place.

Poor Sean! It was super hot that day! I tried to get Dean to go help him, but he insisted Sean didn't need help. But really he did – He was running up and down the hill taking arms full of stuff to set up. When I called him to say we were ready, he said, *"I'm not done yet!"* He was out of breath, so I sent Dean! Sure enough – he needed help! He was hot and sweaty by the time he was done setting up. *I'm surprised we didn't need to run him to the hospital!*

Sean was ready and Katie went along with the elaborate story I came up with and was *fuming mad* about the person just being dropped off. I played along, and didn't dare smile.

I wasn't quite sure what to expect but I knew Sean had little stations we were to stop by and look at along the way. After we turned the corner I saw them on the side of the road, but it was really hard to tell what they were from a distance. As we came up to them, I asked Katie, "What is all that stuff up there by the road." She had no idea but at least she stopped complaining about how mad she was at the person in the fictional story.

We stopped by station where there were pictures of her and Sean on their first date. When she saw what the pictures were, *instantaneously,* she figured out that she was going to be proposed to. *Immediately,* she wanted to go back and shower. *LOL, TOO LATE* . . . I was the driver and we were *NOT* going back; we were only moving forward.

There were a few more stops along the way, and then we got to Sean. It wasn't as secluded as he had hoped for, there were people at the park that day, and they all watched as he got down on one knee. After he stood up, they kissed, and all the people clapped and cheered.

Back at the house, Sean called his parents, and they drove out to our lake house. We all congratulated each other and then discussed when and where the wedding should take place . . . this happened only hours after the engagement ring was accepted. Nobody wanted to wait another year for them to plan a wedding. So they (we) picked August 11, 2018. They were engaged on Memorial Day weekend, and two and a half months later they would get married.

The planning moved fast!! I began texting family and friends on that Sunday to get the ball rolling. Sean called the Bible teacher that had taught both of them in high school and asked him if he would officiate (We might have changed the date if he wouldn't have said yes). Next came the hotels, photographers, flowers, ect. Then it was decided to hold the ceremony in our yard.

If you have ever planned a function that had many moving parts that needed to come together in a short amount of time, you understand this situation. Here's a strange thing about me – I like a lot of moving pieces. I loved being a wedding photographer, with all the people running around trying to get things done quickly with a lot of chaos! I can juggle a lot of things at once. It reminds me of this quote, "If you want to get something done, ask a busy person."

I prayed that God would help me get the things done that needed to get done and to remember what was truly important. Katie and Sean getting married was the main thing, not if all the chairs were the same color, or if the trees were trimmed, or if we had the right audio speakers for the ceremony. So many details, but only one main objective! God made Himself very evident in all the plans which kept me very calm!

Have I mentioned yet, that *ALL* of the bridesmaids and *ALL* of the groomsmen – all twelve of them – had this one weekend available? The bridal party alone being available on the same weekend is a sheer miracle, let alone adding in all other professionals, services, and venues. It was incredible how everything fell into place. I should also tell you that the start of the Iowa State Fair was that same weekend. Hotels should not have had vacancies. – The fair is a big deal. People from small towns across Iowa plan their vacations around the fair, so it is a very busy time throughout the metro area! This should have been a huge problem, but God made miracles happen!

Only put off until tomorrow what you are willing
to die having left undone. - Picasso

The other thing we had to schedule was a bridal shower. Did I mention that Katie, her fiancé, and most of her bridesmaids lived in Minnesota which is three and a half hours north of us? Katie had a good attitude because she knew that not everyone who was invited would be able to change their schedules to attend the shower or wedding due to the short notice. Many people already had their summers planned.

The day of the shower was June 30th, only four days before the highlight of the summer, the Fourth of July!!! As much as I wanted them to get married and have a bridal shower, I really wanted to enjoy that week at the lake. But I had to remember . . . it wasn't about me. The shower was held at our home in Ankeny, which meant I would have to skip Friday night at the lake to get everything ready in the morning.

The soon-to-be-bride had a great time and we managed to keep the shower moving along! Of course, when you're the host, you have to wait for all the guests to leave. Then the cleanup starts all over again. Did I mention that our house was on the market to sell at this time? So when you leave, it has to be clean. – It seemed like every time it was dirty or messy . . . they wanted to show it.

After the house was spotless again, I sat down for a few minutes and chatted with Katie and a couple of her bridesmaids that stayed in town to finish a few more details for the wedding. By mid afternoon, I was back on the road to the lake – it was nice to relax and gather my thoughts. The shower was over, and we only had a few more major things to get finished up before the big day.

The relaxation did not last long!!! The beautiful day turned into an evening of rain. It rained at the lake and *poured* in Ankeny where we lived. Rain!!! *Do you remember 2018?* . . . I bet half of America does. If not, you were very fortunate – there was so much rain that year it flooded from Hawaii all the way to Florida. No exaggeration! . . . Look it up.

All of June had been rainy. – Ponds and lakes were full and the ground was soaked. The night of June 30th, Des Moines and the surrounding area received 11" of rain in two hours. *YES . . . TWO* hours!

We have had the same backyard for twenty-five years but, we have never had water in either of our homes. We have a creek that follows the property line of our yard and it does overflow occasionally. That week we had received rain every day, except the day of the bridal shower.

That night had become chaotic, both Dean and I received many calls from people telling us how bad it was in Ankeny, including Katie. Maybe if my head hadn't been whirling with all the calls and information, I would have known that our house was in *BIG trouble!* "MOM!!! It's really raining!!!" I suddenly realized, I was *still* on the phone with Katie. "The creek is rising, and the pond is already full, and I can see water coming up," she said. We have had water in the yard so many times, and most of the time it's not that big of a deal; a dirty driveway and yard until it rains again leaving piles of branches that don't wash away. *Little inconveniences.* Our driveway floods occasionally so you can't drive down it, but it only lasts a couple of hours. The creek begins about five miles up the road from a natural spring, so it's not like a river that has a lot of tributaries flowing into it. It comes up and then goes down fairly quickly. I have been at our house with running water flowing all the way around it on more than one occasion. It's like being a princess in a castle with a moat. I was not worried. *YET!* I told her to keep an eye on things and keep us informed.

Twenty minutes later, she was on the phone telling us the creek had come up five feet! *YES!* You read that right – five feet in twenty minutes. It was no longer just the yard that we were concerned about. The house was now being threatened by the flood waters. My head was whirling again. This is the same yard where Katie is getting married in less than two months! We told her not to worry; the radar showed the storm was about over. Five minutes later, she called again and said the floor drain in the garage had water coming up through it. We sit on a slab with no basement, a drain goes across the garage and into the office part of our home. We also have drains in our kitchen and the bathrooms. This was going to be a mess!!! I know I mentioned earlier that I like a lot of action and moving parts, but this was not my idea of fun.

Katie and her bridesmaids, Sara and Megan, went into action. –They proceeded to lift everything they could off the floor. This is when I pulled my head out of the clouds and thought through what needed to be saved. I started on what I thought was important and then Dean got on the phone and told them the items in his office that needed rescued. It was so hard we weren't there to help – we could only imagine what was going on, and couldn't do a thing to help the situation. *This is when you know that you are NOT in control of anything!!* I do know that, but in these kinds of circumstances you *really know!*

While the girls ran around the house trying to save anything they could see, the power went out. We told them to go upstairs and go to bed. There wasn't anything that they could do in the dark, and we didn't want them to get hurt. The rain had let up – the damage had already been done.

I would like to tell you at this point in the story that I had turned it all over to God. But that wouldn't be true! I had given God 90% of the situation but the other 10% I took to bed with me. Sleep did not come fast that night. I prayed a lot and thought about other things I could have saved. Romans 12:12 says, "Rejoice in our confident hope. Be patient in trouble, and keep on praying!" I know it's hard to rejoice in these kinds of circumstances, but I knew it could be so much worse, and God would be with us.

> **Ripple:** Think about a time you had to totally depend on God, a time when you were not in a place where you could help the situation. Reflection is a good thing, but sharing that experience with others in a conversation or writing it out so others can read it is even better. Ask people their stories and tell them yours. Make sure to stress you relied on God or that you should have! (Children and grandchildren need to hear our God stories!)

In less than two months, Katie would be married in our backyard. When the yard started flooding, I worried about how much work the yard would take to clean up. If you have ever gone through a *major* flood, there is a lot of cleaning that goes on afterwards. Our yard and three miles up the creek is very wooded, so the branches and sticks end up somewhere. Part of it stays in our yard, and of course some of our branches and debris went to someone else's yard. Five months later, I still found treasures in our yard. (I found a lawn trailer that hooks to a mower.) Our yard is connected to the yard of the person that bought our former house. They found a dead cow on their side of the yard! (*I was glad I didn't have to deal with that!*) But the yard would be secondary.

On the drive home the next morning, we noticed we were not the only ones awake early that Sunday morning. Piles of wet items were already on curbs and the water had receded to the ditches and low areas. When we arrived home, our driveway water had not receded as fast as normal. We parked on the road and waded across the eight inches of water still flowing through the low area in front of our house. (This was not rushing water so no worries about getting swept away!)

When we arrived, Katie and her friends were already up and cleaning. There was a coating of slick mud all over the floor that they were trying to mop up as fast as they could. I think the girls thought I was going to have a meltdown when I saw the mess in my ***CLEAN*** house. Remember, I had cleaned before and after the bridal shower. *It was definitely no longer* *clean!!!* Our home had furniture on the counters, things stacked on top of the furniture, and shoes on the kitchen counter. We had stuff everywhere except for where it was supposed to be.

At this point, I wanted to cry at all the wasted time spent on cleaning our house and knowing I was going to have to clean it all over again! (*Why?* ... *couldn't it have happened when my house needed cleaned!*) I had an hour of prayer on the ride home and knew I would be reflecting the Lord in front of the people that would be around. I was determined to be on my best behavior because God would see us through this mess. It was what it was ... *A MESS!*

> *There is a great difference between worry and concern. A worried person sees a problem, and a concerned person solves a problem. - Harold Stephens*

While I was assessing the situation, my phone rang. It was my family and a few others that wanted to come and see what the storm had done and to help where they could. It wasn't that bad once you looked past the furniture and stuff scattered everywhere. The water had only been less than an eighth of an inch deep – what was left was a skim of slime, the furniture had not been damaged. Since the floor on the main level was slate, it would be fine too. Dean's office side was carpet so it needed ripped out. Good news – he wanted new carpet.

Where to start? ... This is where most people struggle. They look at any problem and get so overwhelmed that they don't know where to start. Our garage has a sealed floor and it was covered with a slime of mud, – it was like walking on ice! Hosing out the garage so you could walk and *NOT* slip was priority number one! We didn't need anyone to go to the hospital while we cleaned.

I will spare you the details. It was a mess of wet stuff! During the cleanup, I was asked over a dozen times how I felt. Personally, I was very grateful! – The girls had picked up and saved so many things! None of the furniture was damaged. I was thankful that it was only a skim of water. If we had a basement, we would have lost everything in it. That's when I started thinking ... *really, was this all that bad?* I do not live in a third world country. When those countries flood, they lose family members, their livestock, and crops, and their homes are destroyed. I don't live in a poverty stricken area where everyone around me doesn't have enough to make it. That became my answer. Do you know how many people around the world have it so much worse?? People who don't have insurance. *OH MY!!! . . . Was our insurance going to cover this??* I had not thought about insurance until that moment, but I was determined not to complain because we could afford to cover the losses. I also knew we were not the only ones affected by this storm and many would be financially strained! After my reasoning, God settled a peace in my heart, and there wasn't anything left to do but clean.

Monday came – we had the driveway pressure washed and the indoor slate floor steam cleaned. We had fans, including a big barn fan, and all the dehumidifiers running that we could borrow. There was still a mess, but nothing that couldn't wait until the next week. Remember, this was the week of the Fourth of July. We typically stay at the lake from Friday through the Fourth to Sunday. The Fourth was on a Wednesday that year, which meant a whole week at the lake. We left everything running, and headed back to the lake . . . *BIG MISTAKE!* Here's some flood advice. I don't care how much water you get, drywall is like a big sponge and soaks up water the instant it gets wet. Plus, it was dirty water and it smelled. We returned and realized it wasn't going to dry and that we were going to need to take the trim boards off and cut the drywall up six inches.

Our insurance company and adjuster treated us very fairly. They saw that the water came up through the floor drains first, so they covered our expenses. We had to cut into the walls, so we had a decision to make. When you hold an outside wedding in Iowa, you need to have a backup plan. *In case it rains!* Our back up plan was the inside of our lodge. There was only six weeks until the wedding and we worried that The Lodge would not be put back together in time for the wedding. The insurance company told us we could leave the living area in tack. We started the construction on the garage and the office side, which nobody would be in except Dean and his new secretary, CJ. Vicky, the secretary that had been with us for fifteen years, had decided to retire on the first of June. – *She had perfect timing!* CJ spent her first few weeks of her new job with a lot of construction workers, fans, and dehumidifiers!

We had a disaster company come in and dry out the living area, but the walls are all wood paneled, so the moisture wouldn't come out. But, it wasn't for the lack of trying! We had over seventy-four fans flowing and at least six of the really big industrial size dehumidifiers running. It was so loud in the house, you had to yell at the person standing next to you. It sounded like you were on the tarmac of an airport, standing next to a big jet liner ready for take off!

The machines ran for about a week which was pretty *annoying!* I could go outside to escape the noise during the day, but unless you unplugged all the machines, it was unbearable because seriously, it was *LOUD!* Everywhere you went, you had to walk around a machine or step over cords. During this mess, I read a devotional that was from James . . . did I mention yet – this is my favorite book of the Bible? And have I mentioned that God has a real sense of humor? The verse I read the day that I was at my wits end was James 1:2-4 which says, "Dear brothers and sisters, when troubles of any kind come your way, consider it an opportunity for great joy. (Great joy!!! ☺) *For you know that when your faith is tested, your endurance has a chance to grow. So let it grow for when your endurance is fully developed you will be perfect and complete, needing nothing."* I didn't have a really bad attitude, but I'm sure it needed to be improved but, after I read that verse . . . I laughed! (Nobody could hear me!) I pointed up to Heaven, shook my head, and kept laughing! Fine . . . at least when I was done with this struggle, I figured I was going to be perfect!!! ☻

We tore out the base board and six inches of drywall, cleaned it, dried it, and put the office and garage back together. It took almost the entire six weeks to do that. – It was good we didn't try to do all of the house!

Would you believe we had to water the grass the week of the wedding? We did! It didn't rain again until the wedding was over. Guests arrived early and ended up in the main room of the lodge. It was a good decision to wait to repair that side. Unless people knew that the lodge had flooded, they could not tell by looking around the property. We praised the Lord for all the help He gave us with the planning, how smoothly everything went, how beautiful the wedding, weather, and the bride was!

The Monday after the wedding, the demolition started again. This time much more was involved. The drywall behind the wood panels was still moist and mold had crept up two feet. When you have a solid wood panel, you can't cut at the two foot mark. So, all the wood wainscoting, floor trim, and in some cases, window trim, and other trim boards had to be taken out and the drywall had to be cut out behind the paneling. *It was twice as much work as the office and garage.*

We had workers coming and going for weeks which was not fun. I may have made this situation sound like it was easy, but I kept out 90% of the problems we encountered along the way.

While I was at The Lodge, I had little to no privacy, and I had to listen to some music choices I would not have picked. (The workers had their own ideas about music.) Being stuck at home with workers all day was not my idea of a good time. I know that doesn't sound very nice, but every time I did leave, I had to call workers to come back and finish the jobs they said they were done with. *I was not being picky.* When I wasn't there to watch, they took shortcuts that were obvious. I was respectful since people were watching, but you can *expect* to have a job done well.

On the positive side, I was able to hand out several gospel tracts, cookies, water, and even gave a few copies of *The Purpose Driven Life* books to workers. There were many God conversations along the way, but the Lord was glorified the most with my attitude and response when people would ask how I was doing. I would answer, "The Lord provided us with an insurance company that covered it, some people don't have insurance. In worse cases, food sources and sometimes family members are killed during floods. I told them I was blessed! People don't think about how blessed they are until they think about how bad it can be."

People will know Jesus - by your actions. Me

People watch to see how Christians respond to tragedies in life – how they react when their world is falling apart. Sometimes our actions are the best way to glorify the Lord. Going through this circumstance made me much more generous to help people financially that go through hard times. Several times that fall, people dealt with flooding and storms in different parts of our country. Samaritan's Purse requested donations to help those that didn't have insurance, and we were able to give more since we did not have to deal with our own expenses. It also made me aware of how to better serve people that go through things like this.

> **Ripple:** Take a step back from any situation you are in. Are you reflecting Jesus? Are you giving Him glory?

One of the sad things that I experienced with this situation was the lack of support or help with what we were going through. The people that helped on the very first day were the only people that helped! No one offered a meal while my kitchen was a disaster. Nobody offered physical labor. Maybe they assumed that the insurance company would cover all the workers. But the lack of offers and support did leave me a bit discouraged. I'm not judging anyone. It just made me more reflective as to my own lack of responses in the past. It made me think of all the times I had failed to help someone with *MY* support or help. Calling, text messages of support, or sending a nice card telling them that you are thinking of them and praying for them can be such an encouragement. This was a lesson learned for myself! When people are going through a crisis, no matter what it is, give them support. You don't have to be with them to love on them, but if at all possible, a physical hug can't be beat!! Romans 12:13 says, "When God's people are in need, be ready to help them. Always be eager to practice hospitality."

> **Ripple:** Encourage someone that is going through a rough time. Make or buy a meal. Write an encouraging note, or stop by and let them know you have time, and have them put you to work or run an errand for them.

God can be glorified in our messes! Face it, life happens, and things do not not always go the way you plan. But you can take the bad things that happen in your life and give it to God and let Him work it out for His good purposes.

GOD JUST GIVES YOU WHAT TO SAY!

I served with Stonecroft Ministries as the chairperson for several years. The responsibilities included leading the planning team meetings, hosting and introducing the speakers at the luncheon, and finding the features. For a year I had wanted to take a step back into a limited role, but nobody on the team wanted to take my position. I don't like leaving an empty spot if possible, so I looked for my replacement! Fortunately, God placed my friend Carolyn on my mind. After a little convincing, she agreed to be my co-chair. *Seriously, she was the chair;* I just jumped in where she needed help!

When we traveled, I knew everything would run smoothly without me. Dean and I went on a vacation to Europe and were scheduled to fly home on Sunday. Saturday evening before we had gone to bed, I received a call from Carolyn – I knew it was her number because her name appeared on my phone screen . . . but I didn't recognize her voice. This was unusual since we talked frequently. She called to tell me that I would have to host the luncheon on Monday. We had discussed that I had not planned to go, since I would be traveling all day Sunday. She knew if I did come, it was only for support, since I would be jet lagged. Normally, Carolyn was on top of things and would have remembered this, so this was weird!

I tried to explain my circumstance, that I was still in Europe. *She was arguing.* We had eighty-four people registered to attend the luncheon, and if I missed my flight or had problems getting home, it would be a problem for those at the luncheon with no hostess. *Still arguing!* She should have known this! Finally, she said, "I'm going to the hospital and someone will have to host the luncheon, and that is you." I could tell she was agitated, (Carolyn is very sweet, so this was not like her at all!!) I stopped arguing. I said, "That's fine, go take care of yourself. – I'll handle it. – I pray you get better."

After we hung up, I called our team to find out if anyone knew what was going on. None of them did. I called Karen because she was in charge of Stonecroft in Iowa. I asked her if she would host the luncheon. She said yes, and we then discussed the Carolyn situation. I went to bed with all the pieces put together. The team knew I would be at the luncheon even if I was sleepwalking as long as we made our connections. Karen would be the host, and I told them to pray for Carolyn. We made it home late on Sunday afternoon, we didn't sleep well that night and I was a walking zombie at the luncheon.

So many things went wrong that day – satan wasn't happy about what is going on. It was the largest attendance we had ever experienced at one of our luncheons. The record had been set only a month earlier with seventy-three in attendance. We had eighty-four.

It was hot, the air conditioner wouldn't keep up, the speakers in the back of the room were not working properly, so people had a hard time hearing, we were short on food . . . and my friend, the co-chair, was not at the luncheon; she was in the hospital! This would have been a day to celebrate with such a large attendance, but that didn't seem to be that big of a deal anymore.

Even before leaving for the hospital, Carolyn had put together materials needed for the luncheon. The next day her daughter-in-law came by the restaurant and dropped off the stuff before she headed to the hospital. She told us that the situation with Carolyn did not look good.

I know when I say this that people will doubt, but the Holy Spirit gives me insights at times of things that are going to happen. This was one of those times. I knew deep in my soul that I was not going to see Carolyn again – God had pressed it upon my heart.

When I first took over this chapter of Stonecroft, I had asked everyone on the team to have five of their friends to be prayer partners that would continually pray for our luncheons all month long. I truly believe that the prayers for our group were what made us grow so fast! When everything seemed to be under attack from the enemy that day, I pulled out my phone and texted my five prayer partners and asked them to pray. I then sat on the floor in the corner, out of the view of the audience, and prayed while our feature speaker talked.

> **Ripple:** If you don't have a prayer partner, ask a friend if you could be their prayer partner and they be yours. I've had multiple prayer partners, and life is much better when you can call on a friend to pray!

The luncheon started with Karen welcoming everyone, making the announcements, and explaining why Carolyn was not there. Then she introduced the feature speaker, who is an attention grabber. Someone that comes and showcases their business or shows us some kind of DIY's (Do-it-yourself). For example: in the spring we like to have local greenhouses come and show us how to use planters to brighten up our outside living spaces. They are a warm-up for the luncheon and then the gal with the spiritual talk comes on after her. That morning, our feature was from one of our local boutiques, Funky Zebra. The owner started speaking – I'm in the corner on the floor praying. I wasn't listening to her at the beginning of her talk because I assumed it was about the boutique. *She was supposed to be talking about clothes.* But this morning, of all mornings, she talked about how you need to tell the people around you how special they are to you. She had been dealing with some personal things and her heart was heavy. She asked everyone at the luncheon to stand up and say to the person next to them that they were loved and told them hug. (Had I not been praying and had been fully alert, I would have been concerned about where this talk was going. As a matter of fact, I don't know what I would have done. *This was NOT the protocol!* (I was glad that Karen was in charge that day.) *THIS WAS SO OUT OF THE ORDINARY!!!* . . . This had never happened before, not even with the speakers. After the hugging was done, the speaker told the audience that the reason we should hug and tell people how we feel is because we never know if we will get the opportunity to tell them again. (When she finished saying that, I knew it was the Holy Spirit's way of giving me confirmation that I would not see Carolyn again until Heaven. – I kept this to myself.)

Fast forward five hours – I received a text message from Carolyn's husband that she had indeed gone to Heaven. Two days later he texted me again and asked if I could speak at her funeral. What a way to start the first week back in town!! Of course, I said yes, and he asked that I keep the speech to two or three minutes since there would be several others that would speak. Carolyn had served the Lord well and was involved in many different ministries. I talk a lot and two to three minutes is not very long. But, I think it's only respectful to do what I'm asked to do. That week while I biked and prayed, I asked God to help me know what I should say. He impressed upon my heart that I needed to give that same challenge that the featured speaker had given only days earlier at the luncheon.

Again . . . I need to learn not to argue with God so much . . . BUT, I did. I said to God, "REALLY?" "You want me to tell people to stand up and hug each other at a funeral???" This is *W A Y* out of the ordinary for a funeral and for my husband that likes to stick with tradition and doesn't like to do things out of the ordinary. Dean looked nervous when I told him that I was going to speak at the funeral – since he would be there. I can't imagine what he would have thought if he had known that I was going to tell people to stand up and hug. (Well, . . . yes I could imagine that . . . *oh boy.)*

After two days of God continuing to tell me to repeat that speech given at the luncheon and the hugging part, I went into Dean's office and told him not to try to talk me out of what God had told me to do. *Actually . . .* I didn't tell him what God had told me to do. I didn't tell him or anyone what the plan was! I knew if I told anyone God's plan they would try to talk me out of it, and for good reason, *BUT* I knew God had told me to do it.

You will be amazed. *I did not read this in a book!!!* I know you're shocked, but I had heard this in a sermon the year before from Nehemiah chapter two. Nehemiah received news that Jerusalem's walls had been torn down while they had been in captivity. He was broken-hearted. He began to fast and pray to God. Later, he made a plan to start rebuilding the wall. God helped him secure time and resources to get the job done and then he set off to Jerusalem. When he arrived in town, he did NOT tell the people right away about his plan. He went out with a few scouts at night to check out all the damage. The next day he told the city planners the plan to rebuild. (Sometimes you have to get the plan that God gives you in your head and heart before you can execute it or tell anyone.) I asked prayer partners and friends to pray for me that the speech I would give would glorify the Lord and that I would have confidence to give it. The night before the funeral, I wrote a few things out about Carolyn and about what the speaker at the luncheon had said only four days earlier. I rehearsed it three times and timed it. It was two minutes and I knew that the standing and the hugging would take about a minute. It was set. *I SLEPT . . .* I knew this was what God wanted.

The next day as I headed to the funeral, my stomach ached. I asked God one more time, "Are you sure you want me to have people stand up and hug each other at a funeral? Is this my ludicrous idea or is this yours?" (I'm not without my own ideas!) I really wanted to be sure it was His. Again He said, "Yes, HUG!" Okay . . . okay . . . I'll do it.

Dean and I rode separately to the funeral which was only about a mile away from our home. He had a meeting to go to after the funeral, and I would stay for the reception. We didn't see much of each other that morning. In fact, I didn't sit with him either. I sat up towards the front of the church next to one of the gals that is in my Bible/book study – she was on the Stonecroft team also. I was naughty and did what I probably shouldn't have done. I asked her to read my speech and pointed to the hugging part at the end. She took a look and said, "Yep, that looks good." So much for backing out.

I know this is petty and I have since let this go, but the pastor who told me not to have the Bible study in my home so many years earlier was at the funeral, which made me feel even more insecure about my speech.

When it was my turn, I marched right up to the podium and looked out over the crowd. I couldn't see my husband, which was good because I knew that this speech and the hugging thing was going to make him a bit uncomfortable, which makes me uncomfortable. Who did I see? Let me tell you how life intertwines. It was a lot of my past friends. Parents that had been at the Christian school where our children had first attended. (Carolyn had been the school's principal when we first transferred to that school.) This woman had made such an impact on people's lives – many there were from the school. (It felt like a class reunion.) And people from the Stonecroft luncheons. There were many that I didn't know, but the ones I did . . . already knew my personality. *I was ready* – let the speech begin. I spoke about my friend Carolyn and the luncheon that she should have hosted on Monday. I shared about our speaker and how serendipitous her talk was that day – how she told us that we are not good about sharing our feelings with the people we know and love – how we never know if we will get the opportunity to tell them the next time we see them – and then what she did after that. I stated the fact that I knew what I was about to do was out of the ordinary at a funeral, but God had laid it on my heart to do it. I said, "Will you please stand and tell the person next to you that you love them and give them a hug?" They hugged! I also think there were many that shed a few tears!

My speech was a matter of only three minutes. I think I was the only one that got the memo that we were supposed to keep our speeches short, or maybe I was the only one that was told that! I sat down knowing that this funeral wasn't about me or what I said. – It was about Carolyn. (Which in all honesty, she would have loved what I said! Carolyn would have never wanted her whole funeral to be about her. She would have been the first to say . . . *GLORIFY HIM!*) Deep in my heart I knew it was about being obedient to God and what He wanted me to do.

At the reception, many people told me they were impressed that I was bold enough to follow the leading of God. Even people that didn't know me, expressed how impressed they were with what I said and did. You know what? Without being prideful, I was too. I had obeyed God, even though it was so out of the ordinary. Sometimes we have to step out in faith. I'm not always comfortable before and during the requests, God lays on my heart, *BUT* when it's all done and I did what I was asked to do – it's an amazing feeling! Maybe it's like when people parachute out of an airplane. I have no desire to do that, but I'm sure there is the fear, amazement, and a sense of accomplishment when it's all done. *That's how I felt!*

> *They are not dead who live in the lives they leave behind. In those whom they have blessed they live a life again. - Eleanor Roosevelt*

Do you ever think about your own funeral? I have! Ecclesiastes 7:2-4 says, "Better to spend your time at funerals than at parties. After all, everyone dies – so the living should take this to heart. Sorrow is better than laughter, for sadness has a refining influence on us. A wise person thinks a lot about death, while a fool thinks only about having a good time." This is one of many verses that reminds us that this life is not all there is. Our thoughts should be about what is eternal.

I remember going to a funeral of one of our daughter's classmates during her junior year. That funeral impacted me. I didn't know her or her family, but her death was a tragic accident that happened in a blink of an eye. Her funeral seemed like that of an older person's funeral from the songs they sang and even her printed program. I decided after her funeral to plan my own.

My plans get updated periodically. The first pastor that I chose to speak at my funeral, Bill, moved away and time and space put a gap in our relationship. The next pastor I asked was Pastor John, but he went to Heaven before me. Both these men knew me well and had a passion for the Gospel and the spread of it. Currently I have a friend that is a women's leader and speaker. (Of course, she just moved out of town!) Only God knows who will speak at my funeral, but I have a plan!

> *Don't be afraid of death. Be afraid of the half-lived life. - Laird Hamilton*

I tell you this not because I have an obsession with dying, but let's face it . . . *we all will die!* I want the person that does my funeral to be very clear that it is not to be about me but it's to be about God. It needs to be a message to people that have not placed their faith in Jesus Christ; how they need to be prepared for their own death and the eternity beyond that. It needs to be a message to Christians, to make sure they are spreading the good news of Jesus Christ. I have the songs I want sang and by whom. The extra books, devotionals, and gospel tracts that I didn't have time to get into people's hands, need to be handed out after the funeral. Maybe? I will have everyone stand up at my funeral and hug. I'll leave that up to God!

> **Ripple:** Write out a funeral plan. Think about the songs and verses you would like used. Put it where someone knows where to find it. Or, you could make copies and discuss it with others. You could use your plan as another God conversation.

QUESTIONS

1. Have you ever had to plan an event in a short period of time? What?

2. Did you see God working with you in the planning? How?

3. Give an example of a time you KNEW the situation was out of your control and in God's?

4. Have you ever represented God in a hard situation to further the kingdom in some way? How?

5. Have you ever helped someone going through something hard? How?

6. Has God ever asked you to say or do something out of the ordinary? What?

7. Have you ever spoken at a funeral? For whom?

8. What was the worst message that you have heard at a funeral? What was the best one? Why?

9. Have you ever thought about how you would like your funeral to be? In what ways?

10. Who is on your heart currently that you need to reach out to and connect with?

11

—⚬⚬⚬—

The Ripple that Won't Stop!

COVID

I was almost finished with this book when the Coronavirus pandemic hit. We were in Florida at the time and honestly everything seemed fine for a month. The virus had been in China and seemed to be contained there far from home.

Our daughter who was married the year before was making plans to go to Europe for her honeymoon. They decided to go to Italy. This was mid February 2020, and she was ready to book the tickets. She called to ask her father-in-law about his airline miles he had offered, and he told her that he didn't think going to Italy at that time was a good idea. She then called to ask me what I thought . . . I wasn't caught up with the news, she needed to ask her father.

I needed to get up from writing and stretch my legs anyway, so I turned on the news, and across the headlines it said that Italy was getting hit with the Coronavirus too, but it didn't look too bad . . . yet. (If you remember, Italy was hit really hard with the virus!)

I thought to myself, "Isn't this just like the flu?" Every year the flu hits and nobody stops traveling because of it. Remember, I don't take the flu too lightly since it's what started the whole MS chapter. You can't stop the flu; but you can take precautions. I was on the fence about the decision, with one leg on the side of . . . just go. My personality leans more towards faith than fear . . . but, fear was starting to win. Once the father-in-law stated his opinion, his son Sean went along with it, and the decision was made.

Dean and I watched the news at night, and it would give counts as to how many died due to the virus. This is going to sound awful, but people do die every day, and at the time the count was trickling in – five in Italy and twenty-five in China. If you went with the numbers, it didn't sound very bad, considering how many died on Florida roadways that day and nobody stopped driving. When you compared it to the flu, the numbers were way low. But this was just the beginning of the whole covid ordeal.

At first the reporting seemed to make this crisis more about a political thing. Honestly it doesn't matter what side you vote on, both sides were going at it, which was really annoying, so I turned off the television. I ignored the news and kept writing, and reading.

We were headed to the Keys with a couple of stops along the way. Our son and one of his roommates were coming down to spend time with us, and I didn't think much about the virus. Things in Florida seemed normal . . . but there was a report of a cruise ship that had Americans quarantined in China. A few days later, I overheard talked about another cruise ship off the West Coast, with passengers being quarantined for two weeks. Suddenly, everywhere we went, the conversations were about how horrible it would be to be trapped on a cruise ship.

We drove to Key West, and the guys flew in. The place was packed with travelers, restaurants were full, and the sidewalks were crowded. I found time to write by the pool, while I watched the cruise ships pull into port. *GREAT!* I'm here with all those sick people on the cruise ships. After five days in Key West, the guys' flights home went smoothly, and we headed north towards Fort Lauderdale.

By this point the news encouraged people to stay home if they could. Spring break travel was discouraged. All the doctors interviewed discussed washing your hands.

Our oldest daughter and one-year-old grandson had plans to visit us for a few days. – Our youngest daughter felt left out, so she came too. The couple of days we were in Pompano without them, we ran around to some thrift stores, bought groceries, and did laundry. Everywhere we went, things seemed normal. Stores were fully stocked and people were living their lives. Wednesday night, before the girls arrived, we ate at a restaurant with about two hundred people. Most of the people were seventy or older – the place was packed!

The news reported that the people who had been quarantined on the cruise ship were being let off, but they were keeping them isolated on military bases. Hand washing and distancing was being pushed. Washington State was hit hard by the virus and other states started to have more cases pop up, but the numbers were still low.

The Democratic Primaries were going on by this time and the news was so negative I turned it off again. I kept reading and writing. At night, I would have text conversations with my brother – he would tell me how out-of-hand it was in Iowa. Stores closing, people buying up all the food, and no toilet paper! Every night he told me that you couldn't get toilet paper. I assured him that this was nonsense since everything in Florida seemed normal.

Day 1 – The girls arrived from different locations at the airport in Fort Lauderdale and there seemed to be no problems. They were glad to be in the warmth and everyone was excited to see Jan, our grandson. This was the first nice weather day in a week so everyone was outside by the pool and on the beach.

Everything seemed to be normal. We went to the store to get food for our daughters. Everyone seemed to be shopping like usual. All the shelves were still stocked. *Except* . . . I forgot to look for toilet paper to see if they had any. I didn't need it, I just wanted to tell my brother I would ship him some from Florida.

> *I've learned life is like a roll of toilet paper. The closer it gets to the end the faster it goes! - Andy Rooney*

Day 2 – Saturday night we ended up at the same restaurant that Dean and I had eaten at a few days before the girls arrived. We were worried we wouldn't get in since it had been so busy on Wednesday night – we were seated right away. Strange! Business in three short days dropped seventy-five percent. This was a big restaurant. Days before, there were over two hundred and fifty people; now it was down to around seventy-five on a Saturday night!

That's when things started to change. More and more conversations on the elevator were getting negative. People were telling families not to come to Florida. Just stay home. The people around the pool talked about the beach shutting down . . . *WHAT??? How can you shut down a beach?* I called Dean and asked him if he knew about beaches being shut down. He said, "Yes, they shut down the beaches in Miami because of all the spring break kids, and they shut the bars down also." He said, "They want to keep more distance around the kids and for them to not take any virus back home with them." Some colleges stated that if the students went on spring break, they couldn't come back to class until they quarantined at home for two weeks after getting back in town. Seriously . . . things started to change daily! Next they shut down all cruise ship travel, and then the most unimaginable thing happened in Florida . . . *Disney shut their gates.*

Day 3 – After that, things happened at warp speed – they shut down colleges for a month and were going to online learning. Then our oldest daughter, Abby, who is a school teacher, started receiving calls and texts from colleagues telling her they might shut down all the primary schools. They didn't shut them down that morning, but after dinner, she received the call that she wouldn't be returning to work. Her husband called and said he too would be working at home.

It wasn't long after Abby received her calls that our youngest daughter, Katie received a call from her husband. He informed her he would be working remotely, immediately. Katie was really sad because *NOW* she was the only one working. Her job was to provide information to pharmacists about the product she represented. This meant she would be around sick people in all the local pharmacies.

Dean was also getting calls from our property manager and his secretary, and received emails from tenants wanting to know what his contingency plan was with the virus. *What does that mean?* We were sure that this was the tenants' way of asking us if they have to pay rent if they close down their stores?

Our conversation that night was about whether Abby and our grandson should just stay with us another week. She could fly home from some other airport up the coast, or if things got really bad, we could drive her home.

When we arrived back at the hotel from dinner, we watched the news. It seemed people all of a sudden were in panic mode. Restaurants and fast food places were allowed pickup and drive-through service only. After much discussion, we decided they both needed to fly home before they shut down air travel, plus we didn't know if hotels were going to stay open. Katie didn't have an option since she still had to work. *LOL*

Day 5 – The next morning the girls and I went to breakfast – we were practically by ourselves. People must have scattered overnight. We talked with our waiter and asked what his thoughts were. He thought that everything was being blown out of proportion! Then he told us they were going to shut the beaches down. *THAT"S LUDICROUS!!!* Vacation was getting strange, but it was still sunny and warm.

Day 6 – We played on a beach with very few people and celebrated Jan's one year birthday. People had vanished, with the exception of a few. The original plan was that Dean and I would make our way home in a week at a leisurely pace. I knew he was concerned that he wasn't at home and in the office to see what was really happening. (Seriously, he really can do everything from his phone and computer.)

Day 7 – The decision was made that Dean would take the girls to the airport since there wasn't much room in the vehicle with all their luggage. I stayed at the hotel to pack and then I went on my bike ride. During my prayers, God impressed upon my soul that I better enjoy it because I was going home. During my ride back, the girls both called me from the airport. Katie said, "The airport is a madhouse. I'm glad I only have a carry-on bag. Everyone with suitcases are being held up." Then Abby called. She was in a panic because she had Jan and the suitcase, and they weren't letting her check in. She had to wait with her bag until an hour before flight departure. Jan needed to be fed, she still had the suitcase, and didn't know how she was going to handle it all. I was on my bike . . . *What was I going to do?* I said, "I will pray." She said, "I'll call Dad."

Just as I was rolling up to the hotel on my bike, Dean called and told me what a mess it was at the airport and that he had Abby's suitcase. She made him come back and get it so she could go up to the gate. He said, " We will take it back home with us, and we would get it back to her at Easter time." After all these calls, my hopes of staying in the warmth were quickly fading. I asked Dean before he left for the airport what our plans were. He told me we'll go up the road a few hours, stay there for a couple of days and then make our way home. *BUT,* I knew things were quickly changing all around me – I had a feeling this virus was going to mess with the plans!

Dean called and was on his way back from the airport. He said to get everything packed up, and that he would be there in ten minutes – I could arrange the car while he made a few calls. He sounded like he was in a hurry, so I had the stuff waiting by the curb when he pulled up. He hopped out, and I started loading the car. He came down ten minutes later with his suitcases and said, "Go up and get your suitcase so we can get out of here!" I knew going up the elevator that "Let's get out of here," meant we were going home but, there was still hope.

I climbed in the car. Dean was on the phone with my brother Jay, our property manager. They talked about what was going on in a fast and anxious manner. Dean kept talking and driving as he headed towards the interstate which was not the way I wanted to get to our next stopping point, which happens to be my favorite stopping point on the whole trip! I wanted to drive up the coast. Then, Dean made another call, and it sounded like he was canceling our hotel reservations. I still hoped that the cancellation was for the hotel a couple of days up the road. When he hung up the phone, I finally asked, "What's the plan?" He said, "We are going home. – This is getting way too chaotic. – I need to be home to handle all of our tenants."

STOP!!! That was not the plan, two hours ago. I was kind of upset – I would have sat out in the sun longer – I would have ridden my bike longer. Of course, I didn't say all of that . . . but, when I did open my mouth, I knew that I should have kept it shut!! I mentioned that he told me we were going up the coast to stay at Jensen beach. *WELL . . . we all know how that conversation went.* It wasn't long, it wasn't uplifting, and we didn't talk for about six hours other than when I would say I had to go to the restroom or needed something to drink. He listened to the radio about Covid and political stuff. I read my book.

I decided I was going to have a pity party, or at least I wanted to have one. But, just like all the other times, God wouldn't let me. Yes, I was sad that I totally missed my favorite part of Florida. We had cut our vacation short, and Dean and I were in a tiff, *but* God kept reminding me of how good I had it all winter. I kept replaying everything everyone else was going through. I wanted to pout for a while, but no! How could I when on the elevator that morning, I ran into a family in a scramble to get back home to Canada. They had young kids and had just arrived in Florida two days earlier to catch their cruise. Of course once they got to Florida, their cruise had canceled and the beaches were shutting down.

Ripple: What pity party should you end? Make a list of all the blessings you can be thankful for. Encourage others to make a list also — compare them. Or make this a game for children or grandchildren to see who can write twenty things they are thankful for the fastest.

I also thought about March Madness basketball and the kids that had worked so hard to get to the tournaments that they don't get to compete in. They talked about canceling all college graduations. Four years and then you don't get the grand finale? I thought of all the high school seniors that wouldn't get to attend Prom. I know in the grand scheme of things, this stuff is shallow. But, it is still sad. (Later it was worse with no weddings, funerals, and Easter celebrations!)

I haven't talked about a book for a while, so let me tell you about another one I read and kept thinking about. *The Things We Couldn't Say* by Diet Eman. (I should have read it before our European trip, we went to many of the places the author mentioned.) It's a true story of Diet as a young seventeen-year-old in the Netherlands when Hitler invaded her country. She ended up in the Dutch Resistance along with her fiance. They risked their lives to save their county and the Jewish people that lived there. It was written by her as an adult, but she had kept a diary during the war. She wrote about her feelings as a seventeen-year-old during the war. Her faith in God grew stronger every day, but she also had times when she was very discouraged and disappointed with the Christians she knew. They wouldn't help her due to the fear they had of keeping their own lives safe. It was really interesting to read how grown up she sounded as a seventeen year old risking her life for God and others. It made me wonder if I was a strong enough Christian that I would have risked my life for others.

Since I had read it only months prior to the pandemic, it was still fresh in my mind. I reasoned that as bad and chaotic as the world was, it wasn't as bad as Europe during the war. We had sickness and had to cancel or delay things we thought were really important. But, there were no bombs or people trying to kill us. What we were going though was a major inconvenience! So the pity party ended after five minutes!!! I really appreciate the fact that God doesn't let me linger with self absorption for long periods of time. God reminds me that I have it good compared to others, and that I need to stop being so shallow.

A week later, Abby, Jon, and Jan, all came to hang out at our house. Both parents had to work from home and since grandma didn't work, I was the built-in babysitter. Ohio had more cases of the virus than Iowa, so they decided to hang out with us. While they were with us, the government kept shutting things down every day. First we were going back to work in two weeks, then three, and then four. Then it was April 30th. (I added to this sentence so many times!) Things really did not start to open up until the end of May and even then they were still canceling things. They even canceled Fourth of July parades.

Honestly, life seemed like it does during the holidays . . . with no gift wrapping! Our house was a mess, there was extra food in the fridge so you couldn't find anything you wanted, and our other kids would stop by to see Jan.

CJ, my husband's secretary, was still coming to work on Dean's office side of The Lodge, and I would see our neighbors out fishing in our pond. The only thing that wasn't normal was I usually had time to write, read, and volunteer but that was hard to do with everyone there.

I feel like I need to suggest you relax here. (Because people were getting really tense!) There was a lot of space around my house, and everyone had their own area. Most of those who stopped over were staying home so it was safe to see each other since we had already been together.

People were getting paranoid. Occasionally during the day, I would watch the news to get the number of victims that had died due to Covid, see the list of all of the businesses and upcoming events that were canceled, and watch politicians argue about the handling of the situation. But if I listened too long, it made me angry. The questions that reporters would ask at press conferences (and then re-ask the same dumb question in another way) did not help get them an answer. – Nobody knew how this situation would work out. During one press conference, the US Surgeon General, Jerome Adams, described the coming week as a "Pearl Harbor moment and 9/11 moment, only it's not going to be localized, it's going to be happening all over the country." *Who says that when people are already on edge,* especially when he had NO CLUE if that was really going to happen? Plus, the number of cases were on the way down! *(He ended up being VERY wrong!)* Finally, I stopped watching the news – and my life was more peaceful!

> *Rather than ask God to change your circumstances, ask Him to use your circumstances to change you.* -- Max Lucado

A few days later, I walked by a friend's house. She came out to visit with me at a social distance and told me she was very concerned. She had read a news article that Bill Gates wanted to chip everyone to know if people had received their vaccinations against diseases like Covid. I told her it sounded like the *"Left Behind"* book series coming to life. She also asked what I was going to do about it. I said, "What can I do? . . . I'm going to pray more, witness more, and do whatever to get God's word out! . . . I'm not going to panic." She was not the only one who talked about multiple conspiracies. We had a shortage of coins – the government wants us to only use credit so they can track you. The elections were rigged – either way you voted. The next president would take us down. Oh, and food is running low – you'd better stock up!

I won't lie, I did entertain a few of these myself! And hey, maybe by the end of this book we will know how this all turned out. I did stop and make a plan or two about what I would do if Christians started being persecuted in the United States. (Hey, it was so bad with certain states not letting churches meet that some churches went to Walmart to hold services. Walmart was able to be open!)

After two weeks of being worried (I don't use that word often!), I finally realized that I couldn't do much about it and that I was trying to save myself and *NOT* relying on God to protect me. All my plan making was getting me sidetracked from what the true purpose of life is. We are here to become more Christlike, to glorify the Lord, and share the gospel with others. I knew if I was worried and scared, there were a lot of people having similar issues. I used my fear to fuel my desire to get God's Word into people's hands.

My mom, who has underlying health issues, didn't want to come to my house to see her great-grandson. We wanted her to sit out in the sun and watch him from a distance. To her credit, she did come with much persuasion and watched him from the car. Of course she went to McDonalds drive-thru and bought a Diet Coke before she came. So she had to pay and touch the cup. Even if you sanitize it, you still touch the germs. (This was before the masks!) Listen, this is how things were. It never made sense! *COMMON SENSE WAS GONE!!!!*

You can't take risks out of life! There is a risk in everything we do — driving our cars, going to shopping malls, and even walking down the stairs. Life is a risk most people are willing to take.

If we are bored in life, we took the bait of safety and quit living. Maybe that's why some Christians are bored. There's no more risk! I'm not saying I risk my life here in America when I witness to people or when I try to push Christians out of their comfort zone. But there is an adrenaline rush when you don't know how a person is going to respond. Maybe Christians need to put themselves out there more! I bet the people that were on the front lines during the virus pandemic were *NOT* bored! I bet at night they felt like they were doing something that made a difference in people's lives!

Two weeks before we left Florida, I had contacted the study group, to see if everyone would be ready to start again the first of April. Six of the ten said yes.

I contacted the study group when we made it home and asked if they were ready to start earlier. Only two of us were willing to meet. I could kind of understand why they didn't want to meet, but I had a large enough space to accommodate at least a ten foot space between them. Also during this time the Stonecroft luncheons had been canceled so I couldn't volunteer there either. Then my excitement turned towards the women's shelter and seeing the gals that were still there, including the gal I mentored. They were on *TOTAL LOCKDOWN!* Nobody could leave the shelter because of Covid. None of the volunteers could go in. (Sad note: some of the gals were so upset with being in lockdown that several left. Even the gal I mentored. I tried to convince her that things were bad everywhere, but she thought she knew best. It was another loss due to Covid!)

Ripple: Look into volunteering for a Christian organization in your community or for your church. Maybe be a mentor to someone.

After Abby's family went home, I had time on my hands. Of course I tuned in to see what was happening in the world through the news. I felt defeated! With all that was going on, I began to feel that satan was winning the battle in people's lives. There was so much fear and so little hope. People were isolated and lonely. Maybe my personality goes back to my cheerleading days with the defense cheers – cheering people on to victory or at least some offensive cheers! But something inside me knew that I was *NOT* about to let satan take anymore ground than he already had! . . . *How could God use me during a pandemic?*

I couldn't volunteer or lead a study, but my neighbors were all home, and we had a really nice spring! I made friends with all my neighbor kids. (I'm ready to adopt some more!) There are six who are old enough to roam around the pond. First, I handed out cookies. (Yes, I asked their parents!) Then came Easter baskets – In the baskets, I put sidewalk chalk, bubbles, stickers, and of course more cookies. Next came May Day baskets. (Eventually the parents started coming outside more. I think they were getting bored, too.) A few of the kids helped me clean up all the sticks in the yard to have a big fire. This was fun, and they did get more cookies for helping! They were able to ride in the utility ATV mule so it wasn't all work! Plus, at the bonfire we made s'mores, and a few parents came!

Ripple: Make May Day baskets and Easter baskets, or do a little treat for the kids in your neighborhood. Include a little note that says God loves them and a few other Christian items. Adults like gift baskets, too!

I used my phone as a tool and encouraged Christians at home. I sent several text messages to Christian friends to see how they were growing in the Lord. New Year's Day 2020 (before Covid), I asked some of my Christian family members and friends what their New Year's resolutions were. I specifically asked them how they planned on growing as a Christian. It was interesting to me to see how people responded. Of course, some did not respond – which is okay. Some people don't set goals or reflect on their spiritual lives. I wrote the resolutions of those who responded in my prayer journal (the one I keep the prayer requests from the waiters and waitresses), and I told them I would pray for them to keep their goals. With the prayer journal in hand, I texted each of those that responded and asked them how they were doing with reading their Bibles, memorizing scripture, or other such goals.

If you're looking for excuses, you will always find one. - Mark Batterson

This was the first time I asked people about New Year's goals, and it worked great. I know people don't think someone would really pray about their request, but I did every week! Some, of course, had let their goals slip but thanked me for the reminder and the encouragement. People want to be encouraged, and I like to encourage! I also asked them what they were doing to further the kingdom of God during the shut down. This is a question a lot of Christians don't like to be asked, because they know they should be doing something but they either don't know what to do or they choose to stay focused on other things. (I know this kind of comment will rub several people the wrong way, but sometimes the truth hurts.) I did have several friends who reached out and wrote letters to family members about the gospel and others that went and picked up groceries for family and neighbors. We swapped good ideas and put a little more effort into our actions. (Side note: I used my phone because I don't have Facebook.)

During this time I listened to several church sermons while cooking dinner, eating, and cleaning up afterwards. I could finish a whole church service. *THIS WAS MUCH BETTER THAN LISTENING TO THE NEWS!!!!* I also sent several sermon links to friends, encouraging them to do the same thing. This is something I will continue to do. I also started listening to podcasts from Focus on the Family, while I was weight lifting instead of listening to the news. I could finish a podcast in the amount of time it took to exercise.

While listening to one during a trip south – it was about marriage and how differently men and women think. We laughed because we had been married for thirty-two years, and we both thought it was just a "Dean thing" or a "Jennifer thing" and we found out it was a "woman or man thing". After I had listened to these podcasts for six months, I was amazed that our marriage lasted . . . we had done so many things wrong! But from the beginning of my marriage, I have prayed daily that our marriage will last a lifetime. So really it was a "God thing!" I now send the ones I listen to that I think someone will enjoy or learn from to newly married or new parents. I even send them to friends to send on to their children.

> **Ripple:** Listen to one extra sermon per week. Look up your favorite Christian author who is a pastor or one of your former churches you have attended!
>
> **Ripple:** Listen to a podcast once a week. Look up Focus on the Family or other Christian podcasts.
>
> **Ripple:** Send one encouraging text message each week, and let someone know you are thinking of them! On New Year's Day, ask children, grandchildren, family members, or friends how they are going to grow spiritually that year. Then pray for them all year long!

Next, I decided to focus my time on my neighbor ladies. I figured the kids had been hanging around each other for a couple of weeks, so we had each other's germs. So I asked if they would like to do a book study on Eternity as a group. Yeah, I know!!! I chickened out a few times before I asked, and then I reread some of the things I had written and it pumped me up. It was called, *One Heartbeat Away . . . Your Journey into Eternity* by Mark Cahill. I was nervous as I went house to house with a title like that, but I did it!

Seven ladies took books, and five came just about every week. We all connected well and had great discussions. At the end of the study, I was able to give one of the gals a Bible, and a devotional to each of the ladies that showed up most of the weeks.

While I was working on my book, a worker at our home asked me what I was doing. I told him about my book, and he admitted that he was questioning his faith! I briefly explained about my crisis of faith. I happened to have one of the Heartbeat books with me since I needed to read it for the study. We talked about what it was like to have a relationship with God. He had gone to church as a child but had started having doubts now that he was in his upper twenties. He listened, and I told him to pray and ask God to make Himself known to him as he read. I hope another seed was planted!

That same day, I was hanging around a gal who talked to me about my book. I happened to say that it isn't about having religion but a relationship with Jesus Christ. It's about asking God into your life. She told me that her husband had said that same thing to her. She continued to tell me about his experience. I told her if she wasn't sure if she had a relationship with Jesus, she should make sure. (She goes to church, but I'm not sure if it preaches about asking Christ into their lives.)

I love to plant the seed of God in the hearts of people! I only have stories like this because I pray for divine opportunities to share God's word with others, and courage to speak out during these opportunities. (I do not always speak up at every opportunity!) I'm a work in progress. But think about this. I didn't even have this book done, and I've already used it a few times to share God with others! *That's what all this work is about!!!*

I will admit that with all the cleaning I did during the shut down, I missed some real opportunities! I could have given devotionals out to *all* my neighbors who were home and had nothing to do! I have shelves full of them . . . I pray that I will learn from this situation.

We were now into June – this virus seemed to have people in even more fear! I know by saying this it will make some people angry! I can tell you what makes me angry . . . Christians sitting on the sidelines just like in that book about the war. *Do you remember that Christians, like firefighters, are supposed to rush in and help?* Iowa is known as a friendly place, but the virus had started to make people unfriendly.

People being isolated, masks and social distancing, and lives being disrupted was day-to-day life. If that wasn't enough, then we had to add riots because of the killing of a black man named George Floyd by a white police officer. (The video was horrible.) The killing was senseless and very sad to anyone who saw it. The peaceful protests about the situation were fine, but with everyone's built-up flustration and being cooped up inside away from each other, riots and looting happened all across the nation, even in Iowa, which made it even more disturbing! Let's be honest, the riots were people out of control, who felt they had the right to do what they pleased. Two wrongs never make things right! It was to the point where *doing the right thing was wrong and doing the wrong thing was right!*

To say that life as we knew it had changed before our eyes is an understatement. Part of Seattle, Washington, was taken over by Antifa, a group that is anti-police and anti-government. Then there was a movement to get rid of police officers.

From my perspective things were out of control, and it looked more like the end of the world was getting nearer. I was not the only one that felt this way. In the midst of all the chaos, I had multiple conversations with friends about how strange things were getting and many of them become very fearful. *(That might be an understatement.)* These were conversations about storing up food, different supplies, and having a plan to hide if things became worse. I'm embarrassed to say for a couple of weeks, I started thinking the same way. I took my focus off Jesus – like when Peter tried to walk on water. Matthew 14:28-32 describes when Peter stepped out of the boat to walk on the water to Jesus. He was doing fine until he took his eyes off Jesus and started to sink. That's what I did until I put my focus back on Jesus and His Kingdom to come. *There is NO PLAN that will protect you the way Jesus can.*

I would like to say that 2 Peter 1:3-8 was in my mind, but it didn't come to me until later. I knew I had to stay focused on Jesus or I would sink into despair like some of those around me.

2 Peter 1:3-8, "By His divine power, God has given us everything we need for living a godly life. We have received all of this by coming to know Him, the one who called us to Himself by means of His marvelous glory and excellence. And because of His glory and excellence, He has given us great and precious promises. These are the promises that enable you to share His divine nature and escape the world's corruption caused by human desires. In view of all this, make every effort to respond to God's promises. Supplement your faith with a generous provision of moral excellence, and moral excellence with knowledge, and knowledge with self-control with patient endurance, and patient endurance with godliness, and godliness with brotherly affection, and brotherly affection with love for everyone. The more you grow like this the more productive and useful you will be in your knowledge of our Lord Jesus Christ."

I needed to escape if only for a while from all the turmoil going on! I wanted to be more productive and useful. How do you shine your light as a

Christian if you look like the rest of the world by falling apart? Thank the Lord that the Holy Spirit didn't let me wander away from God for too long!!!

Turning my focus back to God didn't get rid of that annoying thing everyone was talking and thinking about. *NOBODY* . . . could stop talking about *Covid!* It's like when you are in a large room and everything is good, except one large horsefly that keeps buzzing around your head. All you can focus on is that one annoying fly!!! That's what Covid was like! Everytime you tried to focus on the good things, that one fly would buzz around your head and everyone would start to complain again. *Seriously*, you could not have a conversation without someone talking about how annoying Covid was. This is how bad it was. We had a large storm go through Iowa called a derecho, and it caused a lot of damage, but it took everyone's minds off of Covid for about a week. I don't like storms, and seriously, we had *A LOT* of damage to the trees in our yard. We lost two of my favorite trees plus *many* more, but it was such a pleasant diversion from Covid. I really wished, just like with a fly, I could put a quick end to the pandemic!

(I wanted to end my book with the finale of Covid, but it kept on going, even through all the editing process!!)

I don't want to end this chapter on a negative note, so here's what I see that was positive about Covid.

Due to fear:

- I have seen more people willing to have conversations about God.
- I have seen churches and Christian organizations using technology to share the gospel.
- I have seen Christians being more bold in sharing the gospel with people.
- I have seen families slow down and be closer to one another.
- I have made friends with my neighbors.
- I have gotten to see my faith get stronger with all the negativity around me.

I wanted to put the Top 10 Covid jokes here – due to copyright laws you will have to look them up. – They will give you a good chuckle.

QUESTIONS

1. What was your biggest fear? Did you give your fear to God?

2. What was your biggest disappointment with Covid?

3. Did you grow spiritually during Covid? How?

4. Did you ever stop to wonder what God was up to with a WORLD wide event like Covid?

5. What sin did Covid bring out in you?

6. Did you continue to watch or attend church?

7. Did Covid make you pray more or less? Why?

8. How did you see God working during Covid?

9. How did you serve God during Covid?

10. What was your greatest blessing during Covid?

12

—⟋⟍⟍⟋—

A Group with Rocks

WHEN TO STOP

I tried to figure out how a person goes about ending a book about their life when life keeps happening? I was going to end it when Carolyn died and use the funeral story as a warning to go out and share the gospel with everyone since none of us knows when our work here on earth is going to end. Another reason I was going to end it there was because a week after her funeral, her husband and kids started cleaning out all her personal items. The things they didn't want to keep, they gave to me to sort through. They knew that I would use her things to further the Kingdom of God. Some of it we kept for the auction with Stonecroft Ministries. Some of it went to the Hope Ministries Women's Shelter. She had so many brand new cosmetic bags, *I don't have a clue what she was saving all those for,* but I used those for packets for the homeless.

After seeing all the multiples she had and all the things I know she would have used for the Lord – if she would have known that her mission here on earth was done. I took a good long look at all the cabinets full of stuff I had. Days later I started cleaning out all my cabinets. We have so many things that we can use to further the kingdom, but we save it for *"SOME DAY".*

> **Ripple:** Clean out your cabinets — use those things you are saving for someday and bless people with them today!

I started to have doubts about this book. Again, satan kept tormenting me . . . all this work . . . who's going to read it? People are going to judge you for what you say! Nobody wants to read about your personal life! These and many more thoughts kept going through my mind all fall long . . . and I *stopped* writing again! I didn't have a deadline, and I began to believe that what I had written was boring and nobody would want to read it.

> *It's not whether you get knocked down, it's*
> *whether you get up. - Vinnce Lombardi*

This is where telling people what you're doing comes into play!!! I had people praying for me to get it finished. All of a sudden several people asked me how things were going, and I had to tell them that I had stopped writing and how I was feeling about it. When they heard that I had stopped writing, God used those people to encourage me. They said things like, "You can't let this attack from satan stop you," and "That's all this is, you know – it's an attack!!!" or "He is afraid that you do have something to say, that people need to hear." They also told me that they *did* want to read what I had to say. Even my son said, "Mom, you've done all that work, you have to finish it now." This is why it's good to let people know what God is doing in your life. God will use them to encourage you to keep going. I stepped away for a while to get some perspective, and then out of nowhere I received an email.

I had never signed up for any publisher, but I must have searched about writing. Even though the letter was signed by someone other than God, I really believe God sent it to me. It was just what I needed to give me that extra push to get done. – That may be an understatement! The letter started with my name and talked about never underestimating being obedient to God and the *ripple effects* it has to influence many people. It then went on to tell me how my life would be changed in the process. – which I did see many changes in myself during the writing process. I told you at the beginning of the book I would need perseverance. I truly needed it during the editing process. I fought some of the suggestions at first, and then I chose to see them as a learning experience. I learned better ways to communicate my opinions and to soften my approach. (During the editing process, I was required to take out the original letter due to copyright laws and paraphrase it instead, – which you are reading now.)

Then it went on to tell the effects it would have on family members. – I have not seen many of these effects yet since my immediate family gave up on reading my manuscript because of how many times it has been edited. For those that did read the unedited version, they were able to read more of my raw feelings and many more stories that have been cut. It also talked about the impact on future generations of my family. – I will save a few copies of the original manuscript for my grandchildren to read the *unedited* version of me and to see how much editing I required! . . . I also said at the beginning that I was not a writer – the manuscript might prove my point. Then it talked about how after you accomplish your goal of writing a book it will inspire others to achieve their goals in life too. – How bravery is contagious – I found that to be the one thing that so many people would say to me during the writing process. People would tell me how impressed they were that I set out to reach my goal, which I did have to correct several people as to this wasn't my goal, but was an obedience to God. Even so, they were fascinated in the process of starting such a large project, without it being a dream of mine. I was able to share how God kept me persistent on this and the other adventures we had been on together, how being obedient has made me a stronger, more faithful follower of Him. At the conclusion of the letter, it spoke of the people whom I would minister to – those that I know and the people beyond my circle of influence. One of the people that edited my book was a friend's sister from Arizona, Jill. I chose her to read it since she had never met me – to give me a feeling of how she would relate to it's style. Even before it was published, it was read in Arizona . . . and it was also sent out of the country to my daughter's in-laws in Norway. Both of these experiences made me ponder how far this book could reach. Not for myself, but if even one of the ripples that I mentioned starts in another neighborhood, how far could that next ripple go? It was a fun little daydream . . . thinking of someone in Europe with sidewalk chalk writing Jesus Loves You on their sidewalk. You never know what that message could do in someone's heart.

(That's the long version of what the letter said.)

I had my husband and a friend read it. They both told me that I needed to get busy again. I can honestly say that the words in that email were *ALL* the same reasons that I had thought about over the three years it took to write this book, but had never put in writing. *I LOVE HOW GOD CAN INSPIRE YOU IN THE MOST RANDOM WAYS* and give you the words that you have been searching for to inspire others.

I decided that sending out ripples is how I want to spend my life and to encourage others to do the same! Like God says in Hebrews 10:24, "Let us think of ways to motivate one another to acts of love and good works." And if you remember the words from Rhonda who shared God's salvation message with me were, "Now you will want to go and tell others." Rhonda definitely had a ripple effect on me, and I hope I will continue to send out ripples (or maybe waves!) to others. Psalms 90:12 says, "Teach us to realize the brevity of life, so that we may grow in wisdom." I would say this verse sums it up! Really. None of us knows what the future holds here on the earth. That's why we need to make the most of every situation.

> *Life is a lot like a coin. You can spend it any way you wish, but you spend it once. - Lillian Dickson*

Time is so precious. Time with our families, friends, and our brothers and sisters in Christ. How do you invest your time? Where do you invest it? When you think about it, time is more precious than money. You can't make more time, and once it's gone, it can't be reclaimed. Live a life of no regrets. Put first things first: God, spouse, family, and then the things you need to get done. As you begin each day, ask God to use your time for His greatest good. Then thank Him for the sleep you had – in a bed – in a home that's safe. Pray that God gives you opportunities to share the gospel with others during the day. Go for a walk or a bike ride and spend the entire time in prayer to your Lord and Savior. Spend some time reading the Bible! Do good deeds and encourage others to glorify the Lord. At the end of the day, get on your knees and thank the Lord again for the day that He gave you, and pray for your brothers and sisters in Christ that are being persecuted for their faith. Then wake up and do it all over again!

I love what God says in these two verses. Galatians 6:9-10 says, "So let's not get tired of doing what is good. At just the right time we will reap a harvest of blessing if we don't give up. Therefore, whenever we have the opportunity, we should do good to everyone – especially to those in the family of faith." And Philippians 3:12-14 says, "I don't mean to say that I have already achieved these things or that I have already reached perfection. But I press on to possess that perfection for which Christ Jesus first possessed me. No, dear brothers and sisters, I have not achieved it, but I focus on this one thing: Forgetting the past and looking forward to what lies ahead, I press on to reach the end of the race and receive the heavenly prize for which God, through Christ Jesus, is calling us."

TRAILBLAZER CHRISTIANS - GO ROGUE!

As a child, I remember my mother complaining about her life situations, but would never do anything to change them and how much this bothered me. If you don't like something, change it. I'm not a huge fan of changes, but there's not much you can do about it. That is how life works and you might as well learn to embrace it. Otherwise, life will pass you by! Change happens when your kids grow up and move on – there's not a thing you can do but pray and support them. It happens when you get an incurable disease, when you shut down a business, or your child becomes terribly sick. Yes, change is hard, especially when you aren't ready. Embrace the change! Is it hard? *YES!* Lean on God, ask Him what you can learn in the circumstance. Yes, you can mourn the change – there are a lot of circumstances when it is *VERY* appropriate to do that! But that's not what I'm talking about here.

Just because something is a tradition doesn't mean it has to stay that way. *Change can be good!*

> *Do not ask the Lord to guide your footsteps if you are not willing to move your feet. - Sean Patrick Flanery*

My official birthday is February 11th. I have never liked this date because it would either snow, be freezing cold, or everyone was sick. Birthday parties were hard to plan around those three things! I remember my birthday parties as a child. I would invite ten girls and get three to show up. It's hard to get parents to drop children off in a blizzard!

Remember, I don't like being cold! What do you do for a birthday when it's negative ten degrees outside? It's not like summer time birthdays where you can go boating, swimming, or hang outside and eat barbecue! So one year, I decided to change the date of my birthday. Not my age, just my birth month. I switched it to April 11th. April had to be better than February. (*Honestly it wasn't much better.* I should have chosen a summer month!)

I used April 11th for about two years, but people would forget. So I moved it to April 15th (tax day) since nobody would forget that date, *EXCEPT* . . . when it falls on a weekend. Then everyone forgot because nobody pays their taxes until Monday. I celebrated my birthday this way for at least fifteen years. It snowed on April 15th, 2019, I decided to plan on being out of town where it doesn't snow and celebrate it in February again which worked great for 2020! I celebrated in Florida where it was sunny, 85 degrees, and I was able to celebrate it with friends. (I was glad that I made the change. The Covid quarantine started in March and was still going on.)

People told me you can't change your birthday, but I did! Ask all my friends and family.

Ripple: Talk about your traditions with family. See if there are any you should change.

Ripple: Make a list of five things you routinely complain about, then pray about those five things everyday for a month.

Growing up, I also never cared for cake, but every year my mother would get me one. The first year of marriage, Dean wanted to buy me cake. I said, "No, I would rather have a chocolate malt or cookies." And that's what we did. (Of course, I've changed it again, I now get cake for my birthday – carrot cake or sometimes key lime pie.)

Dean was okay with changes in my life, but he wanted to do things in a traditional way with the kids. But they soon caught on that mom didn't do birthday cake. Dean gave in. *Why do something for the sake of tradition if you don't like it?* I remind my husband that we are making our own traditions.

After our oldest daughter was married, I was excited about becoming a grandma. I didn't bug Abby for the first year but after two years of marriage, I was antsy to be a grandma. I could have given up hope after the third year, but instead decided to do something about my lack of grandchildren. I adopted my neighbor's kids. I met their mother Glenda the first weekend she moved in. (She moved next door to the house we would sell.) It was the same weekend of Abby's wedding. Her fiance's relatives and bridal party stayed in the house and pool house. We were living at The Lodge, the place where her reception was held. It is one street over, and we were running back and forth between the two houses on the golf cart. On a few of those rides, I noticed the house up the street had been sold, and there was a woman unloading boxes into the new house by herself. I was too busy to help her at the time – since I had plenty to do myself.

After the wedding, we had several flower arrangements. Everyone was from out of town and it's hard to travel with flowers and water. I welcomed the new neighbor with a beautiful bouquet of flowers and gave her my phone number since they had moved in from out of town. This was my first time welcoming someone into the neighborhood, something I should have done all along (another regret) but will continue with this new tradition!

> **Ripple:** If a new neighbor has moved into the neighborhood within the last six months, welcome them to the neighborhood. (It's never too late to offer kindness!) Give them a basket with goodies, a bouquet, or a DEVOTIONAL! If nobody is new, get something prepared for when someone moves in. Here's another thought: instead of welcoming new neighbors, give a gift to the best neighbors!

That began a beautiful friendship! She called days later and asked if we knew a person that could help with this or that. Of course working with a lot of contractors, we could usually steer her in the right direction. I invited her to a Christmas function at my house, and then continued to invite her to everything that I was involved in.

Over time, I began to mentor this woman (without being asked). I took her under my wing. She came to a few of the Bible/book studies that I held in the summer, and I encouraged her to read her Bible. She also received free advice on raising children and on her marriage.

Glenda doesn't have a close relationship with her mother. She loves her mother-in-law, but she lives out of town. This left a void of a mother figure and grandmother living in the area. Ultimately, this led to the adoption! I would see her and the kids at the bus station in the morning while I was out for my walk or bike ride. We would chat and the boys were always friendly. Then one day I told her I needed grandkids and that her sons would work for me! She said that was fine, and the deal was done. The boys asked me if they could call me Grandma Jen and my husband Grandpa Dean. I said we better stick with Grandma Jen and Mr. Dean since this was not his hair-brained idea.

> *Our day's happier when we give others a bit of our heart*
> *rather than a piece of our mind - Mary Christine Parks*

Abby didn't care for the adoptive grandchildren idea at the beginning. She tried to explain to me that it didn't make sense with Glenda being only about ten years younger than me. I explained that not everything needs to make sense in life. They didn't have a grandma in the area, and I didn't have any grandkids. It seemed pretty logical to me. Also, Glenda has become like a daughter to me. Some weeks she has called or texted me more than my own children!

I know God is okay with this idea since He said it in Ephesians 1:5, "God decided in advance to adopt us into His own family by bringing us to Himself through Jesus Christ. *This is what He wanted to do, and it gave Him great pleasure.*" How many people can you adopt into your family and invest time in? (Abby has since given us a wonderful grandson . . . *BUT HE LIVES IN OHIO!)*

Tommy and Johnny are like real grandkids – the first thing they asked when they found out Abby was pregnant was if they were still going to be my grandkids. I, of course, said, "Yes." (Their second question was asked after Jan (our grandson) was born. "*Who's your favorite grandson* ☺ *Yep! Just like family.*

Guess who has adoptive grandparents in Ohio??? Abby is okay with the arrangement now – since she has adopted a set of grandparents in Ohio. And so, a tradition was born!

(This whole arrangement worked out well for both of us during the Covid outbreak. I had someone to play cards and games with, and Abby had someone that could celebrate Jan's birthday with them.)

If you've read this far, you may have figured out that I'm a sold out Christian. Maybe, even over the top . . . some of my Christian friends question all the time spent on God stuff. I've even heard a negative voice inside my head tell me that I don't have to go overboard with all this Christian stuff. I don't care what satan thinks – but, I will admit that sometimes it bothers me that people think I'm a bit different. I don't do what I do to get myself noticed, butI do it out of my love for Him and for all He has done for me! When I think back to that young fourteen year old girl that was headed down the wrong path, I marvel that He saw so much potential in me and pursued me until I was one of his children! *Why . . . would I not want to live my life for Him. Our Christian lives should* reflect a difference from society!

We shouldn't wear clothes that show too much skin, or watch many of the television shows or movies that are out there, or read the most "popular" books. We should spend time serving God, volunteering with different ministries, trying to keep God as our top priority! We should always be trying to be more like Christ every day. It won't always look the same, but there should be a noticeable difference in us from our society.

Don't be afraid to stand for what you believe in, even if that means standing alone - Andy Biersack

When I started writing this section about being a different kind of Christian, God popped different Christians in my head, ones that haven't always served God the same way the church is doing it, trail blazers! Or people that go rogue. These are people that don't always wait for a committee to decide if doing good is in the budget, or if the church staff wants to take on more at the time.

Here are a few Christians that took things to the extreme or did things in a different way. They knew the definition of the church – is being the hands and feet of Christ.

William Wilberforce – In 1780, at the age of twenty-one, William became a British politician to fight against slavery. Instead of complaining about what he saw as an injustice, he did something about it. He fought for years before the Slavery Abolition Act was passed by the Commons. Three days after the act passed, he died.

Dwight L Moody – A shoe salesman turned evangelist. His passion was for the lost. When he asked his pastor if he could teach a Sunday school class, the church turned him down since they had more teachers than students. So he went out and recruited his own class. He started out with eighteen students, then later rented an abandoned saloon to contain the 1,000 pupils that he had acquired in a year. From there he evangelized in America, Europe, worked with the YMCA, and started a church.

Helen Duff Baugh – The wife of a banker – she knew that not everyone would come to church, so she started hosting luncheons with ladies to share the gospel and to help them grow spiritually. This became known as Stonecroft Ministries. She didn't get the church involved; she saw a need and tried to fill it.

Billy Graham – He did his preaching in big circus tents, colosseums around the world, on radio, and television. He preached the gospel in prisons and in countries that are closed off to the gospel. His gospel message wasn't confined to a building.

William Booth – The founder of the Salvation Army stopped preaching in a church to start offering practical help to the poor and destitute of London. He would walk the streets and preach the gospel to the down and out, and he started soup kitchens and shelters.

Brenda Spahn - She started a transitional center for women coming out of prison. Her story started with six women and has led to an outreach that serves 450 women and children every day, providing substance abuse counseling, drug rehabilitation, meals, childcare, career counseling, and job opportunities to women working to establish successful lives outside of prison walls.

Christine Caine - She Is the founder of The A21 Campaign, which is one of the largest non-profit organizations in the world dedicated to rescuing victims of human trafficking in twelve countries.

Jesus - He didn't join the religious leaders of the day – the Pharisees or the Sadducees. He created His own following. He did things so differently, religious people didn't like Him. He trained ordinary people – He turned water into wine – He spoke to women – He healed people – He cast demons out of people – He raised people from the dead – He saw a need and met it.

People just want to go to church - These people became the church. - Me

Calvary Chapel Church in Fort Lauderdale, Florida is the church we like to attend when we're in that area. Their church has a saying – "Get in the Story." It's based on John 21:25 which says *"Jesus also did many other things. If they were all written down, I suppose the whole world could not contain the books that would be written."* The idea is that God wrote the Bible to share Himself with others. It's His story, *BUT* He uses all different kinds of people to get His story out there. Fishermen and Kings. Women and Men. Rich and Poor. Upstanding and not so upstanding people. We can all be used by God. We all have stories to share with others as to how Jesus changed our lives. The Bible is full of them! We all have different ways to be the church. I've told you a few of the ways that I serve and share His story with others. I hope I have given you some ideas. But, like I said at the beginning, we can't all be Billy Graham, have prison ministries, or foster hundreds of children. We all live in different places and have different interests, so none of our stories will be the same. But we can all be in His story. If you are still looking for ways to serve, ask others what they do. Read books written by other believers – that's what encourages me to keep trying new ways to get His word out there.

On the way out of the property of the church where our children attended preschool, there was a sign that read, *"You are now entering the mission field."* I hope that's what you have gathered from reading my book. Remember, we answer to the audience of One. Run the race to finish what God wants to accomplish *through you! Don't hesitate, the world needs YOU!* Get in the Story! And GO . . . MAKE . . . RIPPLES!

Let me say again that all of the ripples in this book came with time. Some failed and some have been adjusted. None of us will create ripples in the same way. I would love to hear how you have put your ripples into action, spin offs of mine, or ones that I haven't tried yet! You can email me at RipplesForGod@gmail.com

ONE LAST THING: IF YOU LEAVE THIS BOOK ON YOUR SHELF, IT CAN'T FURTHER THE KINGDOM . . . PLEASE PASS IT ON. Don't wait for that someday you may read it again.

QUESTIONS

1. What are you saving for someday that you know you should share or give away?

2. Do you save your Christian books you may "someday" read again?

3. What tradition are you stuck in only because it's a tradition?

4. Are there changes you can make in your life? Name a few.

5. Have you ever welcomed a new neighbor? How? And how did it turn out?

6. Who has lived a life that you would call a trail blazer?

7. Has this book made you any bolder?

8. What ripple have you already tried?

9. How many index cards of ripples do you have to try?

10. What ripple could you add to this book?

Acknowledgments

I want to first thank my Lord and Savior! You have pushed me out of my comfort zone so many times! Each time we go on an adventure I drag my heels BUT I know You are always with me. I have learned so much about who You are and the woman that You are molding me to be. Thank you for always encouraging me when I wanted to give up!

Dean, thank you for all the ways you have let me serve the Lord, for all the ways you have served alongside me. Thank you for always supporting me in every classroom, event, and in this adventure! From the beginning you have supported me, with time and places to write from. Plus you paid to publish this book for me to give away.
(I'm glad God answered my prayer and put you in my life!!!)

Rhonda, thank you for starting the first ripple in my life! Thank you for walking in your sister's room and asking the question, "Do you want to know how to get to Heaven?" The impact that has made in my life and eternity is NOT calculable! And in the lives of others that I have rippled out to and they have rippled out to! It's endless!

Penny, thank you for encouraging me at the beginning of this book.

Gary, thank you for always asking and praying for me and this book from the very beginning.

To the ladies in the Bible/book study group, thank you for listening to my same prayer requests about this book almost being done and for the

encouragement along the way. For again going on another adventure with me and being my study group trial for this book.
(They sat through the unedited version!)

Karen, thank you for doing the BIG part of the editing! Especially when your computer only let you edit one sentence at a time on the last ten pages!

Jill, thank you for the second edit as a person who does NOT know me and my personality! And for adding all of the commas that were missing!

Thank you for all the free editors!!! Lexi, Bill, Sharon H, Amy, Sharon G, and Amy.
I appreciate all the corrections and the suggestions!
(I was too cheap to pay for a professional.)

To my parents who both read the unedited version so I could write about them. And who have both always supported my hair-brained ideas and me.

Thank you to Abby, Jon, Zack, Katie and Sean for supporting me in this adventure! (Jon thank you for saving my manuscript more than once and all your technical support!)
(And since this is my book . . . I also want to say thanks to Jan and William for being my grandchildren!) (And Tommy and Johnny.)

Printed in the United States
by Baker & Taylor Publisher Services